"Among his readers, it has long been a truism that Barth was motivated by a desire to free theology from the epistemic straight jacket in which Kant had left it. Others have talked about Barth's relationship to Kant, but no one has confronted the question as directly, as clearly, and as convincingly as Robert Hand does here. This book is needed reading for anyone who wants to understand how Barth's theology developed and why he ended up where he did."

—**Bruce Marshall**
Southern Methodist University

"In this highly stimulating and original work, Hand makes a fresh contribution not only to Barth studies but also to our understanding of Kantian philosophical theology. With a deceptively light touch, he takes us through a thicket of diverging Kant interpretations before reaching his astonishing argument that Barth and Kant share many substantial elements of convergence. I expect this book to become a standard point of reference for any future discussion of Barth on the vexed question of our knowledge of God."

—**George Hunsinger**
Princeton Theological Seminary

"Hand's work is part of a trajectory in Kant studies which takes seriously the integrity and originality of his religious philosophy. At the same time, it demonstrates Kant's deep influence on subsequent Christian theology. This book is a significant contribution to our understanding of the Kantian background to Karl Barth's dogmatic theology and its distinctively modern shape."

—**Simon Oliver**
Durham University

"Robert Hand is convinced that Kant, with his 'robust, positive Christian theism,' was and still can be a positive influence for Christian thought, especially in the field of theological epistemology. Hand shows convincingly how Barth never completely let go of certain key traits of Kant's epistemology, even as he moved past Kant in his massive treatment on the knowledge of God and its utter dependance on God's own self-manifestation."

—**Christophe Chalamet**
University of Geneva

"This book brings together two unlikely bedfellows: Kant and Barth. Rather than pit them against one another, Hand suggests we rethink the relationship between these weighty figures, building a solid case for several distinctly Kantian epistemological themes that Barth continues to develop and use throughout his various works. Hand does a masterful job of analyzing a massive amount of literature, enhancing the scholarship on the theological thinking of these two prominent men."

—Mary L. Vanden Berg
Calvin Theological Seminary

"*Presupposing God* challenges the view that Barth's engagement with Kant's philosophy and its neo-Kantian interpretations is only of limited *theological* import for Barth's work. On Hand's reading, the philosophical limits Kant places on the scope of finite human reason resonate fully with Barth's theological resistance to claims of 'liberal theology.' Central to this profound resonance between Barth and Kant is a shared theological epistemology, one 'which does not produce knowledge of God but rather receives it.'"

—Philip J. Rossi, SJ
Marquette University, emeritus

"That Kant was an influence on—indeed, an asset to—Barth's theological revelatory epistemology and that Kant can be a helpful influence for contemporary theology may seem to be counterintuitive. This careful work makes the convincing and nuanced case that it is so. Hand simply shows that Barth himself and, indeed, all theology after Kant, simply has to reckon with him, even if only to adapt or refine his assertions. I recommend the careful scholarship that this work represents."

—Ross Hastings
Regent College

Presupposing God

Princeton Theological Monograph Series

K. C. Hanson, Charles M. Collier, D. Christopher Spinks,
and Robin A. Parry, Series Editors

Recent volumes in the series:

Riyako Cecilia Hikota
*And Still We Wait:
Hans Urs von Balthasar's Theology of Holy Saturday
and Christian Discipleship*

Guillaume Bignon
*Excusing Sinners and Blaming God:
A Calvinist Assessment of Determinism, Moral Responsibility,
and Divine Involvement in Evil*

Jeff McDonald
*John Gerstner and the Renewal of Presbyterian and
Reformed Evangelicalism in Modern America*

James P. Haley
*The Humanity of Christ:
The Significance of the Anhypostasis and Enhypostasis in
Karl Barth's Christology*

Karlo V. Bordjadze
Darkness Visible: A Study of Isaiah 14:3–23 as Christian Scripture

Graham H. Twelftree
The Nature Miracles of Jesus: Problems, Perspectives, and Prospects

William M. Marsh
*Martin Luther on Reading the Bible as Christian Scripture:
The Messiah in Luther's Biblical Hermeneutic and Theology*

Benjamin J. Burkholder
*Bloodless Atonement?
A Theological and Exegetical Study of the Last Supper Saying*

Presupposing God

Theological Epistemology in Immanuel Kant's Transcendental Idealism and Karl Barth's Theology

Robert A. Hand

☞PICKWICK *Publications* • Eugene, Oregon

PRESUPPOSING GOD
Theological Epistemology in Immanuel Kant's Transcendental Idealism and Karl Barth's Theology

Princteon Theological Monograph Series 247

Copyright © 2022 Robert A. Hand. All rights reserved. Except for brief quotations in critical publications or reviews, no part of this book may be reproduced in any manner without prior written permission from the publisher. Write: Permissions, Wipf and Stock Publishers, 199 W. 8th Ave., Suite 3, Eugene, OR 97401.

Pickwick Publications
An Imprint of Wipf and Stock Publishers
199 W. 8th Ave., Suite 3
Eugene, OR 97401

www.wipfandstock.com

PAPERBACK ISBN: 978-1-6667-3374-7
HARDCOVER ISBN: 978-1-6667-2867-5
EBOOK ISBN: 978-1-6667-2868-2

Cataloguing-in-Publication data:

Names: Hand, Robert A., author.

Title: Presupposing God : theological epistemology in Immanuel Kant's transcendental idealism and Karl Barth's theological method / Robert A. Hand.

Description: Eugene, OR : Pickwick Publications, 2022 | Series: Princeton Theological Monograph Series 247 | Includes bibliographical references.

Identifiers: ISBN 978-1-6667-3374-7 (paperback) | ISBN 978-1-6667-2867-5 (hardcover) | ISBN 978-1-6667-2868-2 (ebook)

Subjects: LCSH: Knowledge, Theory of (Religion). | Kant, Immanuel,-1724–1804. | Barth, Karl, 1886–1968.

Classification: BT50 .H33 2022 (paperback) | BT50 .H33 (ebook)

VERSION NUMBER 072222

In memoriam
William J. Abraham (1947–2021)

For Kant the question as to whether and how and within which limits the proposition "God exists" is possible . . . is the secret thorn [geheime Stachel] that drives all thinking in the Critique of Pure Reason *and subsequent works.*
—Martin Heidegger

Barth identified that after Kant, theology . . . could never be the same. Any theologian had to come to terms with Kant, to follow in his tracks, or branch out in some way from what he established.
—Colin Gunton

Contents

Preface | ix
Acknowledgments | xi
Abbreviations | xii
Introduction: Wrestling with God | xiii

1   *Tertium Quid:* Kantian Realism | 1
2   The Secret Thorn: Kant and Theology | 29
3   Paths From Kant to Barth: Varieties of Neo-Kantianism | 53
4   *Ad Fontes*: Kant and Barth's Early Theology | 79
5   Presupposing God: Kantian Themes in the *Church Dogmatics* | 111

Conclusion: A Case for Continuity | 135

Bibliography | 143

Preface

THIS IS AN ESSAY in philosophical theology, and my specific focus is the subject of theological epistemology in the thought of Immanuel Kant and Karl Barth. My thesis is that there is a deep consistency between Kant's and Barth's respective theological epistemologies. Both Kant and Barth held that God's existence was not a concept that was subject to argument or demonstration but one that is built into how knowledge works in the first place. They each articulated this assumption in their own nuanced ways, but I will be suggesting that there is a basic consonance between them. In order to support my thesis, I first argue for a number of positive emphases in Kant's critical philosophy and religious epistemology in conversation with modern Kant scholarship. I then narrate how some of these emphases were obscured in Kant's reception in the decades between Kant and Barth, and then the intellectual conditions under which Barth first encountered Kant. Finally, I demonstrate how Barth wrestled with these varying interpretations and continued to utilize Kant with increased sophistication as his thought developed across the Romans commentaries, *Anselm*, and the *Church Dogmatics*. I conclude by suggesting that contrary to many contemporary accounts, Kant can be an asset to theology, not a liability, and that Barth is one of the better available examples of this in practice.

Acknowledgments

MY THANKS TO THE faculty and staff of Calvin Theological Seminary for investing in this project in its initial form as a PhD dissertation, particularly Lee Hardy, Ronald Feenstra, Young Ahn Kang, Lyle Bierma, and John Cooper. The 2018 Barth Graduate Student Colloquium at the Center for Barth Studies at Princeton Theological Seminary also provided an opportunity to further clarify several aspects of my thinking. The J. S. Bridwell Library at the Perkins School of Theology at Southern Methodist University, the Lanier Theological Library in Houston, and the Moody Memorial Library at Baylor University were invaluable resources for research and inspiration.

The faculty and students at LeTourneau University were also a source of consistent encouragement and challenge, particularly my friends Viktor Roudkovski, Kelly Liebengood, and Steve Mason. Thanks also to Greg Bock at the University of Texas at Tyler for going out of his way to create opportunities to explore some of the specifically philosophical issues involved in my argument through various guest lectures and panel discussions. The 2017 Midwest Regional meeting of the Society of Christian Philosophers also provided a forum for me to present and refine some of my reflections on Kant in particular.

My family has faithfully supported my intellectual and many other interests over the years, especially Al and Melanie Hand, and Mike McDonald was an important companion for the final stretch of the project. I cherished the curiosity and excitement of my daughters, Genevieve and Emmi, as I worked through the various stages of writing and publication. My wife, Michele, selflessly allowed for time and space for me to complete my work over many years and has been an irreplaceable partner for this journey and so many others.

Finally, this book is dedicated to the memory of William J. "Billy" Abraham, who encouraged this project far beyond the call of duty. The future of the church catholic and the Wesleyan tradition in particular is brighter thanks to his mind and ministry.

Robert A. Hand
Easter 2022

Abbreviations

A	Karl Barth, *Anslem: Fides Quaerens Intellectum*. Translated by Ian Robertson. London: SCM, 1960.
CD	Karl Barth, *Church Dogmatics*. Edited and translated by Geoffrey William Bromiley and Thomas Forsyth Torrance. Edinburgh: T. & T. Clark, 1957–88.
CPR	Immanuel Kant, *Critique of Pure Reason*. Edited and translated by Paul Guyer and Allen W. Wood. Cambridge: Cambridge University Press, 1997.
CPrR	Immanuel Kant, *Critique of Practical Reason*. In *Practical Philosophy*, edited and translated by Mary J. Gregor, 133–272. Cambridge: Cambridge University Press, 1996.
ER	Karl Barth, *Epistle to the Romans*. Translated by Edwyn C. Hoskyns. Oxford: Oxford University Press, 1968.
GN-K	Frederick Beiser, *Genesis of Neo-Kantianism, 1796–1880*. Oxford: Oxford University Press, 2014.
KB	Eberhard Busch, *Karl Barth: His Life from Letters and Autobiographical Texts*. Minneapolis: Fortress, 1997.
LPT	Immanuel Kant, *Lectures on Philosophical Theology*. Translated by Allen W. Wood and Gertrude M. Clark. Ithaca, NY: Cornell University Press, 1986.
R I	Karl Barth, *Der Römerbrief*. Zurich: TVZ, 1919.
R II	Karl Barth, *Der Römerbrief 1922*. Zollikon–Zürich: Evangelischer Verlag, 1940.
Religion	Immanuel Kant, *Religion within the Limits of Reason Alone*. In *Religion and Rational Theology*, edited and translated by Allen W. Wood and George Di Giovanni, 39–216. Cambridge: Cambridge University Press, 1996.

Introduction
Wrestling with God

THIS PROJECT IS CONCERNED with the question of whether and how knowledge of God is possible, and I have a particular interest in how Immanuel Kant and Karl Barth attempted to answer this question. The choice of Kant and Barth is not arbitrary; their respective statures in modern philosophy and theology are well established on their own terms, but Kant was also one of Barth's primary intellectual influences. My impression is that Kant influenced Barth's theology in a unique manner, but this is a complicated claim because Kant's role in modern Protestant theology is a contested one. Kant, and interpretations of him, have been used to advance a number of theologies Barth either was or would be opposed to. Contemporary theologians will most readily associate Kant, for instance, with thinkers such as Gordon Kaufman.[1] It is furthermore common to find Kant dismissed in some of the most influential contemporary historical-theological surveys as an Enlightenment philosopher who was theologically agnostic, reduced theology to ethics, or both, or simply as a forerunner to modern Protestant liberalism. This is the case with Roger Olson's account, for instance, in *The Journey of Modern Theology*. According to Kant, Olson states, "there can be no knowledge of God in the strictest sense of knowledge," and "Kant killed metaphysics and limited reason to the realm of appearances [and] restricted religion to ethics."[2] In Olson's *The Story of Christian Theology*, Kant's primary role in the development of Christian theology in the last three centuries was, with Hegel, as a precursor to Schleiermacher and modern Protestant

---

1. Kaufman's use of Kant is most clearly stated in *God the Problem*; *An Essay on Theological Method*; and *The Theological Imagination*. In *An Essay on Theological Method*, Kaufman states that both the concepts of God and world, for Kant, are imaginative constructs that have no bearing on experience (25), and Kaufman mentions his deep indebtedness to Kant in *In Face of Mystery*, 195. J. Patrick Wooley argues that Kaufman's debt to Kant runs even deeper than Kaufman himself realizes in "Kaufman's Debt to Kant," 545. Christopher Insole suggests a more accurate term for Kaufman's theological antirealism is simply *atheism* in "Gordon Kaufman and the Kantian Mystery," 101–19.

2. Olson, *Journey of Modern Theology*, 87, 91.

liberalism.[3] In the widely used text *The Story of Christianity*, Justo González suggests, "Kant's significance for religion and theology . . . go far beyond his rather uninspired attempts to ground religion on morality. His philosophical work dealt a deathblow to the easy rationalism of his predecessors, and to the notion that it is possible to speak in purely rational and objective terms of such matters as the existence of God and the future life."[4] González suggests elsewhere that "in typical rationalist fashion, Kant sees religion as having the sole function of assisting in the moral life," and similar to Olson, portrays Kant as the precursor not just to Schleiermacher but also Ritschl.[5] Alister McGrath likewise sees Kant's role in the development of Christian theology as a forerunner of Schleiermacher and Ritschl, as do Stanley Grenz and Roger Olson.[6] Grenz and Olson conclude, "The theology produced by Kant's method remained anthropocentric. . . . The transcendence of God is easily lost in the voice of the categorical imperative found in the depths of human 'practical reason.'"[7] Kant, it would seem, is not only irrelevant to a historically orthodox Christian theology but potentially even a liability to it.

And yet Barth somehow found an ally in Kant. Given that Kant has been used primarily in theology for projects that reached such different conclusions than Barth's, and given that he is often portrayed as a liability to theology, how could this be? What about Kant's critical philosophy would have been useful for Barth's theology? What is Kant's actual relationship to positive religious claims? What were the reigning assumptions about Kant in the early twentieth-century German theological academy that Barth would have received, and how did Barth ultimately understand and incorporate Kantian themes in his theological method?

My thesis is that there is a deep consistency between Kant's and Barth's respective theological epistemologies, and Kant's philosophy provided the general architecture that enabled Barth's theology to be as uniquely influential as it is. The deep consistency is that both Kant and Barth held that God's existence was not a concept that was subject to argument or demonstration but one that is built into how knowledge works in the first place. They each articulated this assumption—this theological epistemology—in their own nuanced ways, but I will be suggesting that there is a basic consonance between them. I believe Barth learned this explicitly from Kant, and it enabled him to articulate his theology in the way that he did.

3. Olson, *Story of Christian Theology*, 540–54
4. González, *The Reformation to the Present Day*, 195.
5. González, *From the Protestant Reformation to the 20th Century*, 342.
6. McGrath, *Historical Theology*, 3, 193, 221, 232.
7. Grenz and Olson, *20th-Century Theology*, 31.

In order to support my thesis, I will first address particular questions about Kant in chapters 2–3. The first matter I will account for the extent to which Kant's transcendental idealism can be considered realistic rather than antirealistic. The precise character of Kant's transcendental idealism is still very much open for discussion, and it will be important to clarify where exactly my own reading of Kant fits into the landscape. I will begin with Peter Strawson's publication of *The Bounds of Sense* in 1966, which popularized readings of Kant's transcendental idealism that emphasized a strong disjunction between reality and our knowledge of it.[8] This was challenged by Henry Allison's so-called "deflationary" account in *Kant's Transcendental Idealism*, which suggests that Strawson's division between appearances and things in themselves is less pronounced than Kant claims.[9] Ultimately I will be commending a third option—a moderately realist account of Kant's transcendental idealism that is similar in kind to that of Lucy Allais's recent formulation: "An account of mind-dependence that does not involve existence in the mind, and which is compatible with thinking that mind-dependent appearances are grounded in the way things are in themselves."[10]

The second issue I will address in Kant studies is that of Kant's relationship to positive theological claims. The portrayals of Kant I mention above would not lead one to believe this is possible. In recent decades, however, some Kant scholars have suggested that Kant is more amenable to theism than many of his past interpreters have suggested. When Kant states, for instance, "It is one of the worthiest of inquiries to see how far our reason can go in the knowledge of God" (*LPT*, intro.), this suggests that there is more to Kant's story than meets the eye.

While recent interest in Kant's positive theology has generally revolved around his *Religion within the Bounds of Reason Alone*, in this project I will also be examining Kant's theism in the first and second Critiques, where the possibility of the knowledge of God not only figures significantly into Kant's program but even appears as the "highest independent good" (*CPrR*, 1.2.6). Martin Heidegger would even go so far as to suggest, "For Kant the question as to whether and how and within which limits the proposition 'God exists' is possible . . . is the secret thorn [*geheime Stachel*] that drives all thinking in the *Critique of Pure Reason* and subsequent works."[11] If we hold Kant his own standard, that is, "to see how far reason can go in its knowledge of God," it is remarkable just how thoroughly theological reason's quest

---

8. Strawson, *Bounds of Sense*, 15–46.
9. Allison, *Kant's Transcendental Idealism*, 3–19.
10. Allais, *Manifest Reality*, 16.
11. Heidegger, "Kants These über das Sein," 455.

can actually be. The picture of Kant I hope emerges will be one consistent with Allen Wood's suggestion that "despite Kant's generally critical stance toward the transcendent metaphysics of the rationalists and scholastics, he remained quite sympathetic to traditional theology on many points."[12]

After considering these questions in Kant studies, I will turn to questions regarding Barth's reception of Kant and how I understand him to be utilizing Kant in his theology. It is widely recognized in Barth scholarship that Barth's debt to Kant runs deep, but how and to what extent this is the case remains an open question. One challenge to understanding Barth's relationship to Kant is the emergence of neo-Kantianism, which governed how Kant was understood in late-nineteenth- and early-twentieth-century Germany. I narrate these developments at length in chapter 4. Barth's initial understanding of Kant came from this tradition, particularly Hermann Cohen's and Paul Natorp's idealistic interpretation of Kant through Barth's Marburg teacher Wilhelm Herrmann. Although Barth would state that "the first book which really moved me as a student was Kant's *Critique of Practical Reason*" (*KB*, 34), Barth's interest in Kant was not limited to his student years or to his early period; he continued to wrestle with and understand Kant deeply, such that Heinz Cassirer would inquire, "Why is it that this Swiss theologian understands Kant far better than any philosopher I have come across?"[13] The answer to that question, Colin Gunton suggests, is that "Barth identified that after Kant, theology (and for that matter, philosophy) could never be the same. Any theologian had to come to terms with Kant, to follow in his tracks, or branch out in some way from what he established."[14] I address these matters in chapter 5.

These observations raise the question of how exactly Barth incorporated Kant's ideas into his own theological epistemology, which I continue to discuss in chapter 6. Bruce McCormack suggests, "To the extent that Barth concerned himself with philosophical epistemology at all, he was an idealist (and more specifically, a Kantian)" and also that "all of his efforts in theology may be considered, from one point of view, as an attempt to overcome Kant by means of Kant, not retreating behind him and attempting to go around him, but going through him."[15] D. Paul La Montagne has proposed more recently that "Barth uses a foundationalist epistemology, Kant's, in a postfoundational way because he finds it necessary if he is to remain faithful

---

12. Wood, translator's introduction to *LPT*, 10. Wolterstorff's "Is It Possible?" is another important resource for this discussion that I will address in the conclusion.

13. Letter from Ronald Weitzman, March 20, 2001, as reported in Gunton's introduction to Barth, *Protestant Theology in the Nineteenth Century*, xvi.

14. Gunton, *Barth Lectures*, 13.

15. McCormack, *Karl Barth's Critically Realistic Dialectical Theology*, 465–66.

to the object of his discourse."¹⁶ Colin Gunton, on the other hand, views Barth's strategy for using Kant as one of reversal: "My view is that on the whole Barth is trying to outdo Kant, so to speak. But as ever when you try to outdo someone else they continue to shape your thought. . . . Barth changes the Kantian pattern because he wants to say not that the mind shapes the object but that God shapes the mind."¹⁷

For both Kant and Barth, God's existence is not a concept that was subject to external argument or demonstration but rather one that is built into the way knowledge functions. For both of them, questions surrounding God's existence and epistemology proper were intimately related, even inseparable, and one cannot sufficiently explain one without eventually referencing the other. Neither of their theological epistemologies, in other words, happen to have certain incidental theological features but rather are necessarily theological by definition. Barth's use of this strategy in his theology has deep roots in Kantianism, and I intend to show that Kant's philosophy can be an asset to theology rather than the liability it is often taken to be, and that Barth's theology is one of the better available examples of this in practice.

---

16. La Montagne, *Barth and Rationality*, 12.
17. Gunton, *Barth Lectures*, 135.

I

Tertium Quid
Kantian Realism

MORE THAN TWO CENTURIES after the publication of the *Critique of Pure Reason*, the precise character of Kant's transcendental idealism is still an open question.[1] Defining Kant's transcendental idealism is not simply a question of abstract knowledge in general, however, either for my own purposes or for Kant's. In Kant's case, the question of knowledge in general is inseparable from knowledge of God, so it will be necessary to clarify Kant's transcendental idealism first before proceeding to where exactly knowledge of God fits into his epistemology, which I will address in the next chapter.

My purpose in this chapter is twofold. First, I will outline some (but not all) of the basic elements of Kant's transcendental idealism as they appear in the first Critique. In order to emphasize some of the most important parts of Kant's system, I will first devote some time to elaborating two important occasions of Kant's work: dogmatism and skepticism, particularly David Hume's. Second, I aim to clarify some of the primary contemporary interpretive options for Kant's transcendental idealism. Peter Strawson's publication of *The Bounds of Sense* in 1966, for instance, popularized readings of Kant's transcendental idealism that emphasized a strong disjunction between reality and our knowledge of it.[2] This was challenged by Henry

---

1. Ameriks, "Recent Work on Kant's Theoretical Philosophy," and Ameriks, "Kantian Idealism Today," particularly the latter, both still serve as standard surveys of the major issues and figures involved in interpreting Kant's transcendental idealism, as well as his *Interpreting Kant's Critiques*. Strawson, *Bounds of Sense*, remains a defining moment in the contemporary history of interpretation of Kant's transcendental idealism. Henry Allison shifted the conversation considerably with *Kant's Transcendental Idealism*, but Strawsonian readings still have their proponents, for instance, Guyer, *Kant and the Claims of Knowledge*, and Langton, *Kantian Humility*. Other significant resources for these issues include Adams, "Things in Themselves"; Findlay, *Kant and the Transcendental Object*; Höffe, *Immanuel Kant*; Wilkerson, *Kant's "Critique of Pure Reason."* An up-to-date survey of the many complications that will be involved in making a realist claim about Kant's transcendental idealism in particular can be found in Allais, *Manifest Reality*, 3–36.

2. Strawson, *Bounds of Sense*, 15–46. The most notable contemporary proponents of Strawsonian readings are Guyer, *Kant and the Claims of Knowledge*; Langton, *Kantian Humility*.

Allison's so-called "deflationary" account in *Kant's Transcendental Idealism*, which suggests that Strawson overstates his case.[3] Ultimately, however, I believe there is a third option that takes account of the most data possible—a moderately realist account of Kant's transcendental idealism that follows Lucy Allais's recent formulation: "An account of mind-dependence that does not involve existence in the mind, and which is compatible with thinking that mind-dependent appearances are grounded in the way things are in themselves."[4]

Two Important Occasions of Kant's First Critique

Before proceeding to my own summary of Kant's transcendental idealism, it is important to recall some of the circumstances surrounding the first Critique. It was a response to a variety of early modern philosophical developments, chief of which were what Kant refers to as dogmatism and skepticism. Both were unsatisfactory to Kant for different reasons. It should first be noted that dogmatism, for Kant, did not necessarily denote *religious* dogmatism specifically but rather philosophies based on unexamined premises. Dogmatism, for Kant, is "the presumption of getting on solely with pure cognition from (philosophical) concepts according to principles, which reason has been using for a long time without first inquiring in what way and by what right it has obtained them." Epistemological presuppositions should be subject to self-examination, but dogmatism skips this step; it is "the dogmatic procedure of pure reason," in other words, "without an antecedent critique of its own capacity" (*CPR*, B xxxv). This was Kant's chief concern with Leibnizian philosophies and also Leibniz's student Christian Wolff, who played a direct role on Kant's development and was central to scholarly discussions of metaphysics in the mid-to-late eighteenth century.[5] Wolff in particular, according to Gary Hatfield, was problematic for Kant

---

3. Allison, *Kant's Transcendental Idealism*, 3–19.

4. Allais, *Manifest Reality*, 16. Allais's reading, although recent, has a long and stable history in the German interpretive tradition, and Christopher Insole suggests that it can be traced back to the 1780s and 1790s, specifically to Jena interpreters such as C. C. Schmid, Johann Erhard, Franz von Herbert, and Friedrich Niethammer. See Insole, *Intolerable God*, 96n6, as well as Ameriks, *Kant and the Fate of Autonomy*, 64–66.

5. See in particular Wolff, *Theologia naturalis method scientifica pertracta*; Wolff, *Psychologia empirica*; Wolff, *Philosophia rationalis*. See also Kuehn, *Kant*, 67–85. On Kant's relationship with Wolff, see Grapotte and Prunea-Bretonnet, *Kant et Wolff*; and also Dyck, *Kant and Rational Psychology*, esp. chap. 2. On Kant and Leibnizian philosophy specifically, see Jauernig, "Kant's Critique of the Leibnizian Philosophy," 41–63; Kaulbach, *Die Metaphysik des Raumes bei Leibniz und Kant*.

because Wolff "admitted empirical propositions into metaphysics,"[6] but sensory experience is, for Kant, a dissatisfactory criterion for metaphysics. The Leibnizian-Wolffian rationalist tradition was problematic for Kant from early in his academic career, and while he devoted much of his early work to criticizing it, he would still refer to Wolff as "the greatest among all dogmatic philosophers, who gave us the first example . . . of the way in which the secure course of a science is to be taken" (*CPR*, B xxxvi–xxxvii). And yet, as Otfried Höffe notes, Kant remained dissatisfied with dogmatists "because they force upon us certain fundamental assumptions."[7]

Hume's skepticism, on the other hand, was a particularly important influence on Kant's system and worthy of elaboration at some length in order to later clarify Kant's positions on the same issues. In his 1739 *Treatise of Human Nature*, Hume takes as his starting point a concern over what he perceives to be growing confusion regarding what exactly can be known by human beings. Hume, like Kant, was particularly concerned with the confusion caused by the abstractions of "dogmatists" and metaphysicians. In order to cut through the confusion, Hume proposes, memorably, to "march up directly to the capital or center of these sciences, to human nature itself" and restrict his inquiry to empirical sense-data only.[8] From this vantage point, Hume believes, we can sort out what confusion remains. The most important distinction Hume introduces in the *Treatise* is that between *impressions* and *ideas*, where "impressions" are whatever sense-data present themselves to a knowing subject, and "ideas" are the cognitive copies of those sense-data we assimilate into our knowledge.[9] Hume's diagnosis is that there is too much speculation about ideas abstracted from their impressions, and his solution is to clarify that relationship. Belief, therefore, is a lesser form of knowledge than cogitation—if indeed it counts as knowledge at all.

Hume was dissatisfied with the *Treatise*, and he composed the *Enquiry concerning Human Understanding* in 1748 as a sharpened and intensified version of the ideas in the *Treatise*. He continues to make a sharp distinction between empirical and speculative knowledge and rejects abstract

---

6. Hatfield, introduction to Kant, *Prolegomena to Any Future Metaphysics*, xvii.

7. Höffe, *Immanuel Kant*, 32.

8. Hume, introduction to *Treatise of Human Nature*. Guides to Hume's epistemology include Baier, *A Progress of Sentiments*; Church, *Hume's Theory of the Understanding*; Danford, *David Hume and the Problem of Reason*; Flew, *Hume's Philosophy of Belief*; Fogelin, *Hume's Skepticism*; Gawlick and Kreimendahl, *Hume in der deutschen Aufklärung*; Malherbe, *La philosophie empiriste de David Hume*; Maund, *Hume's Theory of Knowledge*; Pears, *Hume's System*; Stern, *Faculty Theory of Knowledge*.

9. Hume, *Treatise*, 1.1.1.1.

philosophy as irrelevant.[10] One of the most significant refinements in the *Enquiry*, and one that he has come to be perhaps best known for, is that he rejects not only metaphysical speculation *but also* unnecessary *empirical* speculation, for instance regarding the relationships between ideas—in other words, causation itself. Hume's argument is that knowledge of causation involves generalizations beyond "original sentiments"—a topic I will return to below—therefore we are restricted from claiming that we have knowledge of them.

The precise way in which Hume organizes sense experience in the *Enquiry* bears further examination. In section 2, Hume poses an issue that will govern his more particular concerns throughout the remainder of the *Enquiry*: the discrepancy between original sentiments—that is, sense data arising from direct experiences—and our recollection of and reflection on those experiences. "There is a considerable difference between the perceptions of the mind, when a man feels the pain of excessive heat, or the pleasure of moderate warmth, and when he afterwards recalls to his memory this sensation, or anticipates it by his imagination. These faculties may mimic or copy the perceptions of the senses; but they can never entirely reach the force and vivacity of the original sentiment."[11] This is hardly an abstract issue only, however; it is a fundamental problem of human experience: our ideas about the world around us do not always correspond to what is actually there. We cannot always say with complete confidence, in other words, that our belief *about x* necessarily corresponds exactly to *x*.

Hume takes matter a step further, however, and notes that our knowledge of the world is not only static but dynamic, and in our attempts to make sense of our experience of not only objects but also dynamic events, we impose categories of relation between the various ideas that we derive from original sentiments. Hume suggests that three relations in particular govern our understanding of relationships between ideas: resemblance, contiguity, and cause and effect.[12] The relation of cause and effect is a matter of particular concern for Hume. The first step toward an answer, Hume suggests in section 4, is that causative belief naturally arises from experience and not from reason.[13] To suggest through reason that one event causes another would be unjustified. Our ideas about impressions are already prone to confusion as it is; why risk further confusion, Hume seems to be saying, by imposing a potential confusion back onto those impressions?

10. Hume, *Enquiry*, 1.11.
11. Hume, *Enquiry*, 2.1.
12. Hume, *Enquiry*, 3.2.
13. Hume, *Enquiry*, 4.7.

Hume therefore wants to restrict cause and effect to experience. At the end of section 4, we find that he is still dissatisfied with his own answer to the question of the precise nature of the inferences we draw regarding cause and effect. In section 5, part 1, we arrive at the basis of causal beliefs: *custom* or *habit*, which stops short of asserting that one event indeed *causes* another event. Rather, Hume states, it becomes *customary* for us to do so after repeated observation: "Whatever the repetition of any particular act or operation produces a propensity to renew the same act or operation, without being impelled by any reasoning or process of the understanding; we always say, that this propensity is the effect of *Custom*."[14]

Why exactly is it important for Hume to say this? Recall his guiding concern in the *Enquiry*: ideas are notoriously prone to confusion, that is, we are often wrong about what we think we know to be the case. This is particularly true for Hume in the matter of causation: even though we may observe two events in exact succession ninety-nine times, the possibility of the one-hundredth succession turning out differently still remains. In order to be properly modest about our knowledge of the relationship between events and allow for potential derivations, therefore, it is best to avoid imposing the category of causation onto the events and instead acknowledge *that* some sort of conjunctive relationship obtains but stop short of claiming to know the exact nature of its operations. While Hume takes particular aim at causation, his general concern seems to be restricting our knowledge to experience in order to rid it of "prejudices, which we may have imbibed from education or rash opinion."[15]

Elements of Kant's First Critique

Like Hume, Kant takes as his starting point the philosophical confusion of his time and seeks to remedy it through his own project. Unlike Hume, however, Kant takes aim not only at dogmatists *but also* skeptics such as Hume himself; in Kant's mind, dogmatism and skepticism were both equally irrational, as were enthusiasm, fanaticism, superstition, and atheism.[16] The

---

14. Hume, *Enquiry*, 5.5.
15. Hume, *Enquiry*, 12.1.
16. Hume is often characterized as a skeptic simpliciter, but it is important to note that he was engaged primarily in *academic* or *mitigated* rather than dogmatic skepticism; see Fogelin, *Hume's Skepticism*, chaps. 1–2; Jessop, "Hume's Limited Skepticism," 3–27. On Kant and Hume, see Beck, *Early German Philosophy*; Beck, *Essays on Kant and Hume*; Guyer, *Knowledge, Reason, and Taste*; Kuehn, "Kant's Conception of 'Hume's Problem,'" 275–93; Lovejoy, "On Kant's Reply to Hume," 380–407; Malherbe, *Kant ou Hume*; Stern, "Metaphysical Dogmatism, Humean Skepticism, Kantian Criticism," 102–16.

solution, for Kant, is *criticism*, "the preparatory activity necessary for the advancement of metaphysics as a well-grounded science" (*CPR*, B xxxvi). The problem common to most philosophies of his era, Kant argues, is that they fail to establish exact correspondence between subjective knowledge and the objects it knows through concepts. The best attempts at doing so, those of Locke and Hume, both run aground in their own ways:

> The first of these two famous men [Locke] opened the gates wide to enthusiasm, since reason, once it has authority on its side, will not be kept within limits by indeterminate recommendations of moderation; the second [Hume] gave way entirely to skepticism, since he believed himself to have discovered in what is generally held to be reason a deception of our faculty of cognition.—We are now about to make an attempt to see whether we cannot successfully steer human reason between these two cliffs, assign its determinate boundaries, and still keep open the entire field of its purposive activity. (*CPR*, B 128)

Kant's solution to this dilemma was to settle reason's *internal* contradictions *apart from* experience, that is, to seek how much *a priori* knowledge we can have and whether synthetic *a priori* knowledge in particular is possible. This is what Kant intends by the term *critique*—an evaluation of knowledge itself insofar as that is possible. Evaluating pure reason's internal structures can prevent needless skepticism, dogmatism, and so on. Several elements of the first Critique are essential in understanding Kant's transcendental idealism: intuitions, the transcendental discovery and deduction of the categories, the refutation of idealism, and the fourth paralogism. I will consider each one in turn before turning in the next section to metaphysical and epistemological readings of Kant's transcendental idealism.

Intuitions in the Transcendental Aesthetic

According to Kant, human cognition stems from two sources: sensibility (*Sinnlichkeit*) and understanding (*Verstand*) (*CPR*, A 15/B 29). Kant's strategy in the first Critique is to separate sensibility and understanding for heuristic purposes and examine their operations individually. The first part of the Transcendental Doctrine of Elements, the Transcendental Aesthetic, is devoted to the former, and the second part, the Transcendental Logic, is devoted to the latter as well the faculty of reason (*Vernuft*). Kant defines sensibility as "the capacity (receptivity) to acquire representations through the way in which we are affected by objects" (*CPR*, A 19/B 33). Understanding, by contrast, is an active faculty that "thinks through" (*durch den Verstand aber werden sie gedacht*) what it receives from sensibility (*CPR*, A 19/B 33). "In the transcendental aesthetic," Kant states, "we will therefore first isolate sensibility by separating off everything that the understanding thinks through its concepts" (*CPR*, A 22/B 36).

"All thought," however, "must, <by means of certain marks,> ultimately be related to intuitions." Intuitions (*Anschauungen*) are an important building block in Kant's system and also a source of confusion in discussions of his transcendental idealism.[17] It is important to clarify that the term *intuition*, for Kant, does not denote something like a personal hunch, instinct, or impression, for instance, "My intuition is that it will rain tomorrow." Rather, for Kant, the term *intuition* is a technical term that he defines as "whatever way and through whatever means a cognition may relate to objects, that through which it relates immediately to them, and at which all thought as a means is directed toward an end" (*CPR*, A 19/B 33). Pure intuitions, for Kant—space and time—are the necessary a priori *conditions* that make knowledge possible at all; they are the "condition of the possibility of appearances" (*CPR*, A 24/B 39). Objects do not appear out of thin air; some conditions must be in place before the process of knowledge can occur. In both the first and second editions of the first Critique, Kant identifies two intuitions that are necessary for human knowledge: space and time.

Repeatedly in his exposition of intuitions in the Transcendental Aesthetic, Kant explicitly emphasizes that space and time are *ideal* rather than *real*. This can be deceptive, because readers could be left with the impression that Kant is suggesting, in Berkeleyan fashion, that *all* knowledge is ideal rather than real. He states, for instance, in his General Remarks on the Transcendental Aesthetic, that

> all our intuition is nothing but the representation of appearance; that the things that we intuit are not in themselves what we intuit them to be, nor are their relations so constituted in themselves as they appear to us; and that if we remove our own subject or even only the subjective constitution of the senses in general, then all constitution, all relations of objects in space and time, indeed space and time themselves would disappear, and as appearances they cannot exist in themselves, but only in us. What may be the case with objects in themselves and abstracted from the receptivity of our sensibility remains entirely unknown to us. We are acquainted with nothing except our way

---

17. On Kant and intuition, see Thompson, "Singular Terms and Intuitions in Kant's Epistemology," 314–43; Smit, "Kant on Marks and the Immediacy of Intuition," 235–66; Wilson, "Kant on Intuition," 247–65.

of perceiving them, which is peculiar to us, and which therefore does not necessarily pertain to every being. (*CPR*, A 42/B 59)

Prima facie, this could easily be taken to mean that knowledge itself is not only purely ideal but entirely relative to knowing subjects. In fact, however, Kant is emphasizing the ideal nature of the *intuitions only* in passages such as this, *not* the real existence of objects themselves. Kant assumes the real existence of objects in the Transcendental Aesthetic but denies that space and time are actual entities themselves (*CPR*, A 23/B 38). Rather, he states, "space is nothing other than merely the form of all appearances of outer sense, i.e., the subjective *condition* of sensibility, under which alone outer intuition is possible for us" (*CPR*, A 26/B 42; emphasis added). "Time," similarly, "is no discursive or, as one calls it, general concept, but a pure form of sensible intuition" (*CPR*, A 31/B 47). Space and time, in Kant's system, are conditions that make knowledge possible; according to Höffe, they are "something quite different from all other familiar entities; they are the *a priori* forms of our (human) outer intuition and inner sensing."[18]

Transcendental Discovery and Deduction of the Categories

Intuitions, however, remain unsorted and unstructured. That sorting belongs to the understanding, the second of two stems of knowledge along with sensibility. One of Kant's first major steps in elucidating the operations of the understanding is the transcendental discovery of categories, also known as the Metaphysical Deduction, in the Transcendental Analytic. In this section of the first Critique Kant seeks to establish *which* concepts we have *a priori* with which we make sense of the world around us.[19] "Through concepts," Höffe states, "the material of intuition, which is taken in receptively, is formed into the unity and structure of a determinate object."[20] This section of the first Critique is where Kant distinguishes his program from those of Locke and Hume, who attempted to derive the categories from experience. This is of utmost importance not just for understanding Kant's system, as Wilkerson notes, but for the consequences of epistemology more

---

18. Höffe, *Immanuel Kant*, 63.

19. On Kant's discovery and deduction of the categories, see Aquila, *Matter in Mind*; Becker, *Selbstbewußtsein und Erfahrung*; Chipman, "Kant's Categories and Their Schematism," 36–50; Forum für Philosophie Bad Hamburg et al., *Kantstranszendentale Deduktion und die Möglichkeit von Transzendentalphilosophie*; Heinrich, *Identität und Objektivität*; Hossenfelder, *Kants Konstitutionstheorie und die Transzendentale Deduktion*; Howell, *Kant's Transcendental Deduction*.

20. Höffe, *Immanuel Kant*, 66.

broadly: "If Kant proves that we must apply pure concepts of understanding, he also proves that skepticism about the external world is misplaced."[21]

Kant arrives at the following four categories of the understanding: *quantity* (unity, plurality, totality), *quality* (reality, negation, limitation), *relation* (inherence-subsistence, cause and effect, and community), and *modality* (possibility-impossibility, existence-nonexistence, necessity-contingency).[22] "This is the listing of all original pure concepts of synthesis," he states, "that the understanding contains in itself *a priori*, and on account of which it is only a pure understanding; for by these concepts alone can it understand something in the manifold of intuition, i.e., think an object for it" (*CPR*, A 81/B 106). Note that among the *a priori* concepts included in this list is the category of relation, particularly that of cause and effect. This is a significant departure from Hume, as Kant himself states in the *Prolegomena to Any Future Metaphysics:* "This complete solution of the Humean problem, though coming out contrary to the surmise of the originator, thus restores to the pure concepts of the understanding their *a priori* origin . . . their possibility is founded solely in the relation of the understanding to experience: not, however, in such a way that they are derived from experience, but that experience is derived from them, a completely reversed type of connection that never occurred to *Hume*."[23] Cause and effect are categories proper to reason, not drawn from experience—the exact opposite of what Hume suggests in the *Enquiry*.

The transcendental discovery, however, is still a preparatory phase before Kant reaches the transcendental deduction in the second chapter of the Transcendental Analytic in the first Critique (*CPR*, A 84/B 117). The transcendental discovery lists the concepts of the understanding but stops short of the question of how exactly their objective validity fares when they are put into contact with experience. Here Kant must tread carefully, for although he has suggested that he has surmounted Hume's skepticism by locating certain concepts in the understanding rather than in experience, he must still account for experience nevertheless. One important distinction he makes to this end is that between *transcendental* and *empirical* deductions, or (1) the ways in which concepts in the human mind relate to all objects of experience *a priori* and (2) how concepts are acquired *through* experience and reflection on it (a clear reference to Hume), respectively (*CPR*, A 85/B 117).

21. Wilkerson, *Kant's "Critique of Pure Reason,"* 48.
22. See Höffe, *Immanuel Kant*, 69–73.
23. Kant, *Prolegomena*, 30.

One final piece of Kant's equation is the transcendental unity of apperception, or the unified experience of self-consciousness itself, which is assumed in both the transcendental discovery and deduction. All thought starts with a thinking subject, and a priori concepts are involved in the knowledge of all objects of experience. Consider this definition that appears in B 139 of the first Critique: "The transcendental unity of apperception is that unity through which all of the manifold given in an intuition is united in a concept of the object." Self-consciousness is united to external objects through a priori concepts in the context of intuitions (e.g., space and time). The picture that emerges from Kant's project, particularly in comparison to Hume's, is one in which the knower and the known are distinct but not necessarily estranged (as in Hume).

Refutation of Idealism

Just how exactly and to what extent the knower and the known remain distinct for Kant remains an issue of some contention; indeed, it is the heart of debates surrounding how best to characterize Kant's transcendental idealism. The term *idealism*, after all, is the noun in the term *transcendental idealism*, and *transcendental* is the adjective. So we are dealing with a species of idealism of some sort rather than a species of realism. On the other hand, Kant admits that the term *transcendental* is misleading and suggests in the *Prolegomena to Any Future Metaphysics* that a better term might have been "formal" [*formalen*] or "critical idealism" [*kritischen Idealism*] in order to better prevent confusion between his own system and those of Berkeley and Descartes:

> My so-called (properly, critical) idealism is therefore of a wholly peculiar kind, namely such that it overturns ordinary idealism, and such that by means of it all cognition *a priori* . . . first acquires objective reality, which, without my proven ideality of space and time, could not have been asserted by even the most zealous of realists. With matters standing so, I have wished that I could name this concept of mine something else, in order to prevent all misunderstanding; but this concept cannot be completely changed. I may therefore be permitted in the future, as has already been stated above, to call it formal, or better, critical idealism, in order to distinguish it from the dogmatic idealism of Berkeley and the skeptical idealism of Descartes.[24]

---

24. Kant, "On What Can Be Done in Order to Make Metaphysics as Science Actual," appendix to *Prolegomena to Any Future Metaphysics*, 126–27. The relationship between Kant's and Berkeley's thought remains a contested issue. See Justin, "On Kant's

Kant's idealism is neither pure realism nor pure idealism; it is a combination of both. Kant allows for the existence of real objects but also recognizes that knowing subjects necessarily contribute to the process of knowledge.

From the publication of the first edition of the first Critique, Kant fought against interpretations of his transcendental idealism that overemphasized its affinity with other idealisms. One of the classic loci of his clarifications in the second edition of the first Critique is the Refutation of Idealism, which is placed at the end of the Transcendental Analytic, the same section as the Transcendental Discovery and the Deduction of Categories. It contains some important qualifications concerning how Kant understood his own system.[25]

As in the *Prolegomena*, in the Refutation Kant makes an explicit effort to distinguish his idealism from that of Descartes and Berkeley specifically: "Idealism (I mean material idealism) is the theory that declares the existence of objects in space outside us to be either merely or doubtful and indemonstrable, or else false and impossible; the former is the problematic idealism of Descartes . . . ; the latter is the dogmatic idealism of Berkeley" (*CPR*, B 275). Kant, by contrast, admits that while the knowing mind unavoidably contributes to the process of knowledge, it does not follow that we must necessarily be skeptical of the products of knowledge (Descartes) or reduce the knowability of objects to our ideas of them (Berkeley). Kant rather offers a tertium quid with the following theorem: "The mere, but empirically determined, consciousness of my own existence proves the existence of objects in space outside me" (*CPR*, B 275). With this theorem, I take Kant to be conceding to both Descartes and Berkeley that while idealism plays a role in knowledge, this *facilitates* rather than *complicates* objective knowledge.

How does he support this claim? Kant returns to the initial qualifications about space and time that he makes in the Transcendental Aesthetic: if we encounter something through time and space, this itself *presupposes* the reality of an object outside myself precisely because the role that time and space play in knowledge is to mediate objects to us. This means two related things: the object of knowledge—the outer object that presents itself

---

Analysis of Berkeley," 20–32; Miller, "Kant and Berkeley," 315–55; Wilson, "Kant and the Dogmatic Idealism of Berkeley," 459–75; and the collected essays in Walker, *Real in the Ideal*.

25. On the Refutation, see Bader, "Role of Kant's Refutation of Idealism," 53–73; Chignell, "Can't Kant Cognize His Empirical Self?," 138–58; Dicker, "Kant's Refutation of Idealism," 80–108; Guyer, "Kant's Intentions in the Refutation of Idealism," 329–83; Oberst, "Kant, Epistemic Phenomenalism, and the Refutation of Idealism," 172–201; Turbayne, "Kant's Refutation of Dogmatic Idealism," 225–44.

to us for knowledge—must be real in itself, and it is not simply a figment of imagination. Kant states,

> I am conscious of my existence as determined in time. All time-determination presupposes something persistent in perception. This persistent thing, however, cannot be something in me, since my own existence in time cannot be determined only through this persistent thing. Thus the perception of this persistent thing is possible only through a thing outside me and not through the mere representation of a thing outside me. Consequently, the determination of my existence in time is possible only by means of the existence of actual things that I perceive outside myself. (*CPR*, B 275)

Self-consciousness, in other words, actually assumes the existence of objects; put differently, it is its own sort of evidence for real objects, which are "absolutely requisite" (*CPR*, B 277) for cognition in the "nexus of experience" [*dem Zusammenhange der Erfahrung*] (*CPR*, A 227/B 279). "My own existence," Höffe states, "perceived by inner sense, presupposes something permanent outside of me and hence presupposes the existence of external things. We therefore have experience and not just imagination of external objects."[26]

Fourth Paralogism

Kant still insists, however, that his system is a species of idealism, albeit distinct from that of Descartes's and Berkeley's. He emphasizes this in the Fourth Paralogism of the Transcendental Dialectic,[27] where he appears to potentially contradict some of his earlier comments when he states that "the existence of all objects of outer sense is doubtful. This uncertainty I call the ideality of outer appearances, and the doctrine of this ideality is called idealism" (*CPR*, A 367). Did Kant not just assert in the Refutation of Idealism, however, that objects of outer sense were *requisite* for cognition in the first place? How, then, can he now assert their doubtfulness?

This is a characteristic example of the hazards involved in attempting to navigate a middle way between two conventional epistemological options, which, it is important to recall, is Kant's stated intention in the first Critique.

---

26. Höffe, *Immanuel Kant*, 106.

27. On Kant, Descartes, and the Fourth Paralogism, see Dyck, *Kant and Rational Psychology*, chap. 6; Dyck, "The Divorce of Reason and Experience," 249–75; Kalter, *Kants vierter Paralogismus*; Priest, "Descartes, Kant, and Self-Consciousness," 348–51; Schwyzer, "Subjectivity in Descartes and Kant," 342–57.

In Kant's case, he assumes *both* that objects are requisite for cognition—a realism of sorts—*and also* that there are limitations to what we can know of them as they are in themselves—a basic tenet of idealism of any kind. Kant simply refuses to allow one assumption to negate the other; the process of knowledge is sufficiently complex to allow for both things to be true. "By an idealist, therefore," Kant clarifies, "one must understand not someone who denies the existence of external objects of sense, but rather someone who only does not admit that it is cognized through immediate perception and infers from this that we can never be fully certain of their reality from any possible experience" (*CPR*, A 368–69). Spatial and temporal objects are both transcendentally ideal and empirically real (*CPR*, A 34/B 51). What makes Kant's species of idealism unique among the other idealisms of his time is that it actually also assumes a realism; knowledge is governed by concepts, but this does not negate the reality of external objects: "Thus the transcendental idealist," Kant states, "is an empirical realist, and grants to matter, as appearance, a reality which need not be inferred, but is immediately perceived" (*CPR*, A 371).

A similar potential contradiction is found in just after the Fourth Paralogism in the Antinomy of Pure Reason, where Kant again seems to equivocate on the reality of external things more explicitly when he states, "We have sufficiently proved in the Transcendental Aesthetic that everything intuited in space or in time, hence all objects of an experience possible for us, are nothing but appearances, that is, mere representations, which, as they are represented, as extended beings or series of alterations, have outside our thoughts no existence grounded in itself. This doctrine I call *transcendental idealism*" (*CPR*, A 491/B 519). Once again it appears that Kant is denying that things in themselves possess their own existence apart from the mind of the knowing subject. But as in the Paralogisms, Kant is quick to qualify his position: "One would do us an injustice if one tried to ascribe to us that longdecried empirical idealism that, while assuming the proper reality of space, denies the existence of extended beings in it, or at least finds this existence doubtful, and so in this respect admits no satisfactorily provable distinction between dream and truth" (*CPR*, A 491/B 519). "Kant's break with the subjectivist tradition," Frederick Beiser states, "is final and complete."[28]

---

28. Beiser, *German Idealism*, 110.

Interpretive Options for Kant's Transcendental Idealism

There is hardly a consensus, then or now, on exactly how all of these pieces of Kant's transcendental idealism fit together to form a coherent whole and work together. Hardly so; as Lucy Allais notes, "Despite the centrality of transcendental idealism in Kant's thinking, in over two hundred years since the publication of the first Critique there is still no agreement on how to interpret the position. As Karl Ameriks dryly notes, 'Kant scholarship has yet to be overcome by a consensus.'"[29] All is not lost, however; at least two major interpretive positions have emerged in recent history of Kant interpretation, which I will refer to as "metaphysical" and "epistemological." Metaphysical readings emphasize the discontinuity between our knowledge of objects of experience and things as they are in themselves, and they dismiss Kant's metaphysical claims as incoherent. Epistemological readings are more sympathetic to Kant's metaphysical claims; they allow for more continuity between our knowledge of objects of experience and things as they are in themselves, but they also place an emphasis on the subjective conditions of knowledge. I will summarize each position below before turning to what I take to be a more promising third way proposed in recent years by Lucy Allais.

Metaphysical Criticisms

Metaphysical readings of Kant's transcendental idealism have a long and distinguished history. Some argue that they appear as early as the initial Garve-Feder review (1782), and they also appear in various versions of neo-Kantianism, which I will address in chapter 4. In twentieth-century Anglo Kant scholarship, however, it has exercised a considerable influence on Kant interpretation. P. F. Strawson's *Bounds of Sense*, which I will consider below, has become the standard work for metaphysical interpretations, but it was not without precedent in Harold Arthur Prichard's *The Philosophy of Immanuel Kant*, and it has continued to be advocated in recent years by Paul Guyer and, to a lesser extent, Rae Langton.

HAROLD ARTHUR PRICHARD

Prichard sets a high bar for his project when he indicates that he is interested not just in an examination of what Kant's transcendentalism *means* but whether it is actually *tenable* as a metaphysic. "The elucidation of Kant's

---

29. Allais, *Manifest Reality*, 3.

meaning, apart from any criticism," he states, "is impossible without a discussion on their own merits of the issues which he raises."[30] Prichard rightly identifies God, freedom, and immortality as central metaphysical concerns of Kant's critical project when he states that

> our faculty of knowledge is incapable of dealing with the objects of metaphysics proper, viz. God, freedom, and immortality, for the assumption [that objects must conform to our knowledge of them] limits our knowledge to objects of possible experience. But this very consequence, viz. the impossibility of metaphysics, serves to test and vindicate the assumption. For the view that our knowledge conforms to objects as things in themselves leads us into an insoluble contradiction when we go on, as we must, to seek for the unconditioned; while the assumption that objects must, as phenomena, conform to our way of representing them, removes the contradiction.[31]

This statement contains an incisive summary of an important conundrum in the first Critique: we ask metaphysical questions we are incapable of answering (*CPR*, A vii), and the fact that we face this conundrum in the first place itself suggests the problem of the possibility of metaphysics. Prichard's analysis of where exactly this problem leads, however, has significant ramifications for the integrity of Kant's project.

Prichard identifies two primary problems with Kant's transcendental idealism: (1) its inadequacy to according to its own rules and (2) its insignificance for epistemology. The argument for the inadequacy of Kant's metaphysical conundrum rests on the assumption that metaphysics must operate in Kant's critical philosophy according to the same (or at least similar) principles as mathematics. "The revolution in metaphysics *should have* consisted in the adoption of a similar procedure [to mathematics]," he states, "and advance *should have* been made dependent on the application of an at least quasi-mathematical method of the objects of metaphysics."[32] If the "objects" of metaphysics—God, freedom, and immortality—are to be known in an analogous way to mathematics, we should expect similar results: "since these objects are God, freedom, and immortality, the conclusion *should have been* that we ought to study God, freedom, and immortality by somehow constructing them in perception and thereby gaining insight into the necessity of certain relations. Success or failure in metaphysics would

---

30. Prichard, *Kant's Theory of Knowledge*, iii.
31. Prichard, *Kant's Theory of Knowledge*, 12.
32. Prichard, *Kant's Theory of Knowledge*, 13; emphasis added.

therefore consist simply in success or failure to see the necessity of the relations involved."[33]

What Kant actually does, according to Prichard, is to subsume the metaphysical principles of God, freedom, and immortality into the epistemological *conditions* of his transcendental idealism, where they simply conform to our own minds.[34] "If we wish to think out the nature of God, freedom, and immortality, we are not assisted by assuming that these objects must conform to the laws of our thinking," he states. "We must presuppose this conformity if we are to think at all, and consciousness of the presupposition puts us in no better position."[35] Because Kant's metaphysical questions cannot be answered in the same way mathematical questions can be answered, for Prichard, they disappear into irrelevance in the mind itself. Metaphysics, therefore, collapses under Kant's own rules.

Prichard's second criticism of Kant's transcendental idealism is that it is ultimately epistemologically insignificant. Prichard's central claim on this score is that Kant's "Copernican revolution" is not actually the revolution Kant claimed it to be but rather simply a reversal, or mirror image, of the procedure he presumes to be correcting. "The 'Copernican' revolution is not strictly the revolution which Kant supposes it to be," Prichard states.

> Kant only succeeds in stating the contrary of the ordinary view with any plausibility, because in doing so he makes the term object refer to something which like "knowledge" is within the mind. His position is that objects within the mind must conform to our general ways of knowing. For Kant, therefore, the conformity is not between something within and something without the mind, but between two realities within the mind, viz. the individual object, as object of perception, i.e. a phenomenon, and our general ways of perceiving and thinking.[36]

Kant's emphasis on the epistemological *conditions* of knowledge, for Prichard, *prevents* rather than *facilitates* our knowledge of the objects of perception. Kant must therefore conclude, according to this assumption, "that we do not know this object, i.e. the thing in itself, at all. Hence his real position should be stated by saying not that the ordinary view puts the conformity between mind and things in the wrong way, but that we ought not to speak of conformity at all. For the thing in itself being unknowable, our

---

33. Prichard, *Kant's Theory of Knowledge*, 13.
34. Prichard, *Kant's Theory of Knowledge*, 13.
35. Prichard, *Kant's Theory of Knowledge*, 14.
36. Prichard, *Kant's Theory of Knowledge*, 14–16.

ideas can never be made to conform to it."[37] In addition to being metaphysically inadequate, therefore, for Prichard, Kant's transcendental idealism is also epistemologically irrelevant if our aim is to know things as they are in themselves.

P. F. STRAWSON

P. F. Strawson levies similar criticisms of Kant's transcendental idealism in *The Bounds of Sense*. His central claim is that Kant's transcendental idealism is ultimately self-refuting. Strawson discerns three limiting concepts in Kant's transcendental idealism: two are necessary properties of it, and a third is a self-refuting consequence. They are as follows:

- A minimum epistemological structure—"concepts"—is necessary in order for us to make sense of experience and produce knowledge. (Empiricism violates this rule.)
- Extending those concepts beyond experience is meaningless. (Dogmatic rationalism violates this rule.)
- Kant, however, develops these concepts themselves not from experience but from an allegedly third-person perspective—a perspective beyond the bounds of experience—that is inconsistent with his own objectives. (Kant violates his own rule.)

According to Strawson, therefore, Kant's transcendental idealism violates its own principles. "Kant's arguments for these limiting conclusions," he states, "are developed within the framework of a set of doctrines which themselves appear to violate his own critical principles. He seeks to draw the bounds of sense from a point outside them, a point which, if they are rightly drawn, cannot exist."[38]

What and where is this "point outside the bounds of sense" Strawson discerns in Kant's system? Strawson detects it throughout the first Critique but focuses on the Antinomies (*CPR*, A 546–47/B 574–75), where Kant suggests that self-consciousness is a necessary property of understanding and reason. This is a problem for Strawson because every human being becomes aware of self-consciousness at a particular point in time and space. Yet Kant, according to Strawson, is claiming to have discerned *a*temporal concepts within the confines of temporal self-consciousness. "There immediately arise, on Kant's own principles, the objections, first, that anything which

37. Prichard, *Kant's Theory of Knowledge*, 16.
38. Strawson, *Bounds of Sense*, 11–12.

can be ascribed to a man as a case or instance of such self-consciousness must be something which occurs in time and, second, that it must be consciousness *of* himself as reasoning or recognizing or thinking something, as intellectually engaged at some point, or over some stretch, of time."[39] Kant's attempts at suprasensible knowledge, for Strawson, are themselves necessarily tethered to time and space and never get off the ground. "The identity of the empirically self-conscious subject and the real or supersensible subject . . . is simply assumed without being made a whit more intelligible."[40]

According to Strawson, therefore, Kant's idealism necessarily transgresses the boundaries it sets for itself. Even though that is the case, however, Strawson further alleges that Kant's attempt to draw these boundaries in the first place was actually *unnecessary*. Why attempt to delineate, as Kant did, a *general* transcendental idealism to which all particular efforts at cognition ultimately refer? "I see no reason why any high doctrine at all should be necessary here," Strawson states. "The set of ideas, or schemes of thought, employed by human beings reflect, of course, their nature, their needs and their situation. . . . But it is no matter for wonder if conceivable variations are intelligible only as variations within a certain fundamental general framework of ideas. . . . There is nothing here to demand, or permit, an explanation such as Kant's."[41]

Paul Guyer and Rae Langton

In *Kant and the Claims of Knowledge*, Paul Guyer suggests that Kant's transcendental idealism, particularly its references to non-spatiotemporal things in themselves, is not inadequate, irrelevant, or unnecessary but rather *unsuccessful*: "None of Kant's arguments for the nonspatiality and nontemporality of things in themselves, certainly none of his arguments from legitimate claims of the transcendental theory of experience, succeeds."[42] Specifically, Guyer alleges, "there is not a single sound argument in his mature philosophy which can prove that the forms of intuition and judgment which we know *a priori* are *imposed* on otherwise formless objects of experience, rather than being forms which those objects do possess on their own and in virtue of which *they* thereby satisfy the necessary conditions for our own experience."[43]

---

39. Strawson, *Bounds of Sense*, 248.
40. Strawson, *Bounds of Sense*, 249.
41. Strawson, *Bounds of Sense*, 44.
42. Guyer, *Kant and the Claims of Knowledge*, 335.
43. Guyer, *Kant and the Claims of Knowledge*, 342–43.

Kant's system, for Guyer, is unsuccessful first because it rests on *a priori* presuppositions that Kant never actually succeeds in establishing. Furthermore, the arguments that Kant makes *based on* those presuppositions do not actually ever establish what Kant seeks to argue. Kant's transcendental idealism, for Guyer, is not a *solution* for the epistemological dilemmas Kant discerns in the first Critique but rather precisely those dilemmas writ large: "When [Kant] argued for transcendental idealism, what he swallowed was not the antidote but the poison."[44]

Among the metaphysical readings of Kant's transcendental idealism, Rae Langton's *Kantian Humility* is the most optimistic regarding Kant's project. Langton is not interested in demonstrating, in other words, the inadequacy, irrelevance, superfluity, or failure of Kant's transcendental idealism. Rather she grants Kant the benefit of the doubts that Prichard, Strawson, and Guyer cast on him. "He said that there is a distinction between appearances and things in themselves, that things in themselves exist, and that we have no knowledge of things in themselves. This has seemed to come dangerously close to nonsense . . . that he did not mean quite what he said," she notes. "It seems unlikely, though," she continues, "that a philosopher did not mean to say what he said, when he said it over and over again."[45]

What about Langton's reading of Kant, however, makes it *metaphysical*? The answer is found in the fact that she allows for the hypothetical existence of things in themselves *beyond* the confines of the conceptual apparatuses of human knowledge. "Things in themselves exist, and affect us, *and* we have no knowledge of things as they are in themselves. That is to say, there exist things that have intrinsic properties, and they affect us by means of their forces, and we have no knowledge of their intrinsic properties."[46] What other metaphysical readers of Kant have taken to be contradictory— (1) things in themselves exist; (2) we have no knowledge of things in themselves—Langton takes as complementary. The complementary nature of these premises, for Langton, provide "an explanation for why Kant believes things can be objects of possible experience when they can never be seen, or heard, or tasted, or touched: we have an explanation for Kant's striking realism about *the unseen realm*."[47]

---

44. Guyer, *Kant and the Claims of Knowledge*, 344.
45. Langton, *Kantian Humility*, 2.
46. Langton, *Kantian Humility*, 205.
47. Langton, *Kantian Humility*, 205; emphasis added.

Epistemological Readings

While metaphysical readings of Kant's transcendental idealism have held sway for much of the twentieth century, they have not been without their critics. An initial concern was raised in 1962 with Graham Bird's *Kant's Theory of Knowledge*, which offered a direct rejoinder to Prichard's book by the same name. Robert Pippin advanced a significant epistemological reading in 1982 with his *Kant's Theory of Form*, but Henry Allison's *Kant's Transcendental Idealism*, originally published in 1983 with a revised and expanded edition in 2004, would prove to be the *de facto* text for non-metaphysical, or "deflationary," readings of Kant.

Graham Bird

"Prichard's *Kant's Theory of Knowledge*," Graham Bird states, "provided . . . more genuine philosophical interest and argument than most commentaries on Kant; but he almost always misunderstood Kant's views."[48] Thus begins one of the first offensives against the default metaphysical readings of the twentieth century. Bird's concern with Prichard's reading of Kant is twofold: (1) Prichard's account of Kant's epistemological constructivism and (2) his failure to distinguish between Kant's empirical and transcendental modes of inquiry.

By Prichard's "epistemological constructivism," Bird is referring to Prichard's assumption that metaphysical knowledge, for Kant, works analogously to mathematical knowledge. According to this view, mathematical principles offer a guide to "connecting," or "constructing" the link between, perceiving subjects and phenomena in the physical world. According to Prichard, this is impossible, therefore Kant's system fails. According to Bird, however, Kant never intended to suggest this. Rather Kant makes a distinction between construction and *synthesis*, and even his account of construction, as in mathematical knowledge, was not always intended to be taken literally. "The term 'Construction,'" Bird states, "is explicitly restricted by Kant to use in the context of mathematics (B 867), and elsewhere (e.g. B 741 ff.) is treated as a concept referring quite specifically to mathematics. . . . Kant's account of construction, even in the context of the application of mathematical concepts or models, is not a straightforwardly literal construction of objects in the physical world."[49]

---

48. Bird, *Kant's Theory of Knowledge*, x.
49. Bird, *Kant's Theory of Knowledge*, 7–8.

Bird also raises the important distinction, which Prichard overlooks, between empirical and transcendental inquiry. Previously I suggested that according to Prichard, because Kant's metaphysical questions cannot be answered in the same manner that mathematical questions can be answered, they disappear into irrelevance. Metaphysics, according to this picture, collapses under Kant's own rules. But *does* Kant intend for metaphysical knowledge to operate according to the same, or even similar, rules as mathematical knowledge? Does Kant intend, in other words, for metaphysical principles to be *demonstrable*? Bird rightly suggests that Kant does not in fact intend this. Indeed, he notes that "Kant tried hard to avoid the misleading features of his terminology by explicitly distinguishing his task from that which he believed Locke to have undertaken. In the passage at B 118–20, Kant distinguishes between an empirical enquiry into the origins of ideas, such as Locke's, and a transcendental enquiry into the status of concepts, such as his."[50] Repeatedly in the first Critique, Kant makes it clear that his intention is to pursue a *transcendental* project, not an empirical one. In so doing, according to Bird, "Kant rejects the empirical and chooses the transcendental enquiry. . . . It is plain that Kant spent much time considering what kind of enquiry he was engaged on, and firmly rejected the claim that it was an empirical investigation into the origin of our ideas."[51] Kant's project is primarily transcendental, not empirical.

Robert Pippin

In his *Kant's Theory of Form*, Robert Pippin takes a step back from these details and suggests that many of the disputes in secondary literature on Kant's transcendental idealism are a consequence of a more general failure to appreciate the central concept of *formality* in the first Critique. "Kant's theory of transcendental reasoning and argumentation," he states,

> has been called everything from a discovery of the Absolute to a disguised version of "verificationism." In the face of this diversity, it seemed to me that no progress at all on this issue could be made without a detailed examination, in Kant's terms . . . of the most obvious and fundamental aspect of "transcendental reflection"—its formality, Kant's claim to have discovered only the "forms" of experience.[52]

---

50. Bird, *Kant's Theory of Knowledge*, 10.
51. Bird, *Kant's Theory of Knowledge*, 10.
52. Pippin, *Kant's Theory of Form*, x.

Upon examination, the first Critique is replete with references to the concept of "formality"; indeed, Pippin notes, "this emphasis on formality is probably what most of all distinctively characterizes his theories of a priori cognitive, moral, and aesthetic judgments."[53]

What exactly does Pippin intend by the term "formality"? One approach is to define the term by what it is *not*. Pippin notes that Kant clearly intends to distinguish his project from the epistemologies of Descartes, Locke, Spinoza, and Leibniz, who were all still too closely tied to traditional metaphysical formulations—of mind and substance, for instance—to have really achieved anything truly "new" in epistemology. Kant's formalism, whatever it might be, is "not tied to empirical psychology or to rationalist theories of mind."[54] What of its positive definition? According to Pippin, statements of Kant's such as, "Pure intuition contains therefore simply the *form* under which something is intuited, and a pure concept only the *form* of the thought of an object in general" (*CPR*, A 51/B 75) suggests that Kant is primarily concerned with *how* things are known rather than with the *objects* of knowledge (and by extension, whether we can actually claim to have knowledge of them) per se. Kant's transcendental idealism is, in other words, a method *of* knowledge, not a comprehensive metaphysical system concerned with prescribing and proscribing what can and cannot be known. "Kant means by this notion of form that his analysis will concentrate on *how* human beings experience (insofar as such modes can be established necessarily and a priori) and less on *what* is known."[55]

One of the merits of Pippin's reading is that is redirects the focus of readings of Kant's transcendental idealism away from its metaphysical successes or failures and toward a more modest aim: its *epistemological contours*. In this sense, it "deflates"—in a positive way—the expectations readers might bring to what Kant actually says. If we are expecting a comprehensive *metaphysical system* when we approach Kant's first Critique, we are bound to be disappointed—as, perhaps, Prichard, Strawson, and Guyer have been. If we approach his text with more moderate expectations, however, according to Pippin, we will be in a better position to understand what exactly it was he was trying to convey. Such "deflationary" readings can now lay claim to their own legitimacy thanks to the groundwork of critics such as Bird and Pippin, but the most influential and persuasive deflationary reading in recent years is that of Henry Allison's *Kant's Transcendental Idealism*.

---

53. Pippin, *Kant's Theory of Form*, ix.
54. Pippin, *Kant's Theory of Form*, 4.
55. Pippin, *Kant's Theory of Form*, 8.

Henry Allison

Allison takes as his starting point the familiar fault line in discussions of Kant's transcendental idealism between things in themselves and their appearances to us. For metaphysical interpreters, this discrepancy is the point at which they exit the system. "The manifest untenability of transcendental idealism, as they understand it," Allison states, "has led to some critics attempting to save Kant from himself, by separating what they take to be a legitimate core of Kantian argument . . . from the excess baggage of transcendental idealism, with which they believe it to be encumbered."[56] Of the non-metaphysical readings I have considered so far, Allison's is the most explicit not just is what it denies but also what it affirms: Allison denies the "separability" of Kant's transcendental idealism from the other philosophical insights of the first Critique—a separation that Strawson, Guyer, and Langton affirm in order to salvage the rest of Kant's work from his allegedly incoherent metaphysical claims: and instead affirms its "discursivity": "transcendental idealism is grounded in a reflection on the *a priori* conditions of human cognition (what I term 'epistemic conditions') rather than, as in other forms of idealism (for example, Berkeley's), on the ontological status of what is known."[57] Kant's transcendental idealism, for Allison, is not a grand metaphysical system but rather "a doctrine of epistemological modesty."[58] It does not, pace Prichard and Strawson, *separate* the process of knowledge into two different objects (or "worlds")—the representation of an object in cognition, on the one hand, and the object of cognition in itself, on the other—but rather describes *two aspects* of the same object in the process of cognition.

This distinction between "dual object" and "dual aspect" readings is important grist for Allison's mill, and it is also a fixture of contemporary discussions of Kant's transcendental idealism. It allows Allison to emphasize the *epistemic conditions of* Kant's transcendental idealism—specifically, the categories themselves *as* epistemic conditions—rather than its alleged metaphysical implications. Allison characterizes epistemic conditions as follows: "a necessary condition for the representation of objects, that is, a condition without which we our representations would not relate to objects or, equivalently, possess objective reality."[59] It also allows Allison to emphasize the *objectivating function of* these epistemic conditions, an important

---

56. Allison, *Kant's Transcendental Idealism*, 3.
57. Allison, *Kant's Transcendental Idealism*, xv.
58. Allison, *Kant's Transcendental Idealism*, xvi.
59. Allison, *Kant's Transcendental Idealism*, 11.

correlative feature of Allison's view. This objectivating function, according to Allison, is what qualifies Kant's transcendental idealism as a species of idealism and also what makes it unique; without it, epistemic conditions *simpliciter* would be nothing new. Epistemic conditions are not merely receptive but also actively *contribute to,* or "objectivate," our knowledge of objects itself. The crucial difference of Allison's dual-aspect view is that this objectivating function affects the *subjective conditions of* knowledge rather than the objects of knowledge themselves. Kant's famous statement that "objects must conform to our cognition" (*CPR*, B xvi), for Allison, means that "objects must conform to the conditions of their *representation*; not that they exist in the mind in the manner of Berkeleian ideas or the sense data of the phenomenalists."[60]

Epistemic conditions and their objectivating functions are the twin gears that turn Allison's discursivity thesis, which is the heart of his dual-aspect view. Kant's transcendental idealism, for Allison, involves discursive negotiation between subjective concepts and the objects that present themselves to us for knowledge. "Cognition requires that an object somehow be given to the mind. . . . In Kant's terminology, this means that it must be present (or presentable) in intuition, by which he understands a singular representation that is immediately related to its object."[61] An object's givenness to the mind and the mind's representation of it are two sides of the same coin—two aspects of the same discursive process—not two different coins. This means that "sensibility is merely receptive and, therefore, capable of providing only the raw data for cognition," and "it *also* means that the very possibility of discursive cognition requires that the data be presented by sensibility in a manner suitable for conceptualization."[62]

An important consequence of this way of viewing the central conundrum of Kant's transcendental idealism—as an epistemological rather than metaphysical problem—is that it makes Kant's system "a viable philosophical option, still worthy of consideration."[63] "Deflating" Kant's transcendental idealism of the metaphysical attributes incorrectly attributed to it, furthermore, reveals the intriguing possibility that the central problems associated with Kant's system might turn out not to be problems at all but rather positive conduits to knowledge itself. "That Kant viewed the transcendental distinction between things as they appear and the same things as they are in themselves as a major philosophical discovery is undeniable. It is likewise

---

60. Allison, *Kant's Transcendental Idealism*, 12; emphasis added.
61. Allison, *Kant's Transcendental Idealism*, 13; emphasis added.
62. Allison, *Kant's Transcendental Idealism*, 14.
63. Allison, *Kant's Transcendental Idealism*, 4.

undeniable that he regarded the limitation of cognition to the former as a consequence of this distinction. Nevertheless," Allison continues, "it would be more accurate to say that he viewed this limitation as liberating or therapeutic rather than depressing."[64]

A Third Way: Lucy Allais

Epistemological readings of Kant's transcendental idealism have attempted to salvaged Kant's critical philosophy from its alleged inadequacy, irrelevance, superfluity, and failure. Allison's dual-aspect reading in particular has exercised considerable influence in contemporary discussions of Kant's transcendental idealism, such that readers have typically had to choose between *either* metaphysical *or* epistemological readings. In recent years, however, a third approach has surfaced that suggests readers might not in fact have to make this choice; Kant's transcendental idealism, that is, by definition contains *both* metaphysical *and* epistemological features. This reading has been advanced by Lucy Allais's 2015 *Manifest Reality*, in which she argues that "Kant's position is a careful combination of realism and idealism, and of metaphysical and epistemological claims."[65]

Allais begins her argument by acknowledging that despite the importance of Kant's transcendental idealism for Kant's critical philosophy, not to mention for its significance in early modern philosophy in general, there is still no consensus on how exactly to interpret it. "Recent publications," she notes, "continue to represent such a wide spectrum of views that it sometimes scarcely seems possible that they are all interpretations of a single position, put forward by a single philosopher, primarily in a single book."[66] For the purposes of her project, she notes that interpretations have tended to swing between two pendulums: idealist-realist and metaphysical-epistemological—and there are good textual reasons for each position, as well as varieties of combinations of them.[67] The question then, for Allais, becomes one of *emphasis*. While Kant's project is clearly epistemological, for instance, that does not mean that it is devoid of metaphysical concerns. Hardly so. "While some of Kant's central concerns are epistemological," she states, "his transcendental idealism must be understood as containing substantial metaphysical commitments to the mind-dependence of things as

---

64. Allison, *Kant's Transcendental Idealism*, 19.
65. Allais, *Manifest Reality*, 11.
66. Allais, *Manifest Reality*, 3.
67. Allais, *Manifest Reality*, 5.

they appear to us, and to the existence of an aspect of reality that grounds the appearance of things, and which we cannot cognize."[68]

Allais's objective, then, is to offer a reading of Kant's transcendental idealism that avoids purely deflationary readings, which she takes to avoid the metaphysical dimensions of his project, and also Strawsonian readings, which she takes to overemphasize the discrepancy between non-sensible, non-spatiotemporal things in themselves and their appearances in our cognitive faculties. Instead, she states her position as follows: "I argue for a moderate metaphysical interpretation which sees Kant as holding that the things of which we have knowledge have a way they are in themselves that is not cognizable by us, and that the appearances of these things are genuinely mind-dependent, while not existing merely in the mind."[69] One benefit of this view is that it is able to account for the many subtle distinctions Kant makes throughout the first *Critique*; for instance, he is clearly an idealist of some sort, yet he goes to great length, particularly in the B edition, to distance himself from Berkeley. "He insists," Allais notes, "that his transcendental idealism is also an empirical realism."[70] In the end, she states, "There are strong grounds for thinking that Kant is an idealist who is also committed to the existence of an aspect of reality that we cannot know. There are also strong grounds for thinking Kant is neither a phenomenalist nor a noumenalist. My interpretation accommodates both sides of Kant's thought."[71]

Allais supports her general argument by two sub-arguments, which I will refer to as the *cognition sub-argument* and the *perceptual sub-argument*. The cognition sub-argument has two stages: (1) Kant's transcendental idealism is concerned with *cognition* rather than *knowledge*, and (2) cognition is dependent entirely on Kant's account of *intuition*.[72] The perceptual sub-argument clarifies what *sort* of cognition Kant intends. Emphasizing cognition—*Erkenntnis*—is important for Allais because "what is relevant to whether or not something qualifies as cognition is not whether it has some special kind of justification or warrant, but rather the kind of representation of objects with which it is able to provide us." Why is this important?

---

68. Allais, *Manifest Reality*, 7.
69. Allais, *Manifest Reality*, 9.
70. Allais, *Manifest Reality*, 9.
71. Allais, *Manifest Reality*, 10–11. *Phenomenalism* and *noumenalism* are Allais's preferred terms for referring to metaphysical readings of the Strawsonian variety. Noumenalist metaphysical readings, for Allais, emphasize nonspatiotemporal objects, while phenomenalist metaphysical readings emphasize our mental representations of them (7).
72. Allais, *Manifest Reality*, 11.

Because, she states, "both at the empirical and the a priori level, Kant's primary concern is with what it takes for us to achieve a certain kind of objective representation of the world (cognition), rather than with what kind of warrant is required for knowledge."[73] In order to achieve cognition, we must be actually *acquainted* with objects, and this is possible only through *intuition*, which mediate objects to our cognition: "Kantian intuitions are representations that give us acquaintance with objects, and . . . since he thinks cognition requires intuition, he thinks our cognition is limited to that which we can have acquaintance: what can be presented to us in conscious experience."[74] Cognition through acquaintance with objects through intuition, for Allais, paves the way for her second sub-argument, which is that Kant's transcendental idealism is best characterized on a *relational* rather than *indirect* account of perception, that is, a "mental state . . . which involves the presence to consciousness of the object perceived. . . . The presence to consciousness of the object is part of what makes the mental state the state that it is."[75]

One benefit of Allais's approach is that it is consistent with Kant's own stated intentions at the beginning of the first Critique to forge a middle way between the extremes of dogmatic metaphysics, which lacks epistemological rigor, and the twin errors of skeptical epistemology and idealism, which ignore the possibilities of metaphysics (*CPR*, B xxxiv). Her approach also demonstrates an exegetical fidelity to the text of the first Critique that avoids over- or under-emphasizing certain passages to fit a single, preferred theory. There is an additional benefit, however, that has considerable consequences for interpreting Kant's transcendental idealism: her account of Kant's acquaintance-based cognition allows for positive metaphysical insights. This will strike readers of Kant as a curious claim, but that is due in no small part to the fact that readers of Kant have grown accustomed to having to choose between *either* metaphysical readings *or* epistemological readings. Kant's particular form of idealism, on this account, "is not established by, but rather makes possible, the explanation of metaphysics."[76] Kant's idealism, in other words, allows for rather than prohibits metaphysical insights.

73. Allais, *Manifest Reality*, 13.
74. Allais, *Manifest Reality*, 11.
75. Allais, *Manifest Reality*, 12.
76. Allais, *Manifest Reality*, 300–301. One potential problem with Allais's argument for my own is that her model in *Manifest Reality* only allows for metaphysics within the realm of empirical cognition. It is important to bear in mind, however, that her argument is restricted to the first Critique on its own terms, and she acknowledges that "there is much more to the Kantian position than this, and there are a number of ways in which bringing it in relation to other works will require development of the

Conclusion

Interpreters of Kant's transcendental idealism face a number of challenges. Not only must they take account of Kant's own arguments, which Wilkerson alleges are "badly organized, repetitive, and sometimes contradictory,"[77] but they must also sift through a variety of seemingly irreconcilable secondary readings. Metaphysical accounts have proliferated in the twentieth century. In Prichard's case, the conditions of knowledge Kant identifies obscure rather than facilitate knowledge; we cannot claim to have knowledge of things as they are in themselves, and metaphysics collapses into epistemology. For Strawson, Kant's transcendental idealism transgresses its own strictures. Epistemological readings, by contrast, have called these emphases into question and proposed new interpretive solutions to old dilemmas. Graham Bird addressed Prichard's concerns directly, while Pippin redirects readers to Kant's *method* rather than its precise *results*. Allison, crucially, rejects that Kant's transcendental idealism can be separated from the rest of Kant's system and enjoins readers to consider a "dual aspect" rather than "dual object" view of Kant's project. Recent readings, such as that of Lucy Allais, hold yet more promise for understanding what exactly it was that Kant was trying to do, not least because her reading accounts for *both* the metaphysical aspects of Kant's transcendental idealism *and* its epistemological structure. These are imperative clarifications for understanding Kant's transcendental idealism on its own terms, but as I will argue in the next chapter, they are also necessary building blocks for understanding his views on how and to what extent God can be known.

---

position" (307–8). She mentions his account of the possibility of the freedom of the will specifically, which I take to be a metaphysical issue, and Kant's account of God (and immortality) is closely related to this. Her account, as I read it, does preclude nonempirical metaphysical insights *in the first Critique*, but it does allow for further metaphysical insights to be developed when other texts, such as the second Critique, are taken into account, as Kanterian also notes in *Kant, God, and Metaphysics*, xii. And starting with an account of Kant's transcendental idealism that assumes realism rather than antirealism is an important building block in the process of approaching his metaphysical insights in the second Critique and beyond.

77. Wilkerson, *Kant's "Critique of Pure Reason,"* 47.

2

The Secret Thorn
Kant and Theology

FOR MUCH OF THE twentieth century, readings of Kant's relationship to religion have been overwhelmingly pessimistic on a number of fronts. As Chris Firestone summarizes, the first Critique, allegedly, "cuts off all access to knowledge of God, and, in so doing, demolishes not only the foundations for dogmatic metaphysics, but also the foundations for any kind of positive theology whatsoever."[1] Kant's critical philosophy issues in agnosticism because, as Firestone summarizes, "there exists an impassable boundary between the experience of human beings and the 'reality' of noumenal beings, a boundary so deep and wide that not even the highest possible being—God—could traverse it. If God did traverse it and in some way attempt to become manifest to us, we could never know or even reasonably believe that it was God."[2] God is, at best, a leftover postulate of the critical philosophy that has been relegated to "morally based convictions not amounting to knowledge," according to Strawson.[3]

Such readings largely assume a *metaphysical* reading of the first Critique, however. But as I have suggested in the previous chapter, metaphysical readings are not the only viable readings of Kant's critical philosophy. If a metaphysical reading is *not* assumed, theology takes on a renewed significance not only for Kant's critical philosophy but his entire philosophical corpus. A new generation of readers sympathetic to this interpretation emerged in the 1970s, such as Allen Wood, Michel Despland, and Ronald M.

---

1. Firestone, *Kant and Theology*, 1–8.

2. Firestone, *Kant and Theology*, 2. Additional examples of this line of interpretation include Savage, "Kant's Rejection of Divine Revelation"; Ward, *Development of Kant's View of Ethics*; Cupitt, "Kant and the Negative Theology"; Ray, *Subjectivity and Irreligion*; Yovel, *Kant and the Philosophy of History*; Michalson, *Fallen Freedom*; Wolterstorff, "Conundrums in Kant's Rational Religion"; Wolterstorff, "Is It Possible and Desirable?," 1–18; Quinn, "Christian Atonement and Kantian Justification," 188–202; Quinn, "Saving Faith from Kant's Remarkable Antinomy," 418–33. I will address Wolterstorff's concerns specifically in the final chapter.

3. Strawson, *Bounds of Sense*, 240–41.

Green.[4] Additional alternative readings by Ann Loades, Stephen Palmquist, Bernard Reardon, Adina Davidovich, John E. Hare, and Elizabeth Cameron Gailbraith emerged in the 1980s and 1990s, and at the turn of the century, a renewed effort at rehabilitating Kant's theological significance has been undertaken by Chris Firestone, Nathan Jacobs, James Joiner, Christopher Insole, and others.[5]

In this chapter, my intention is to continue to explore the possibilities that these readings have opened and to emphasize the *positive* theological characteristics of three strategically significant moments in Kant's corpus: the critical philosophy, *Religion within the Bounds of Mere Reason*, and his later *Lectures on Philosophical Theology*. The Kant that emerges from these reflections, I will argue, is an asset to theology rather than the liability he is often taken to be.

God in the Critical Philosophy

The ideas of freedom, immortality, and God occupy a place of outsized importance in Kant's critical philosophy. They occur to the mind as knowing subjects come into contact with empirical reality through reason (*Vernuft*). We are immediately faced with a dilemma, however, according to Kant, because pure speculative reason lacks the ability to specify or define freedom, immortality, and God beyond the initial idea of them. They are questions we cannot answer through pure speculative reason, he states in the preface to the first edition of the first Critique, but they are also questions we cannot avoid asking: "Human reason has the peculiar fate in one species of its cognitions that it is burdened with questions which it cannot dismiss, since they are given to it as problems by the nature of reason itself, but which it also cannot answer, since they transcend every capacity of human reason" (*CPR*, A vii).

Quo vadis? The short answer to this question is that *pure speculative reason requires the supplementation of pure* practical *reason*. Through moral experience, pure practical reason supplies content for the theoretical but incomplete ideas of pure speculative reason, which pure speculative reason then reassimilates into its conceptual framework. This is a complex and

---

4. Wood, *Kant's Moral Religion*; Despland, *Kant on History and Religion*; Green, *Religious Reason*; Green, *Religion and Moral Reason*.

5. Loades, *Kant and Job's Comforters*; Palmquist, *Kant's System of Perspectives*; Palmquist, *Kant's Critical Religion*; Reardon, *Kant as Philosophical Theologian*; Davidovich, *Religion as a Province of Meaning*; Hare, *Moral Gap*; Gailbraith, *Kant and Theology*; Firestone et al., *Kant and the Question of Theology*; Insole, *Kant and the Creation of Freedom*; Insole, *Intolerable God*; Insole, *Kant and the Divine*.

highly nuanced process in general for Kant, and the particular ideas of the freedom of the will, the immortality of the soul, and the existence of God play their own unique roles in his general scheme.

Recall that one of Kant's objectives with the first Critique is to find a middle route *forward* for metaphysics in an age of both enthusiasm and skepticism (*CPR*, B 128). Dogmatic answers to the questions of the freedom, immortality, and God neglect a prior critique of pure reason; skeptics, on the other hand, have an easy way around these questions: because the ideas of freedom, immortality, and God do not arise from sense experience, there is little if anything we can say about them. Kant is dissatisfied with both these answers. Pure speculative reason untethered from experience runs into contradictions and confusion, but pure practical reason requires pure speculative reason to make sense of experience. Kant somehow needs to both (1) steer a middle course between dogmatism and skepticism, and (2) account for what we might call the great "imperial" questions of existence: freedom, God, and immortality. Kant begins to address the first matter through his doctrine of transcendental idealism, which I covered in the previous chapter: by sorting out reason's *internal* contradictions *apart from* experience. For the second matter as it appears in Kant's critical philosophy, I'll first consider the first two sections of the first Critique's Canon of Pure Reason (*CPR*, A 795/B 823—A 831/B 859) and then turn to the second book of the first part of the *Critique of Practical Reason*.

The Canon of Pure Reason

Kant begins the first section of the Canon with a question: what is the ultimate end of the use of our pure reason? (*CPR*, A 797/B 825). The threefold answer is: solving the problems of the freedom of the will, the immortality of the soul, and the existence of God. Kant is not subtle in his estimation of the centrality of these ideas for philosophy: "the entire armament of reason, in the undertaking that one can call pure philosophy," he states, "is in fact directed only at the three problems that have been mentioned" (*CPR*, A 800/B 828). Pure theoretical reason constantly recommends these three questions to us, but as we have seen, it lacks the ability to answer them. The meaning and content of these ideas, then, must come from pure practical reason. For Kant, the locus of practical reason's information about these ideas is in *the moral law* as it pertains to free choice (*liberum arbitrium*).

Kant suggests that all human reason—speculative and practical—asks three guiding questions in its efforts to answer the larger questions of freedom, God, and immortality: *What can I know? What should I do? What may*

I hope? The first two questions are purely speculative and purely practical, respectively. The third question—*What may I hope?*—concerns both speculative and practical reason, and as I read it, it serves as both a bridge between the questions of theoretical and practical reason and pure practical reason's reference beyond itself. Morality, for Kant, has a telos, a transcendent reference: hope. "All hope concerns happiness," Kant states, and "happiness is the satisfaction of all our inclinations" (*CPR*, A 805/B 834—A 806/B 835). The questions of what I should do and what I may hope, in other words, cannot be separated; thus his maxim for human action is not "What makes me happy?" but rather "What will make me *most worthy of* happiness?" Practical reason is not a self-enclosed system; it is driven by the ideal of a highest good—the unity of happiness and virtue—which is by definition bound up with the idea of God and the possibility of future happiness (*CPR*, A 811/B 839). If the highest good is to be realized, God must exist, the will must be free, and the soul must be immortal.

Kant takes it for granted that some sort of basic, objective, necessary, and universal moral order exists, and he does not defend this assumption. As I suggested in the preceding paragraph, he furthermore holds that this moral order has some sort of unified telos and purpose. This, for Kant, presupposes some sort of highest original good, some supreme cause—something that "grounds, conserves, and completes the order of things that is universal though well hidden from us in the sensible world"—and this is where the practical concept of God is to be found in the world of sense. Kant calls this presupposition *moral theology*: "It inexorably leads to the concept of a single, most perfect, and rational primordial being, of which speculative theology could not on objective grounds give us even a hint, let alone convince us" (*CPR*, A 814/B 842). Speculative reason commends the concept to us but cannot demonstrate it; practical reason, on the other hand, finds it to be entirely consistent with its highest and most hopeful and noble efforts: acting in such a way as to be worthy of happiness.

Critique of Practical Reason

We have reached what Kant refers to a "high point" in his system, and he continues the discussion in the second book of the second Critique. Here Kant returns to the ideas of freedom, God, and immortality and again offers them as examples of both the limits of pure speculative reason and its need for practical reason to provide an adequate basis for belief that it cannot acquire through speculation alone. Recall that pure speculative reason, for Kant, is not self-sufficient; it is only one part of an incomplete "circuit" that is completed by practical reason (*CPrR*, pref.). The concept of freedom in particular, Kant states, is even the cornerstone of pure theoretical reason, but pure theoretical reason cannot affirm it; it is dependent on practical reason for this. Pure reason is tethered to practical reason, and this is not a negative thing for Kant; rather it prevents speculative reason from engaging in metaphysical "mischief" (*CPrR*, 2.2.3).

Practical reason presents what Kant refers to as *postulates* to theoretical reason, which theoretical reason then assimilates into its transcendental categories. Postulates, for Kant, are necessary in order for reason to complete its theoretical-practical circuit; they provide the practical content for speculative concepts. Transcendental concepts without practical postulates are simply empty concepts; practical reason supplies this content for the transcendental concepts. Postulates, Kant states,

> give objective reality to the ideas of speculative reason in general (by means of their reference to what is practical) and justify its holding concepts even the possibility of which it could not otherwise presume to affirm. These postulates are those of immortality, of freedom considered positively (as the causality of a being insofar as it belongs to the intelligible world), and of the existence of God. The first flows from the practically necessary condition of a duration befitting the complete fulfillment of the moral law; the second from the necessary presupposition of independence from the sensible world and of the capacity to determine one's will by the law of an intelligible world, that is, the law of freedom; the third from the necessity of the condition for such an intelligible world to be the highest good, through the presupposition of the highest independent good, that is, of the existence of God. (*CPrR*, 1.2.6)

Kant's Deontological Theism

This is an important juncture in Kant's critical philosophy: he has just stated that the existence of God is to be *presupposed*, and this is worthy of further consideration. Postulates qua postulates fall short of apodictic certainty, but they are necessary to belief; in Kant's system, it becomes subjectively necessary to believe things that cannot necessarily be proven because pure speculative reason lacks content, and practical reason needs beliefs to invest experience with meaning and validate moral experience. Kant actually goes so far as suggest that practical reason not only *can* postulate freedom, God, and immortality to pure speculative reason but is actually *obligated* to do so: "There is in us not merely the *warrant* but also the *necessity*, as a need connected with duty, to presuppose the possibility of this highest good, which, since it is possible only under the condition of the existence of God, connects the presupposition of the existence of God inseparably with duty; that is, *it is morally necessary to assume the existence of God*" (*CPrR*, 1.2.5; emphasis added). According to Kant, we have an epistemic *duty* to believe in God as a condition of practical reason itself. I call this duty to believe in God Kant's *deontological theism*.[6]

An instructive contrast to this disposition is that of John Locke, who also describes epistemological duty in the fourth book of his *Essay*, but the requirements are quite different in kind.

> Faith is nothing but a firm assent of the mind: which if it be regulated, *as is our duty*, cannot be afforded to anything, but upon good reason; and so cannot be opposite to it. He that believes, *without having any reason for believing*, may be in love with his own fancies; but neither seeks truth as he ought, nor pays the obedience due his maker, who would have him use those discerning faculties he has given him, to keep him out of mistake and errour. . . . This at least is certain, that he must be accountable for whatever mistakes he runs into: whereas he that makes use of the light and faculties God has given him, and seeks sincerely to discover truth, by those helps and abilities he has, may have this satisfaction in *doing his duty as a rational creature*, that though he should miss truth, he will not miss the reward of it. *For he governs his assent right, and places it as he should, who in any case or matter whatsoever, believes or disbelieves, according as reason directs him*. He that does otherwise, transgresses against his own light, and misuses those faculties, which were given him to no other end, but to search and follow the clearer evidence, and greater probability.[7]

Locke sets the requirements for belief *outside* reason; reason assesses the rationality of beliefs before they are assented to, and one must provide evidence for a belief before holding it. This view is commonly known as

---

6. Deontologism in epistemology refers to what if any *duties* or *obligations* one might or might not have to justify certain claims prior to holding them to be true or false. What obligation do I have, in other words, to demonstrate my reasons for believing something to be the case? See Alston, "Deontological Concept of Epistemic Justification," 258, 293.

7. Locke, *Essay concerning Human Understanding* 4.27.24; emphasis added.

evidentialism, which suggests that belief in God is guilty until proven innocent; the burden of proof rests on theists to demonstrate evidence for their beliefs.

These are high standards for belief in God. Indeed, many have argued they are too high. Nicholas Wolterstorff has helpfully placed Locke in historical perspective by noting that

> for centuries European humanity had resolved its moral and religious quandaries by appealing to its intellectual inheritance—its tradition. By Locke's day and in Locke's place this tradition had split into warring fragments. Thus on the cultural agenda there was the question: How should we form our beliefs on fundamental matters of religion and morality so as to live together in social harmony, when we can no longer appeal to a shared and unified tradition? This anxious question motivated Locke's *Essay concerning Human Understanding*. . . . Knowledge, said he, is "short and scanty." How are we to pick our way when we find ourselves forced, as we all are, to leave the small clearing of knowledge and enter the twilight of belief and disbelief?[8]

This was an urgent issue, and yet Locke's standards found a life of their own after the time they were most needed.

> Locke was the first to develop with profundity and defend the thesis that we are all responsible for our believings, and that to do one's duty with respect to one's believings one must, at appropriate junctures and in appropriate ways, listen to the voice of Reason. Reason must be one's guide. . . . Locke was the great genius behind our modern ways of thinking of rationality and responsibility in beliefs. And Locke's vision became classic: for many, compelling; by some, contested; by no one, ignored. Locke, on this issue, is the father of modernity. . . . For doing one's best, as Locke understood it, consists of setting aside all unverified tradition and getting down to "the things themselves."[9]

Who or what is the object of Locke's epistemological obligation? To whom or what does one have a duty to justify one's beliefs, in other words, specifically religious beliefs? According to Locke, I am obligated to myself and my rational faculties to regulate the religious beliefs I hold by faith, which, this passage seems to infer, are so often irrational or at least have a tendency to run that risk. Beliefs seem to be guilty until proven innocent.

---

8. Wolterstorff, *John Locke*, x.
9. Wolterstorff, *John Locke*, xvii.

I noted above that in Kant's system, it becomes *subjectively necessary to believe things that cannot necessarily be proven* because pure speculative reason lacks content, and practical reason needs concepts. "The moral law led to a practical task that is set by pure reason alone and without the aid of any sensible incentives, namely that of the necessary completeness of the first and principal part of the highest good, morality," Kant states, "and, since this can be fully accomplished only in an eternity, it led to the postulate of *immortality*. The same law must also lead to the possibility of the second element of the highest good, namely happiness proportioned to that morality, and must do so as disinterestedly as before, solely from impartial reason; in other words, it *must lead to the supposition of the existence of a cause adequate to this effect, that is, it must postulate the existence of God as belonging necessarily to the possibility of the highest good*" (emphasis added). According to Kant we arrive at the existence of God as a necessary component of the moral life. "The highest good in the world," he continues,

> is possible only insofar as a supreme cause of nature having a causality in keeping with the moral disposition is assumed. Now, a being capable of actions in accordance with the representation of laws is *an intelligence* (a rational being), and the causality of such a being in accordance with this representation of laws is his *will*. Therefore the supreme cause of nature, insofar as it must be presupposed for the highest good, is a being that is the cause of nature by *understanding* and *will* (hence its author), that is, God. Consequently, the postulate of the possibility of the *highest derived good* (the best world) is likewise the postulate of the reality of a *highest original good*, namely of the existence of God. (*CPrR*, 2.2.5)

Like Locke, one has a doxastic duty to oneself. But unlike Locke, theistic belief is not a secondary belief that must pass through the primary tribunal of reason before it is accepted. It is a fundamental, a priori belief that must— *must:* that is, it is obligatory—be assumed as a component of reason itself.

Kant's enduring contribution to epistemology is his effort to settle epistemological conflicts by locating them in the mind's a priori concepts. But there is more at stake here with this particular issue. Kant manages to demonstrate that belief in God is not a secondary belief that must pass through reason before being assumed. It actually must be assumed first as a precondition of practical reason itself. According to Kant, the concept is already there, and our obligation is to clarify it and promote it tangibly through pursuing "the good." Belief in God, for Kant, is not something that needs to be defended in Lockean fashion, but neither is it something that needs to be defended against having to be defended in the first place: we have a duty to assume it in our reasoning. Locke suggests we are obligated to prove things before believing them; Kant suggests we are obligated to believe things that we cannot necessarily prove, such as the existence of God, "the possibility of which no human understanding will ever fathom although no sophistry will ever convince even the most common human being that they are not true concepts" (*CPrR*, 1.2.6).

Religion within the Bounds of Reason Alone

"The traditional approach to interpreting Immanuel Kant," Chris Firestone states, "understands his philosophy to put a debilitating boundary line between knowledge and faith. So complete is this separation in the *Critique of Pure Reason* that a realist religious faith is thought to lack any meaningful grounds in reason whatsoever. . . . Faith is effectively dead on arrival in Kant's critical philosophy."[10] The picture I hope has emerged of Kant up to this point already departs considerably from many standard accounts. Louis Loeb even goes so far as to suggest that these interpretations are a distortion of the evidence, and Firestone and Nathan Jacobs have continued the critique of this traditional narrative by reexamining Kant's most explicit theological work, *Religion within the Limits of Reason Alone*.[11] As Allen Wood states, "Much careful and fruitful labor has been devoted to the analysis of the subtle argumentation of Kant's epistemology and moral philosophy; but his philosophical outlook as a whole, his view of the world and man's place in it, is often grotesquely caricatured, or dismissed."[12]

In the previous section I suggested that according to Kant's critical philosophy, the existence of God is an epistemological presupposition we are morally obligated to assume. In this section, I will consider Kant's *Religion* and suggest that his understanding of redemption in particular—a specific religious belief, not merely belief in God in general—is not as radical a departure from traditional understandings as it is commonly assumed to be. My argument will begin with and emphasize his understanding of the extent of evil in book 1 of *Religion*. Kant's arguments for a "moral" solution to this evil, particularly in book 2, have caused many to dismiss him on this subject as one of the first in a long line of modern thinkers

---

10. Firestone, "Rational Religious Faith," 77. A chief proponent of this interpretation of Kant is Michalson, *Fallen Freedom*.

11. Loeb, *From Descartes to Hume*; Firestone and Jacobs, *In Defense of Kant's "Religion."*

12. Wood, *Kant's Moral Religion*, 1.

who reduce religion to ethics. Consider his description of the extent of evil, however: "We call a man evil . . . not because he performs actions that are evil (contrary to law) but because these actions are of such a nature that we may infer from them the presence in him of evil maxims" (*Religion*, 71). Furthermore, "This propensity to evil is here ascribed (as regards conduct) to men in general, even the best of them," and "evil can be predicated of man as a species" (*Religion*, 80). Kant does not like to say that we can know that evil can be predicated of humanity *a priori* (*Religion*, 80), and he dislikes certain notions of Adamic inheritance (*Religion*, 85). Nevertheless, it is significant that he acknowledges the universal and inescapable presence of evil in each individual human being without exception, which suggests a need for a solution. This, I argue, is generally consistent with the basis of traditional Western understandings of redemption, which are predicated first on a *problem*.[13] Kant acknowledges that there is a problem, and this separates him from later, perhaps less traditional accounts of atonement (e.g., Ritschl) that are less eager to acknowledge a problem in the first place.

Kant's Problem

Religion within the Boundaries of Mere Reason assumes the concepts of Kant's critical philosophy, particularly the distinction between speculative and practical reason.[14] At the very outset of this text, Kant distinguishes himself from both complete, fatalistic pessimism and radical moral optimism (*Religion*, 69). He goes on to state that his interest in *Religion* is finding a "middle ground"—a familiar term from the critical philosophy—between these two extremes and accounting for the fact that humans are capable of both moral good and evil. Kant's case rests on at least one crucial assumption: the freedom of the will to choose either good or evil, right or wrong.[15]

---

13. By "traditional Western understandings of redemption," I have in mind the consensus that (1) evil entered into the world through the free choice of Adam; (2) we inherit that disposition from Adam; and (3) we bear a responsibility for that evil. While Augustine would make this particularly explicit, it can be discerned in the pre-Augustinian fathers as well, according to Kelley: "Though falling short of Augustinianism, there was here the outline of a real theory of original sin. The fathers might well have filled it in and given it greater sharpness of definition had the subject been directly canvassed in their day. A point on which they were all agreed was that man's will remains free; we are responsible for our acts." Kelley, *Early Christian Doctrines*, 347. On Augustine, see in particular *On Grace and Free Choice*, 180–81. Kanterian concurs that Kant can rightly be associated with this tradition; see Kanterian, *Kant, God, and Metaphysics*, xv.

14. See Wood, *Kant's Rational Theology*, 25–78.

15. On Kant and freedom, see Mulholland, "Freedom and Providence in Kant's Account of Religion, 77–102.

"The ground of evil cannot lie in any object determining the power of choice through inclination, not in any natural impulses," he states, "but only in a rule that the power of choice itself produces for the exercise of its freedom" (*Religion*, 70–71).

Although we have freedom of choice, Kant qualifies this by acknowledging that we have a propensity to choose evil over the good. Interestingly, he suggests that this propensity is universal: "By propensity (*propensio*) I understand the subjective ground of the possibility of an inclination (habitual desire, *concupiscentia*), insofar as this possibility is contingent for humanity in general.... We can further add that the will's capacity or incapacity arising from this natural propensity to adopt or not to adopt the moral law in its maxims can be called the good or the evil heart" (*Religion*, 76–77). The universal character of the human propensity to will evil leads Kant to speak of "a kingdom of evil," that is, something so pervasive that it exceeds the sum of its parts.[16] Kant identifies the beginnings of this "kingdom" in a traditional location: Adam. "A Kingdom of Evil was thus set up here on earth in defiance of the good principle, and all of Adam's (natural) descendants were subjugated to it—and this with their own free consent, since the false show of this world's goods diverted their gaze from the abyss of perdition in store for them" (*Religion*, 118–19). Kant does not specify *origin* of evil; the answer to this question, in any case, would be the province of speculative rather than practical reason. It should be noted, however, that this does not necessarily place Kant outside the Western tradition noted above, which itself is not settled on the exact mechanism(s) of transmission. The point of agreement was *that* evil descended from Adam, not *how*.

Kant's Solution

"The human being," Kant states, "is nevertheless in this perilous state through his own fault; hence he is bound at least to apply as much force as he can muster in order to extricate himself from it" (*Religion*, 129). What is Kant's solution to the problem of "extricating" ourselves from moral evil? "If a human being is corrupt in the very ground of his maxims"—in other words, if evil is so hopelessly pervasive—"how can he possibly bring about this revolution by his own forces and become a good human being on his own?" This appears unlikely, but God's moral commands seem to imply responsibility. "Yet duty commands that he be good, and duty commands nothing but what we can do. The only way to reconcile this is by saying that

---

16. Pasternack discusses the extent of evil in Kant's *Religion* in more detail in "Kant on the Debt of Sin," 30–52.

a revolution is necessary in the mode of thought but a gradual reformation in the mode of sense (which places obstacles in the way of the former), and [that both] must therefore be possible also to the human being" (*Religion*, 92).

The precise mechanisms of redemption lie beyond the purview of practical reason. Practical reason, however, can grasp moral concepts, and it is through these concepts that what we can know of redemption can come into view. The presence of these moral concepts is no trivial matter, however: "There is one thing in our soul which, if we duly fix our eye on it, we cannot cease viewing with the highest wonder, and for which admiration is legitimate and uplifting as well. And that is the original moral predisposition in us, as such" (*Religion*, 93). Moral problems, both general and particular, require moral solutions, and not simply on a superficial level. Thus "a human being's moral education must begin, not with an improvement of mores, but with the transformation of his attitude of mind and the establishment of a character, although it is customary to proceed otherwise and to fight vices individually, while leaving their universal root undisturbed" (*Religion*, 92). Humanity's moral predicament is more pervasive: "Does not the thesis of the innate corruption of the human being with respect to all that is good stand in direct opposition to this restoration through one's own effort? Of course it does, so far as the comprehensibility of, i.e. *our insight into*, its possibility is concerned" (*Religion*, 94; emphasis added).

We are commanded to improve our moral situation even as we know that efforts toward that improvement are insufficient, and it is imperative to note that for Kant, this cul de sac requires *divine assistance* through what Kant refers to as "a prototype." "It is our universal human duty to elevate ourselves to this ideal of moral perfection, i.e. to the prototype of moral disposition in its entire purity.... But ... it is better to say that that prototype has come down to us from heaven, that it has taken up humanity" (*Religion*, 104).[17]

Christ is this prototype of moral perfection for Kant, but it would be a mistake to identify Kant's version of Christ with moral influence theories of atonement, which restrict the identity of Christ to morality only. Similarly, it would also be a mistake to dismiss Kant's solutions so far as "Pelagian," as many readers of *Religion* have.[18] Kant is saying that although Christ descends to our moral world as a moral prototype, this role as moral prototype does not necessarily exhaust his identity. Christ as moral prototype, viewed

---

17. See Michalson, "Moral Regeneration and Divine Aid in Kant," 259-70; Firestone and Jacobs, *In Defense of Kant's "Religion,"* 165.

18. See Palmquist, "Kant's Ethics of Grace," 530-53. See also Mariña, "Kant on Grace," 379-400; as well as Palmquist, *Kant's Critical Religion*, esp. 189-216.

in this light, might simply be something like divine accommodation in moral guise.

> In the practical faith in this Son of God (so far as he is represented as having taken up human nature) the human being can thus hope to become pleasing to God (and thereby blessed); that is, only a human being conscious of such a moral disposition in himself as enables him to believe and self-assuredly trust that he, under similar temptations and afflictions (so far as these are made the touchstone of that idea), would steadfastly cling to the prototype of humanity and follow this prototype's example in loyal emulation, only such a human being, and he alone, is entitled to consider himself not an unworthy object of divine pleasure. (*Religion*, 104–5)

Note Kant's language of "hope," "faith," and "trust," which is different from "knowledge." Moral perfection is not something we necessarily attain, and certainly not in any salvific sense on our own terms. Redemption would be the province of speculative theology, and that is not something we can claim to know with absolute certainty. Rather this is something that we *hope* for. Any ultimate end to the kingdom of evil will have to be brought about by God, not us, but we are able to participate in the progress of goodness through the faculties of morality and freedom (*Religion*, 121).

I believe the problem of moral evil and its solution as identified by Kant is compatible with traditional Christian teaching on the subject. This is not to say that it is *identical* with it, but the tradition itself admits of varying emphases. The thread that holds the tradition together is the necessity of divine assistance even in the decision to direct the will toward the good. Kant does not preclude this in *Religion*. It is simply the province of speculative reason rather than practical reason, and speculative reason can only know so much. Our responsibility is first to what we know, and in this case, we know that we have a tendency to evil and that we have the freedom to will otherwise. Traditional understandings of redemption share a common problem and a consensus *that* Christ is the answer to that problem, but not necessarily a common understanding of *how* precisely that solution works out per se. Kant certainly meets this requirement, and thus I suggest that on this important score, he is not necessarily as unorthodox as he is commonly assumed to be.[19]

---

19. McCall supports this reading of Kant's *Religion* in "Christology," 213–27.

Lectures on Philosophical Theology

Kant has now suggested that belief in the existence of God is obligatory, that human beings are inclined toward evil, and that Christ, the prototype, is the answer to this problem. In his *Lectures on Philosophical Theology*, Kant returns to many themes found in the *Critique of Pure Reason*, but the *Lectures* also offer material that is not found elsewhere, such as discussion of some of the traditional proofs of God's existence, clarification of some of his earlier, more complex views, and perhaps most important, explicit statements regarding his *positive* beliefs concerning God, such as providence, creation, and the divine attributes. I will examine each part of this important text in order to demonstrate that Kant's interest in theology persists well beyond the contested ground of the critical philosophy and *Religion*. Indeed, as Robert Merrihew Adams notes, the *Lectures* are "surprisingly rich" and "astonishingly luxuriant," particularly given the constraints of the first Critique.[20]

Transcendental Theology

The *Lectures* are divided into two primary parts, again corresponding to the faculties of speculative and practical reason: "Transcendental Theology" (i.e., speculative reason) and "Moral Theology" (i.e., practical reason). Kant begins the *Lectures* with a thorough examination of what knowledge speculative reason can yield. There are three concepts of God within the faculty of speculative reason according to Kant. First is the concept of God as *ens originarium* ("original being"), according to which God is a general, underived being. God *ens originarium* is a pure concept, that is, it is disconnected from other beings, isolated from the natural world; God *ens originarium* exists by and for himself. (Kant will later refer to this concept in his discussion of "cosmotheology," which conceives of God as the highest perfection.) The second speculative concept of God is *ens summum* ("highest being"), according to which God possesses every conceivable property and attribute of being. Kant derives the subsidiary concepts of originality and necessity from this concept, and it serves as the basis of ontotheology. Third and finally is the concept of God as *ens entium*, "the being of all beings." In contrast to the concepts of "original being" and "highest being," according to this concept God is the being from which all other being is derived, the ground of all other being. God is thus "omnisufficient." These three concepts—*ens originarium* ("original being"), *ens summum* ("highest being"),

---

20. Adams, "Things in Themselves," 811, 813.

and *ens entium* ("being of beings")—form the basis for all speculative theological knowledge and correlate to its three main branches: cosmotheology, ontotheology, and physicotheology.

Ontotheology

Kant first considers ontotheology. Ontotheology, for Kant, assumes rather than seeks to establish God as an *ens realissimum* ("most real being") because human reason needs a standard against which being can be defined. God as *ens realissimum* is the ideal that regulates our own concepts of being, which are necessarily incomplete. "An *ens realissimum* is something which contains all realities in itself. But existence is also a reality. Hence the *ens realissimum* must necessarily exist. Thus if someone were to assert that God does not exist, he would be negating in the predicate something which is included in the subject, and this would be a contradiction" (*LPT*, 58). Kant's next question is whether anything can be predicated of the God of ontotheology. If so, how can we know? How do we proceed? How are they arranged and prioritized so that they do not obscure the pure concept of being? In other words, can we know God as anything other than a concept? If not, speculative knowledge is of little use. We are in a precarious position with respect to predicates, however, because the only predicates we know arise from our sense experience of the external world. Kant's caution on this matter is to "carefully separate out everything sensible inhering in my representation of this or that reality, and leave out everything imperfect and negative. Then I must ascribe to God the pure reality which is left over" (*LPT*, 52). Even with this complication, the investigation itself, for Kant, is a worthwhile—even necessary—endeavor, for it enables us to determine the limits of and regulates our theological reason. "This investigation will also be of great utility to us in that it teaches us to know God as far as human reason is capable of this knowledge. It gives us convenient rules as to how we are to speak of God, and what we are to say of him. And it will recommend caution and care to us, so that nothing creeps into our concept of God which is contrary to his highest reality" (*LPT*, 50).[21]

"Being" is not itself a predicate for Kant; it is not something that can be predicated of or added to another concept. Being, rather, merely *is* the existence of things themselves. Kant gives the example of the phrase "God is omnipotent" (*LPT*, 59). In this phrase, the word "is" is misleading; it gives

21. Palmquist summarizes this notion as follows: "Such regulative usage implies nothing about how we are to go about gathering empirical knowledge, but only about how we are to structure our beliefs about the source of the ultimate unity of that knowledge." Palmquist, "Kant's 'Appropriation' of Lampe's God," 93.

the appearance of an additional predicate when it is actually already assumed in the word "God." It is syntactically necessary in order to introduce the concept of omnipotence, but it is not an additional predicate of the word "God." The concept of being, which is already assumed in the word "God," also assumes anything that can be predicated of it.

And yet speculative reason demands predicates. To attempt to speak of God in terms other than being and without predicates "cancels" the very concept of God itself. And to "cancel" the concept of God is to cancel the ground of all possible predicates. We cannot speak of God without predicates, and we cannot speak of predicates without the concept of God. A "most real original being" is therefore a necessary presupposition for Kant because it contains within itself the possibility of all things; God as *ens realissimum* is not an object external to other things—a being among beings—but the ground and condition of all being. It is a necessary rational concept from which all concepts proceed. The existence of God is a concept speculative reason must assume but at the same time cannot prove: "The totality of what speculative reason can teach us concerning the existence of God consists in showing us how we must necessarily hypothesize this existence. But speculative reason does not show us how God's existence could be demonstrated with apodictic certainty" (*LPT*, 69). Kant takes the matter further, however, and argues not only that the concept of God is integral to the structure of speculative reason but also that God is a *substance* external to the world and defined by the following attributes (predicates): unity, simplicity, and immutability. Kant also argues (against pantheism) that God is by definition *ens a mundo diversum*, "external to the world in an intellectual way," and (against Stoicism and neo-Platonism) *ens extramundanum*, "being not belonging to the world," that is, entirely outside the world.

Cosmotheology

Having identified God as necessary hypothesis for existence, Kant considers the concept of God within the sphere of human existence as the foundation of experience. Kant refers to this endeavor as *cosmotheology*, which assumes a theistic concept of God as "the supreme intelligence, as a highest being who is author of all things through understanding and freedom" (*LPT*, 81). As *entis realissimi*, the most real being, God must possess the faculty of knowledge. Kant establishes the faculty of knowledge in the being of God by suggesting that because individual beings possess the faculty of knowledge, *therefore* the *entis realissimi* must possess the same faculty. Kant reasons from the particular to the general rather than the other way around. He states,

> We have in addition a stronger ground of proof that God has a faculty of knowledge, a ground derived from the constitution of an *entis realissimi*. And a ground of proof derived from that always has more strength than grounds of proof taken merely from the concept of an *entis realissimi*. We argue that an *ens originarium* containing within itself the ground of the possibility of all things must have a faculty of knowledge because it is the original source of beings which do have this faculty (for example, man). For how could something be derived from a being unless this original being itself had it? Thus the original being of all beings must have a faculty of knowledge. (*LPT*, 83)

If God possesses the faculty of knowledge, Kant suggests, this implies that God also possesses a will by which he actualizes all possible things. Kant suggests that God takes unique pleasure in the actualization of things despite the fact that God is by definition self-sufficient. This pleasure from actualizing all possible things is the impetus for the act of creation, "the greatest whole of everything possible, that is, the *summum bonum finitum*, the most perfect world" (*LPT*, 98).

Physicotheology

Kant continues the discussion of God's will in his third and final section on speculative concepts of God, physicotheology, in which God is the *ens entium*, the "being of all beings." Because God is outside of and distinct from the world, God is not bound by space and time. God's will is therefore free from all constraint. He is not determined by anything and in his self-sufficiency is not compelled by anything to alter himself. God's will is part of this unlimited freedom. "Hence if we want to think of the concept of divine freedom purified of every limitation, then it consists in nothing but the complete independence of God's will both from external things and from inner conditions" (*LPT*, 104–5).

If God is not constrained to create, can we reason from creation back to its author? Kant frames the issue of physicotheology in particular in the form of a question: "From the purposive order of nature can one infer an intelligent author of this order?" (*LPT*, 99). Even if God were the cause of the natural order, the mechanisms of causation would not be apparent to us. Nevertheless, as in the case of Kant's arguments for ontotheology, existence requires us to assume the existence of God. Apart from this assumption, conversation regarding the natural order doesn't even get off the ground. We are incapable of proving God's existence with apodictic certainty, but it is no less needful for that fact.

Moral Theology

Speculative, or "transcendental," theology can only take us so far in our knowledge of God. It can identify the idea of God, whether through ontotheology, cosmotheology, or physicotheology, as a necessary hypothesis for existence, but that concept will always lack specificity as long as it remains a transcendental concept. The second half of Kant's *Lectures* are devoted to "practical" or "moral" knowledge of God, that is, the realm of experience. Unlike transcendental proofs for the existence of God, these realities are "apodictically certain," that is, we have immediate knowledge of them—indeed, they are the realities through which we view all else.

The Moral Attributes of God

Kant first speaks of "moral faith" in God. By this he means a faith that is grounded in moral experience rather than in speculation. In moral faith God is no longer a hypothesis but a "necessary postulate" of practical experience and the laws of nature. Indeed, "morality not only shows that we have need of God, but it also teaches us that he is already present in the nature of things and that the order of things leads to him" (*LPT*, 110–11). In transcendental theology God remains indeterminate; in moral faith God become determinate. Kant identifies three "moral attributes," or "moral perfections," for God: *holiness, benevolence,* and *justice*.[22] These are not arbitrary attributes for Kant; he argues that together they exhaust the moral concept of God. He defines them—and their relationships to each other—as follows.

> *Holiness* is the absolute or unlimited moral perfection of the will. A holy being must not be affected with the least inclination contrary to morality. It must be impossible for it to will something which is contrary to moral laws. So understood, no being but God is holy. *Benevolence* is an immediate well-pleasedness with the welfare of others. Pure and complete benevolence is to be found nowhere but in God. For every creature has needs which limit its inclination to make others happy; or at least these needs limit its ability to make such use of these inclinations

---

22. On Kant's "ethical postulation" as an example of his theological constructivism, see Davidovich, "Kant's Theological Constructivism," 325–40.

that it may have no regard at all for its own welfare. But God is independent benevolence. He is not limited by any subjective ground, because he himself has no needs. His *justice* is fundamentally only a negative perfection, because it limits his benevolence in the measure that we have not made ourselves worthy of it. God's justice therefore consists in the combination of benevolence with holiness. In other words, one could also call it a *true benevolence*. (*LPT*, 114)

The problem of evil falls under the moral rather than transcendental concepts of God for Kant. This is rooted in the fact that among all the creatures, humanity has the unique ability to employ reason in the service of moral decisions and therefore develop good and bad character. This ability is itself a gift from God, but it remains with individual agents to decide how they will use this ability. Kant identifies this ability as *freedom*. God bestowed humanity with talents and capabilities but also "animal instincts" and "senses" that we must learn to control. Thus, Kant argues, we are created "predisposed" to goodness and perfection, but we must labor to attain these states. The reverse is also true, of course; if we must labor to cultivate perfection through the free exercise of our will, this also implies that we have the freedom to *not* cultivate perfection, which is simply another way of saying that we have the capacity for evil. Kant states,

> Man himself had to be responsible for this development, through the cultivation of his talents and the goodness of his will. Endowed with great capabilities, but with the application of these capabilities left to himself, such a creature must certainly be of significance. Much can be expected of him, but on the other hand, no less is to be feared. He can perhaps raise himself above a whole host of will-less angels, but he may also degrade himself so that he sinks even beneath the irrational animals. To begin his cultivation he must step forth out of his uncultivated state, and free himself from his instincts. (*LPT*, 116)

This is the root of the problem of evil for Kant: humanity's freedom to neglect, avoid, or otherwise refuse its capacity for the development of moral perfection. The more humanity strives toward perfection through reason, the less influence evil has in the world. God does not will evil; God wills the moral perfection of humanity through humanity's free exercise of its own will toward this end. Evil "arises as a by-product" (*LPT*, 118) of humanity's struggle to overcome its uncultivated animal instincts.

The Nature and Certainty of Moral Faith

God, freedom, evil, and human morality have now already become so intertwined in Kant's arguments that God is a necessary postulate. "I cannot say that it is probable that God exists. Such an expression would be unsuited to the dignity of this knowledge" (*LPT*, 121). He furthermore states that "it is improper too because no analogy between God and the world is thinkable" (*LPT*, 121). We have arrived at a concept of God that is both intertwined with practical human realities and fully transcendent from them, and there is a measure of certainty about this. Kant calls this "practical conviction," and it "gives us far more satisfying prospects than dry speculation can ever yield" (*LPT*, 122). Practical conviction is distinct from "dogmatic conviction," which is associated with transcendental theology and speculative knowledge. Moral faith rests on practical conviction, so much so that it would be absurd for any truly rational person to deny it. Kant refers to this as the *absurdum practicum* of moral faith.

Kant has now established the foundation on which to make further positive statements about the character and attributes of God, and he moves into a discussion of God's justice and blessedness. Regarding God's justice, Kant argues that this can be understood in one of two ways: (1) justice within the realm of nature and experience or (2) the justice of a God who stands apart from the world and pronounces judgments on it from the outside. Unsurprisingly, Kant is interested in the former conception primarily because the latter belongs to the realm of speculation and therefore is beyond the realm of practical knowledge. We are by definition already acquainted with the concept of justice within the order of nature and experience, and we should not speculate beyond it. Similarly, we should not speculate about God's positive attributes either; God's positive attributes should remain "connected" to our own positive concepts. Take the state of happiness, for instance. We cannot ascribe a state of happiness to God arbitrarily; there is no speculative warrant for this predication. We can, however, infer God's blessedness from our own experience of happiness; our happiness is transitory and impermanent, but God, the very personification of the perfection of the moral laws we experience, is supreme, eternal blessedness.

The Causality of God

God is intimately connected with the world through moral laws but remains transcendent from it. This connection with the world is the locus of Kant's discussion of God's "causality," a term he uses to encompass the theological concepts of *creation*, *providence*, and *governance*. Once again Kant seems to go out of his way to distinguish his views on this matter from Spinozism and Neoplatonism. He first rejects what he refers to as a *systema inhaerentiae* in which God is represented *as* the world itself. He associates the *systema inhaerentiae* with both Spinozism and ancient pantheism. He then rejects a version of what he refers to the concept of God as the *ens extramundanum*, in which God's relationship with the world is *necessary*. He associates this concept with Neoplatonic emanation, in which substances derive from each other in succession (*crassior*) or emanate directly from God (*subtilor*). Kant then affirms a second version of the *ens extramundanum* he refers to as the *systema liberi arbitrii*, in which God is both *extramundus* and free to create independent substances. "It would be absurd to think of God as homogeneous with the totality of the world," Kant states, "because this would wholly contradict the concept of an *entis originarii*. For, as we have shown above, an *ens originarium* has to be isolated from the world. Hence there remains to our reason only the opposite system of causality, the *systema per libertatem*" (*LPT*, 133).

Now that Kant has established God's independence from the world, he is in a position to further specify God's identity as creator. He insists on referring to God as an *author* rather than an "architect" who merely creates the forms of things. As an "author," God creates not only the "forms" but also the "substance" of the world itself. And precisely because he creates the substance of the world, he is invested in its perfection. God achieves the perfection of the world "in accordance with the nature of things" and "along with the rational creature's worthiness to be happy" (*LPT*, 139). God is not interested in *either* the physical perfection of the natural world *or* humanity's moral perfection; as the author and creator, God is interested in both. The combination of the perfection of the natural (or physical) and moral orders leads to the best possible world.

The horizon of the unity of the physical perfection of the world and the moral perfection of humanity constitutes Kant's teleology, which he refers to as "a universal system of all ends" (*LPT*, 140). "Just as there is a physical system of ends, in which everything in nature has a reference as a means to some end found in rational creatures, so there is also a practical system of ends, that is, a system in accordance with the laws of free volition" (*LPT*, 143). God's *providence* over this universal system of ends consists of three separate but complementary functions: (1) providing, (2) governing, and (3) directing. Kant summarizes these three functions as follows: "God's *providing* consists in the institution of the laws according to which the course of the world is to proceed. God's *governing* is the conservation of the course of the world in accordance with these laws. And God's *directing* is the determination of individual events in accordance with his decrees" (*LPT*, 152).

Describing these specific functions of providence does not negate human freedom, however. Kant thus states that God "governs as a monarch, but not as a despot" (*LPT*, 156). God's intentions for humanity and the earth humanity inhabits are ultimately benevolent and consistent with what is beneficial for practical experience. If it seems otherwise, this is the result of a deficiency in our perception, not in God's intentions themselves. The knowledge of God completes our moral knowledge, but it does not *determine* morality. Moral duties are derived rather from the knowledge of the "system of ends," or from knowledge of the natural order of things, and from these duties we can infer the existence of God as a necessary postulate. Kant suggests that our knowledge of the moral order is similar to our knowledge of the fact that a triangle has three angles. We observe the three angles of a triangle; it is not the sort of knowledge that has to be "revealed" to us. We experience moral laws empirically much in the same way, and it is through these moral laws that God makes himself apparent to us. God is known in this way "in order to provide my heart with conviction, import, and emphasis" (*LPT*, 159). Knowledge of God's providence through natural and moral laws is the "crowning achievement" of our natural knowledge rather than the principle by which the natural order is known.

Revelation

Kant ends the *Lectures* with a brief discussion of revelation. It is of course significant that he places this discussion at the end of the *Lectures* rather than at the beginning. This is consistent with his discussion of providence, however, which is something that is discovered *after* one develops an appropriate awareness of the laws that govern the natural order and the practical moral laws that provide the conditions for our freedom and perfection. One must pass through nature, in other words, in order to discover any sort of knowledge that might otherwise be considered "revealed," for God works concurrently with nature rather than contrary to it.[23] Revelation can be either *internal* or *external*, according to Kant. "External" revelation occurs either through works or words, while "internal" revelation occurs through *reason*, and Kant prioritizes internal revelation over external.

> Inward divine revelation . . . must precede all other revelation and serve as a judge of external revelation. It has to be the touchstone by which I know whether an external revelation is really from God; and it must give me proper concepts of him. . . . The religion of reason always has to remain the substratum and

---

23. Kant discusses "concursus" in his section on providence (*LPT*, 147).

foundation of every investigation. It is according to this religion that the value of verbal revelation must be determined. So it must precede every other revelation and serve as a yardstick. (*LPT*, 162)

Kant's discussion of revelation leaves the *Lectures* on a seemingly unorthodox note, but the precedence of internal revelation over external revelation is simply another way of describing what he has been arguing throughout the *Lectures*, that is, that moral theology known through practical reason rather than transcendental theology is what provides us with specific knowledge of God beyond the limits and generalities of speculative reason alone. "Nature by itself can never give me a complete and determinate concept of God unless I bring reason to its aid," Kant states. "Nature teaches us to fear that being (or more than one) which might have produced the world, but it does not teach us to honor and love God without flattery and as a being possessing every perfection" (*LPT*, 160). Transcendental theology can only generate God as a hypothesis; moral theology identifies God as a necessary postulate.

Conclusion

In this chapter I have considered three primary texts to support a relatively modest claim: Kant is not the liability to traditional theology that he has often been claimed to be. Recent accounts that are sympathetic to this claim have focused on *Religion*. My own account has sought to build on this case and expand the conversation to include Kant's other major works. In the Canon of Pure Reason at the end of the first Critique, we find that Kant assumes the existence of God as a condition of reasoning itself. In the *Critique of Practical Reason*, Kant goes further to suggest that we even have an obligation, a doxastic duty, to believe in God. His *Religion* offers an original take on some specific theological loci, none of which necessarily stray from the broad tradition of reflection on atonement. Finally, his *Lectures on Philosophical Theology* offer a closer inspection of some traditional themes in philosophical theology, including a straightforward consideration of revelation. As Allen Wood states, "[The *Lectures of Philosophical Theology*] show, perhaps surprisingly, that despite Kant's generally critical stance toward the transcendent metaphysics of the rationalists and scholastics, he remained quite sympathetic to traditional theology on many points."[24]

In summary, one will not find in Kant's corpus straightforward doctrinal summaries of traditional Christian belief, but Kant never promised

24. Wood, translator's introduction to *LPT*, 10.

us this, nor should this necessarily imply that his work is incompatible with traditional Christian belief. Interpreting Kant's relationship to theology involves managing expectations as much as the texts themselves: interpreters expecting dogmatic accounts of theology will be disappointed, as will those expecting the agnosticism of metaphysical interpretations. What Kant gives us instead, I suggest, is an unusually sophisticated, detailed, and robust positive Christian theism that successfully steers the middle course between dogmatism and skepticism he intended throughout his corpus. Indeed, as he states in the *Lectures on Philosophical Theology*, "It is one of the worthiest of inquiries to see how far our reason can go in the knowledge of God" (*LPT*, pref.).

3

Paths from Kant to Barth
Varieties of Neo-Kantianism

THIS CHAPTER WILL BE primarily historical in nature. It will narrate some of the ways Kant's critical philosophy was received and reinterpreted in neo-Kantianism and how Kant was understood in late-nineteenth- and early-twentieth-century Germany. Barth's initial understanding of Kant came from this tradition, particularly Hermann Cohen's and Paul Natorp's idealistic interpretation of Kant through Barth's Marburg teacher Wilhelm Herrmann. Bruce McCormack states, "There can be no question that Barth found in [Marburg neo-Kantian] idealism an ally, a fellow-traveler for at least part of the way in which he wished to travel."[1] Barth would ultimately break from these received assumptions about Kant in favor of his own reading, and this will prove to be crucial for understanding the role Kant plays in Barth's theological method. Before turning to this subject in the next chapter, it is important to understand the many ways in which Kant was understood—and misunderstood—during the century between his death and Barth's early education. That approximately century-long route from Kant to Barth is not only lengthy and convoluted but also obscured by outdated narratives and counter-histories that must be cleared up before proceeding to how Kant reappears in Barth's theological method.

The standard account of neo-Kantianism is that it appeared as a distinct movement in the mid-nineteenth century, specifically the 1860s. Otto Liebmann's repeated refrain to "return to Kant" ("*also muss nach Kant zurückgegangen werden*") in his *Kant und die Epigonen* (1865) is commonly cited as the inaugural text.[2] Sebastian Luft's 2015 *Neo-Kantian Reader*, for instance, begins with Hermann von Helmholtz in the 1840s as its background, and Luft describes the origins of neo-Kantianism as "the most broadly influential movement of European philosophy between approximately 1850 and 1918. The neo-Kantian movement was inspired by the battle cry 'back to Kant.'"[3]

---

1. McCormack, Review of *Karl Barth*, 305.
2. Liebmann, *Kant und die Epigonen*.
3. Luft, *Neo-Kantian Reader*, xx.

Thomas Willey points to Hermann Lotze (1817–81), whose main works were published in the 1840s and 1850s, as the *precursor* to neo-Kantianism, and he dates neo-Kantianism itself similarly to Luft.[4] Hans-Ludwig Ollig's entry on "Neukantianismus" in the *Philosophisches Wörterbuch* indicates that neo-Kantianism's beginnings are in the second half of the nineteenth century, and Copleston's brief chapter on the topic *begins* with the movement's final stages in the 1870s.[5]

One glaring problem with this narrative is that it leaves the more than a half century between Kant and the 1860s largely unaccounted for. The main reason for this is that this period—the first several decades of the nineteenth century—are dominated by the rise of *absolute* or *speculative* idealism, which was understood to be an improvement on Kant's transcendental idealism. According to this account, Hegelian absolute idealism in particular becomes the period's primary center of gravity. Neo-Kantianism, therefore, appears chronologically *after* the Hegel's idealism falls out of favor and as a consequence of it.

Recent work in neo-Kantianism, however—particularly the work of Frederick Beiser and Klaus Christian Köhnke—accounts for this lacuna and also tells a much different tale of neo-Kantianism's origins.[6] Köhnke emphasizes that what the conventional account describes as beginning in the 1860s in fact constitutes the last two-thirds of a three-stage process that stretches back well before the middle of the nineteenth century. For Köhnke, there is a long and rich "prehistory" prior to the developments of the 1860s that extends from Kant and *ends* in 1848. "That which constituted itself a new movement [neo-Kantianism of the 1860s] and maintained it derived only from Kant and not from post-Kantian philosophy [to 1848] can be far more closely attached to the philosophies that were the predecessors of neo-Kantianism than one has been willing to admit."[7] Frederick Beiser takes matters a step further and suggests that neo-Kantianism not only has a prehistory prior to 1860 but actually *began before* Kant's death in 1804 as Kant's influence began to wane. "The founding fathers of the movement," Beiser

---

4. Willey, *Back to Kant*, 40.

5. Ollig, "Neukantianismus," 327; Copleston, *Modern Philosophy*, 761–73.

6. Köhnke, *Rise of Neo-Kantianism*; Beiser, *Genesis of Neo-Kantianism*. Köhnke's and Beiser's monographs are two of the only full-length, dedicated treatments of the topic of neo-Kantianism, and certainly two of the only ones that offer accounts that improve upon the standard narrative. Other dedicated treatments of neo-Kantianism include Dufour, *Les Néokantiens*; Willey, *Back to Kant*; Ollig, *Der Neukantianismus*; Lehmann, *Geschichte der nachkantischen Philosophie*. Essay collections include Makreel and Luft, *Neo-Kantianism in Contemporary Philosophy*; Warren and Staiti, *New Approaches to Neo-Kantianism*.

7. Köhnke, *Rise of Neo-Kantianism*, 7.

argues, "were Jakob Friedrich Fries (1773–1843), Johann Friedrich Herbart (1776–1841) and Friedrich Eduard Beneke (1798–1854). All defined themselves as Kantians, and all called for a return to the spirit of Kant's teachings. They anticipated, and laid down the foundation for, defining doctrines of later neo-Kantianism."[8]

I approach these conflicting narratives by accounting for two periods: (1) the period leading up to 1860 ("The Rise of Hegel and the Eclipse of Kant") and (2) the period between 1860 and 1914 ("Resurrecting Kant, 1860–1914").[9] The second period is divided into two phases: the "revival decade" of the 1860s and the period of neo-Kantianism's dissemination into distinct schools (1870–1914). In the first section I address both the issue of Hegel's influence and some problems with making it the primary focus of early-nineteenth-century philosophy, particular for neo-Kantianism. In the second section I address some of the standard figures and issues in neo-Kantianism but also attempt to connect them to the previous decades in order to (1) demonstrate that Kant's influence was persistent throughout the nineteenth century, not just beginning in the 1860s, and (2) trace how some the major themes of his critical philosophy were understood in the period between Kant and Barth.

---

8. Beiser, *Genesis of Neo-Kantianism*, 3. Beiser's work will hereafter be abbreviated in the text as *GN-K* with references to page numbers.

9. The nineteenth century was full of important developments in European intellectual history, especially in Germany, that are worthy of consideration. This is particularly true in both philosophy and theology, and I have had to omit some significant figures and movements in the interest of focus. The first and most obvious omission is Friedrich Schleiermacher (1768–1834), an important figure in Barth's development and critic of Kant's but who is less significant for developments in neo-Kantianism in particular. Schleiermacher scholarship, furthermore, has emphasized closer affinities between him and Spinoza and Schelling rather than Kant. See, for instance, Lamm, *Living God*, esp. 159–98; Brandt, *Philosophy of Schleiermacher*, 37. Another omission is the German Romantic tradition in general, which shared some mutual concerns with neo-Kantianism but not enough to merit lengthy consideration in this chapter. On these shared concerns, see in particular Beiser, *Romantic Imperative*. Arthur Schopenhauer is another omission that was more directly involved in responding to Kant after his death and also criticizing Hegel, but he is an outlier in the traditions I am accounting for in this chapter and also had little bearing on Barth's later development. Schopenhauer responds most forthrightly to Kant in the appendix to the first volume of *Die Welt als Wille und Vorstellung*, 1:509–651; see also Magee, *Philosophy of Schopenhauer*, 271n85. Finally, later influential neo-Kantians, such as Ernst Cassirer and Martin Heidegger, have been omitted because Barth had abandoned the movement by the time they came into prominence. Cassirer and Heidegger's meeting in Davos, Switzerland, which not only settled the fate of neo-Kantianism but changed the course of twentieth-century philosophy, has been addressed recently and exhaustively by Gordon in *Continental Divide*, 43–86, 136–214.

The Rise of Hegel and the Eclipse of Kant: Post-Kantian Idealism, 1804–60

Hegel's centrality in the first decades of post-Kantian idealism is considerable. This is due in large part to an account of the first decades of the nineteenth century that emphasizes Hegel's "ascent" to prominence, which begins with Fichte, passes through Schelling, and culminates in Hegel. The language of "culmination" is intentional, for it is both how Hegel viewed his own system and also the role it is often assigned in histories of German idealism. According to Karl Löwith, for instance, Hegel is one of two "end points" ("*beiden Enden*"; the other being Nietzsche) in German idealism, and Hegel's system in particular is "the brilliant culmination of the systems of idealism."[10] In the second part of this section, I will describe the ways that his narrative has been called into question by Klaus Christian Köhnke and Frederick Beiser. Given its significance, however, it is important for this purposes of this chapter to understand how Fichte, Schelling, and Hegel each interpreted and thought they had improved on Kant's idealism before turning to the role they played in the larger narrative of neo-Kantianism in particular. They all played a central role in interpreting Kant in the decades following Kant's death, which influenced the direction neo-Kantianism would take in turn, and which Barth would eventually receive.

Fichte, Schelling, and Hegel: The Hegelian "Ascent" Narrative of Post-Kantian Idealism

The account of post-Kantian idealism that begins with Fichte, passes through Schelling, and culminates in Hegel has exercised considerable influence in accounts of early nineteenth-century philosophy, not to mention the roots of contemporary philosophy as well.[11] "The development of German idealism after Kant," Sally Sedgwick states, "is in large part a story of the various ways in which features of Kant's Critical philosophy get either preserved or transformed in the systems of Fichte, Schelling, and Hegel."[12] This does not mean that they all interpreted Kant in the same way, or even similar ways. To the contrary, they were all territorial about their unique reading of Kant. One common characteristic they did share, however, was

---

10. Löwith, *Von Hegel zu Nietzsche*, 7, 52, translated as *From Hegel to Nietzsche*, xv, 39. See also Dorrien, *Kantian Reason and Hegelian Spirit*, 18; Liminatis, *German Idealism and the Problem of Knowledge*, 1–5; Inwood, *Hegel*, 251.

11. See, for instance, Pinkard, *German Philosophy*, 105–98, 217–305.

12. Sedgwick, "Idealism from Kant to Hegel," 1.

that they all believed that Kant's critical philosophy should be *improved on* and *surpassed*; for all three, Kant's philosophy did not go sufficiently far in its claims. I will discuss each one briefly before considering challenges to the Hegelian "ascent" narrative.

Johann Gottlieb Fichte (1762–1814)

It is difficult to overestimate the force with which Fichte asserted his own version of Kant's idealism, which emphasizes the role of the knowing subject in epistemology. The foundational premise for Fichte's idealism begins with the *ego*. This becomes significant and problematic for Kant's reception because while it sounds vaguely Kantian, it also undercuts Kant's critical philosophy in at least one major way: it eliminates the role of things-in-themselves in the construction of knowledge. Fichte's version of Kant's critical philosophy rejected the notion of "things in themselves" as incoherent. "The Kantianism of the Kantians"—note the use of Kantian*ism* already in Kant interpretation—"indeed consists in a reckless juxtaposition of the crudest dogmatism, which has things-in-themselves making impressions upon us, with the most inveterate idealism, which has all existence arising solely out of the thinking of the intellect."[13] A coherent system of philosophy, for Fichte, must be derived entirely from the knowing subject or entirely from objects; Kant wanted it both ways, and Fichte sought to place the emphasis back on the knowing subject. Lines were being drawn in Kant interpretation before Kant's career was even finished, and Fichte states in no uncertain terms, "Till this moment, there is not one who has understood this book [Kant's first Critique] in anything but a *completely* distorted fashion; they have discovered in it the very opposite system to that which is propounded therein; dogmatism instead of transcendentalism: *I alone, however, understand it aright.*"[14]

Friedrich Wilhelm Joseph Schelling (1775–1854)

Schelling—one of Hegel's roommates in seminary—like Fichte, emphasized subjective experience and would be extraordinarily influential for

---

13. Fichte, *Science of Knowledge*, 56.

14. Fichte, *Grundlage der gesamten Wissenschaftslehre*, translated as *The Science of Knowledge*, 53. On Fichte's epistemology, see Breazeale, *Thinking through the "Wissenschaftslehre"*; Rockmore and Breazeale, *Fichte and Transcendental Philosophy*; Janke, *Fichte*; Kim and Hoeltzel, *Kant, Fichte, and the Legacy of Transcendental Idealism*; Martin, *Idealism and Objectivity*; Österreich and Traub, *Der ganze Fichte*; Zöller, *Fichte's Transcendental Philosophy*.

subsequent philosophy and theology both. In his *System of Transcendental Idealism*, he appeals to Kant's observation that "as soon as a child begins to speak of itself by the word 'I,' a new world appears to open up for it."[15] Unlike Fichte, however, who found himself embroiled in accusations of atheism,[16] Schelling was a theist who located God in subjective experience. For this reason, he is often considered to be the forerunner of existentialism.[17] Schelling's signature fascination was with the concept of freedom, which he suggests is not one metaphysical concept among many but the central metaphysical concept around which all other concepts revolve—and that it had not been fully understood in the history of philosophy until idealism.[18] "Freedom is the one principle on which everything is supported," he states, "and what we behold in the objective world is not anything present outside us, but merely the inner limitation of our own free activity."[19]

Schelling's God is bound up with the mind and is subject to human experience; God, for Schelling, does not know particular outcomes, for instance. God undergoes development and change as history progresses. In striking departure from classical theism, Schelling's God *does* possess potential; if God has the power to end the world, but the world still exists, this indicates to Schelling that God has power that God is not exercising. God, according to Schelling, is a dynamic force, not a static, changeless being. "God himself is not a system," Schelling states, "but rather a life."[20]

Both of these emphases are crucial for understanding developments in idealism after Kant, and one could argue that there is precedent in Kant's critical philosophy for both subjectivism in idealism in general and also a connection between subjectivism and God. Schelling's achievement was what he understood to be a synthesis between Kant's critical philosophy and Fiche's *Science of Knowledge*.

---

15. Schelling, *System des transcendentalen Idealismus*, translated as *System of Transcendental Idealism*, 31. On Schelling's epistemology, see Matthews, *Schelling's Organic Form of Philosophy*; Matthews, *Beyond Presence*, 30–87; Snow, *Schelling and the End of Idealism*; Asmuth et al., *Schelling*; Marx, *Philosophy of F. W. J. Schelling*; Bausola, *Metafisica e rivelazione nella filosofia positiva di Schelling*. See also Kile, *Die theologischen Grundlagen von Schellings Philosophie der Freiheit*; Tillette, *Schelling*.

16. See Estes and Bowman, *J. G. Fichte and the Atheism Dispute*, 1–16.

17. See Tillich, "Existential Philosophy," 44; Fackenheim, *God Within*, 50–52.

18. Schelling, *Philosophische Untersuchungen über das Wesen der menschlichen Freiheit und die damit zusammenhängenden Gegenstände*, translated as *Philosophical Investigations into the Essence of Human Freedom*, 16–17.

19. Schelling, *System of Transcendental Idealism*, 35.

20. Schelling, *Philosophical Investigations*, 62.

Georg Wilhelm Friedrich Hegel (1770–1831)

The specific relationship between actively knowing, finite human subjects is a more complex issue for Hegel, one addressed most famously in his *Phenomenology of Spirit*.[21] In this work Hegel calls the relationship between a finite human mind and the world "consciousness" (*Bewusstsein*), and systematic philosophical reflection on the progress of consciousness is *phenomenology*.[22] Consciousness, for Hegel, is in a constant state of development; it is dynamic, not static. It evolves dialectically as finite consciousness apprehends the infinite in increasing measure until it reaches absolute knowledge. Hegel's epistemology would come to be characterized in post-Kantian idealism as *absolute* or *speculative*—rather than *transcendental*—idealism.

In the *Phenomenology of Spirit* Hegel traces the development of this philosophical consciousness in three distinct phases: consciousness (*Bewusstsein*), self-consciousness (*Selbstbewusstsein*), and reason (*Vernuft*). The first phase, consciousness, concerns the basic, objective relationship between the mind and an external object. "Our approach to the object must . . . be *immediate* or *receptive*; we must alter nothing in the object as it presents itself. In *a*pprehending it, we must refrain from trying to *com*prehend it."[23] Self-consciousness, the second phase of the *Phenomenology*, returns to the effect the recognition of an external object has on the subjective knower. "If we consider this new shape of knowing, the knowing of itself, in relation to that which preceded, viz., the knowing of an other, then we see that though this other has indeed vanished, its moments have at the same time no less been preserved. . . . Self-consciousness is the reflection out of the being of the world of sense and perception, and is essentially the return from *otherness*."[24] There is no self-consciousness prior to consciousness of alterity.

The third phase of the development of consciousness, reason, is of particular importance for post-Kantian idealism. In the same way that there is no self-consciousness prior to consciousness of alterity, for Hegel there is no reason prior to self-consciousness. Reason is the synthesis of consciousness

---

21. Hegel, *Phänomenologie des Geistes*, translated as *Phenomenology of Spirit*.

22. The relationship between a finite human mind and a transcendent infinite object first requires not only a recognition of the transcendent infinite on the part of the finite knowing subject but also the existence of other self-conscious subjects like oneself. The triangulation of these recognitions constitutes what Hegel refers to as *objective spirit*, an important notion that is also addressed in the *Phenomenology of Spirit*. See Taylor's discussion of the Kantian background of Hegel's notion of objective spirit in *Hegel*, chap. 14. A good summary of Hegel's epistemology in general can be found in Westphal, *Hegel's Epistemology*, esp. 51–71; Rockmore, *Hegel's Circular Epistemology*, esp. 16–43.

23. Hegel, *Phenomenology of Spirit*, §90.

24. Hegel, *Phenomenology of Spirit*, §167.

and self-consciousness; the distinct characteristics and limitations of consciousness and self-consciousness are exceeded in this final stage as the knowing subject achieves "universal self-consciousness." Reason does not *replace* consciousness and self-consciousness, however; rather, it fulfills and completes them.[25] The result is "absolute knowledge," which is the ultimate synthesis of knower, known, and the self-consciousness of God.

Challenges to the Hegelian "Ascent" Narrative

Fichte, Schelling, and Hegel have proven to be philosophers of considerable influence and have justly earned their place in the philosophical canon. Each of their attempted improvements on Kant were both unique and prominent. With Fichte, we see an important theme that will emerge in later neo-Kantianisms: an emphasis on the subjective knower and a resistance to the influence of things-in-themselves in determining the outcome of knowledge. Schelling and Hegel are also resistant to Kantian things-in-themselves, but their solutions involve attempts to *integrate* or *synthesize* subjective contributions to knowledge and objects of knowledge. Their influence would wane immediately after Hegel's death, however, and their place in the development of post-Kantian idealism and neo-Kantianism in particular has grown increasingly suspect in recent years. Klaus Christian Köhnke and Frederick Beiser in particular have called into question whether Fichte, Schelling, and Hegel are indeed best characterized as Kantians at all. Their respective concerns are unique and merit further consideration. I will consider each one in turn.

KLAUS CHRISTIAN KÖHNKE AND NEO-KANTIAN "PREHISTORY"

In his history of neo-Kantianism, *Rise of Neo-Kantianism*, Köhnke seeks to revise the standard neo-Kantian narrative, which suggests that neo-Kantianism does not *begin* until after Hegel, and particularly as a *consequence of* Hegel's decline in influence.[26] Köhnke's concern, in other words, is that the standard narrative characterizes 1860s neo-Kantianism as an afterthought,

---

25. This synthesis of finitude and infinity has particular importance for religious knowledge. As Tom Rockmore notes, "The parallel between philosophy and religion is that both treat the real infinite, which is God, from the vantage point of the finite world. There is, hence, a parallel concerning the immediate finite object and the true, ultimate infinite. In effect, for Hegel philosophy and religion concern the same object, the same reality, and are therefore inseparable in this sense." Rockmore, *Hegel's Circular Epistemology*, 88.

26. Köhnke, *Rise of Neo-Kantianism*, xii.

a contingency plan following the decline of speculative idealism. Köhnke suggests that Karl Löwith's *From Hegel to Nietzsche*, "which regards neo-Kantianism as a mere symptom of decline," bears particular responsibility for this assumption, as well as the revisionist readings of the likes of Georg Lukács, Karl Korsch, and Ernst Bloch.[27]

Köhnke's criticism of Löwith is twofold. First, Löwith treats the development of neo-Kantianism in the second half of the nineteenth century as a second-rate intellectual movement that appeared in the void created by the collapse of a vastly more superior Hegelian absolute idealism in the previous decades. Neo-Kantianism, for Löwith, is an inferior development that bridges the gap between Hegel and the twentieth century. Köhnke's second and related criticism of Löwith's project involves the fact that Löwith's starting point is in the twentieth century looking backward rather than in the nineteenth century itself: "Since Löwith's 'real' history of the philosophy of the nineteenth century desired to 'circumscribe' history 'within the horizon of the present' and interpret it 'anew,' it goes without saying that it had to sacrifice the actual course of events to a naïve topicality and present-day perspective—it had to nullify what had really happened so as to provide space for the expression of its own interests, all of which in turn have less to do with the nineteenth century than with the interests of the twentieth."[28] Other standard accounts of neo-Kantianism bear a troubling family resemblance: they "rely chiefly on the neo-Kantians' own expositions of their own history and thus could not obviate the necessity for a critical resifting of the material."[29]

The need for a revised account of neo-Kantianism based on textual evidence is apparent, according to Köhnke, and this is what he seeks to reconstruct in his *Rise of Neo-Kantiansim*. Köhnke divides his account into three phases: (1) prehistory (to 1848); (2) the traditional neo-Kantian program (1850s–1865); and (3) the dissemination of neo-Kantianism into schools. The first phase is of particular importance for the purposes of this chapter, because it gets us closer to Kant himself in a period that is otherwise dominated by Fichte, Schelling, and Hegel. The chief figure during this period for Köhnke is Friedrich Adolf Trendelenburg (1802–72), who Köhnke sees as a vital missing link—the "mediator"—between Kant himself and the traditional period of neo-Kantianism of the mid-nineteenth century.[30] Trendelenburg's lineage in this respect is admirable: he was the last student

27. Köhnke, *Rise of Neo-Kantianism*, 3.
28. Köhnke, *Rise of Neo-Kantianism*, 3.
29. Köhnke, *Rise of Neo-Kantianism*, 6.
30. Köhnke, *Rise of Neo-Kantianism*, 11.

of Karl Leonard Reinhold (1757–1823), who was originally responsible for the dissemination of Kantian philosophy in Germany, as well as a student of Johann Erich von Berger (1772–1833), a student of Fichte's and colleague of Reinhold's. It is also worth noting at this point that in the first half of the nineteenth century, Kant himself had largely fallen out of favor, with a reputation for being a philosopher of mediocre stature; it is therefore significant that Trendelenburg would have been compelled to carry on Kant's legacy at all. That being the case, Trendelenburg did go beyond Kant and introduce the concepts of *becoming* and *epistemological motion*, or Hegelian *development*, into standard Kantian categories of theoretical and practical philosophy, reason, and judgment; indeed, Trendelenburg sees the concept of epistemological motion as a resolution of the Kantian problem of sense perception: "Only through the internal motion of thought," Köhnke states, "can the thinker, by means of pure self-knowledge of thought, also attain to knowledge of the external world."[31]

Frederick Beiser and the "Lost" Neo-Kantian Tradition

Köhnke's work in *Rise of Neo-Kantianism* is a significant step in the right direction in the historical reconstruction of the figures, debates, and issues at stake in Kant's reception in the early nineteenth century as well as later, mid- and late-century developments in neo-Kantianism. Indeed, according to Frederick Beiser, "Köhnke . . . has done more than anyone else to place neo-Kantian scholarship on a sound footing" (*GN-K*, viii). Beiser also suggests, however, that Köhnke's narrative does not go far enough in challenging older narratives of neo-Kantianism that begin in the 1860s with Otto Liebmann's *Kant und die Epigonen*. Beiser suggests, more radically, that neo-Kantianism was well under way even *prior* to Kant's death in 1804. Beiser is interested in "the neo-Kantians before neo-Kantianism, the chief figures of the movement before its formation and division into distinct 'schools,'" and seeks to argue in no uncertain terms that "*the origins of neo-Kantianism go back to the 1790s, even before Kant's death* (1804)" (*GN-K*, 3; emphasis added). This has significant implications not only for understanding neo-Kantianism in general but also specifically for understanding the trajectory from Kant to Barth, specifically by unearthing an additional historical development of central importance: the "lost" Kantian tradition of Jakob Friedrich Fries (1773–1843), Johann Friedrich Herbart (1776–1841), and Friedrich Eduard Beneke (1798–1854).

---

31. Köhnke, *Rise of Neo-Kantianism*, 13–14.

Before I turn to an account of this "lost tradition," it is important to understand Beiser's dissatisfaction with the standard account of post-Kantian idealism. Like Köhnke, Beiser finds fault with Karl Löwith's account of post-Kantian idealism in *From Hegel to Nietzsche*, which pits the neo-Kantians against Löwith's preferred protagonists of the period: Marx, Kierkegaard, and Nietzsche. But Beiser also finds fault with a more recent account, that of Richard Rorty's *Philosophy and the Mirror of Nature*. Beiser states,

> Though Rorty wrote with an air of authority about neo-Kantianism, almost everything he said about it is false, confused, or misleading.... While Rorty is certainly correct to ascribe a crucial role to neo-Kantian in forming much 20th-century philosophy, he ascribes doctrines to the movement that reveal ignorance of its intentions and origins. He maintains that the neo-Kantian conception of epistemology went hand in hand with the theory of the mind as a mirror of nature—though even a partial familiarity with neo-Kantian thinking shows that they decisively rejected that theory. He also states that the neo-Kantian conception of philosophy as epistemology is essentially foundationalist, that it is based on the idea that philosophy can provide grounds for the positive sciences. But the neo-Kantians, virtually without exception, rejected foundationalism. (GN-K, 9)

This is a striking claim, not least because of the influence Rorty's text has exercised in postmodern philosophy. More to the point for my purposes, however, is the possibility that much of what has been received about neo-Kantianism—and thus Kant himself—is not as stable as we might like to think, particularly when it comes to accurately characterizing neo-Kantian epistemology.

For Beiser, debates about Kant begin with the "lost tradition" of Fries, Herbart, and Beneke, who have been largely overlooked in standard accounts of idealism at the end of the eighteenth century and first half of the nineteenth. I have described above how these standard narratives emphasize the speculative idealism that begins with Fichte, matures in Schelling, and culminates in Hegel. One of Beiser's most insightful critiques of this "ascent" narrative, Löwith and Rorty notwithstanding, is that its original architect is *Hegel himself*. Indeed, Hegel saw his own work as "the *telos* of post-Kantian philosophy.... What this history so tendentiously leaves out is its competition, the tradition of Fries, Herbart, and Beneke. For self-serving reasons, Hegel had virtually written his opponents out of history, and his disciples gladly followed him" (*GN-K*, 11).[32] It is furthermore important to

---

32. Beiser points to the final section of the third volume of Hegel's *Lectures on the*

acknowledge that Fichte, Schelling, and Hegel did not appear in an intellectual vacuum; to the contrary, it was precisely out of disputes with other idealisms that Fichte, Schelling, and Hegel emerged. Fries, Herbart, and Beneke were the earliest post-Kantian idealists of the much-longer neo-Kantian tradition that would continue through the nineteenth century well into the twentieth.

Who were Fries, Herbart, and Beneke, and what were their emphases? Fries taught philosophy at Heidelberg and Jena, Herbart at Göttingen and Königsberg, and Beneke at Berlin. While they did not collaborate directly and did not constitute a formal Kantian "school," Beiser suggests that they shared the following six distinguishing characteristics: (1) an allegiance to *transcendental* idealism (i.e., adhering to Kant's original intent rather than seeking to improve on it); (2) a commitment to reforming epistemology through *psychology*; (3) a mistrust of speculative rationalism; (4) a trust in the methods of empirical sciences; (5) an ethics based on aesthetics; and perhaps most important, (6) "an antipathy to the speculative idealism of Fichte, Schelling, and Hegel" (*GN-K*, 11). Taken together, these emphases are a sufficiently significant departure from the Fichte-Schelling-Hegel tradition to constitute a rival idealist tradition.

Methodologically, Fries, Herbart, and Beneke were opposed to the notion that pure thought alone was capable of reaching a priori conclusions, one of the fundamental assumptions of the deductive and dialectical method of Fichte, Schelling, and Hegel. Rather, they retained confidence in the importance of empirical sense data in forming judgments, thus "insisting that pure thinking alone could reach no substantial conclusions and that knowledge must receive its content from experience" (*GN-K*, 12). Fries, Herbart, and Beneke's concerns were therefore *empiricist* and *psychological* in nature rather than *rationalist* and *speculative*. This affected their understanding of Kant in several ways. First, unlike Fichte, Schelling, and Hegel, who *departed from* and sought to *improve upon* the limitations Kantian transcendental idealism placed on reason, Fries, Herbart, and Beneke generally *accepted* its strictures as an asset. Beiser states, "The rationalist-speculative tradition rejected, while the empiricist-psychological tradition accepted, Kant's transcendental idealism in its original intended sense, that

---

History of Philosophy as the locus for this narrative. There, after a lengthy discussion of Fichte and a shorter discussion of Schelling, Hegel declares, "Es ist eine neue Epoche in der Welt entsprungen.... dem Weltgeiste jetzt gelungen ist, alles fremde *gegenständliche* Wesen sich abzutun.... Dies ist nun der Standpunkt der jetzigen Zeit" ("It is a new epoch in the world... the world-Spirit has now succeeded in dismissing all alien *representational* beings.... This is now the standpoint of the current time"). Hegel, *Vorlesungen über die Geschichte der Philosophie*, 459–60; emphasis added.

is, the limitation of knowledge to appearances and the distinction between appearances and the thing-in-itself. Rather than decrying the thing-in-itself as the great weakness of the Kantian system, as Fichte, Schelling, and Hegel had done, Fries, Herbart, and Beneke regarded it as its great strength" (*GN-K*, 11–12).

Similarly, Fries, Herbart, and Beneke generally accepted the *dualistic* outlines of Kant's transcendental idealism—dualisms, for instance, between "understanding and sensibility, essence and existence, form and content"— whereas Schelling and Hegel sought to go beyond them through syntheses, such as *Geist* and nature, for instance (*GN-K*, 12). This led Fries, Herbart, and Beneke to insist on retaining a distinction between theoretical and practical reason—a distinction central to Kant's system but one that Fichte, Schelling, and Hegel sought to erode.

Another major divide between these two traditions is that Fichte, Schelling, and Hegel read Kant's epistemology as a *foundationalist* project, while Fries, Herbart, and Beneke did not;[33] rather, they read Kant's project as a primarily *psychological* or *anthropological* effort, one that sought primarily to *describe* rather than *prescribe* the basic epistemological functions of the human mind. This divide between prescriptive and descriptive interpretations of Kant's critical project is a crucial distinction in the history of neo-Kantianism, and both traditions could find precedent in Kant's writings for their views. Rather than arguing for the superiority of one view over the other, Beiser suggests that

> with the benefit of hindsight, we can see that each tradition had stretched one aspect of Kant at the expense of the other. They had pitted his rationalist and empiricist sides against one another. Reinhold, Fichte, Schelling, and Hegel had taken hold of Kant's rationalist side, namely, the value he placed on systematic unity, on a dogmatic method of demonstration, on a priori principles and reasoning. Fries, Herbart, and Beneke, however, had grasped the empiricist side, namely, his insistence that the content of knowledge be given by the senses, that metaphysics should not transcend the limits of experience, that analysis of concepts cannot provide substantive knowledge. (*GN-K*, 14)

33. Some of the strongest initial criticism of Kant's critical philosophy came from early German Romanticism, for instance, Hölderlin, Novalis, and Schlegel. More accurately, they reacted against Fichte's *version* of Kant's philosophy. But both Fichte and the romantics shared a similar premise: that Kant's philosophy was *foundationalist* in nature. This shared premise is often overlooked in the historiography of this period. The result has been a strong disjunction between rational *Aufklärung* and irrational *Frühromantik*, but recent scholarship emphasizes their common concerns. See Beiser, *Romantic Imperative*, 56.

Which side of this divide Beiser outlines can be said to have interpreted Kant most faithfully is still a matter of dispute. The significance of this interpretive divide for the history of neo-Kantianism—and particularly for the neo-Kantianism Barth would inherit—is threefold. First, it pushes the origins of what we now refer to as neo-Kantianism back to Kantianism itself, that is, as an immediate rather than later historical development. Second, it neutralizes the assumed centrality of the Hegelian tradition in narratives of neo-Kantianism and post-Kantian idealism. Third, it establishes historical continuity with what is traditionally referred to as the "golden age" of neo-Kantianism (1860–1914), which would emphasize, like Fries, Herbart, and Beneke, the empiricist-psychological dimensions of Kantianism rather than the rationalist-speculative tradition of Fichte, Schelling, and Hegel (*GN-K*, 16).

Resurrecting Kant: Neo-Kantianism, 1860–1914

While the first decades of the nineteenth century pose unique historiographical considerations for neo-Kantianism, all the major accounts, from Löwith to Beiser, agree that the period from 1860 to 1914 was the "golden age" for neo-Kantianism. "During these decades, to be at the cutting edge of philosophy, to have a rigorous training in the discipline, meant studying Kant" (*GN-K*, 1). This does not suggest that disagreement was absent from the era. Hardly so. Rather, this was the period that the major figures typically associated with neo-Kantianism were active. I will divide this period into two sub-phases: (1) the revival decade of the 1860s and (2) the period of the schools, which begins in the 1870s and continues until 1914. These developments set the stage for the neo-Kantian ideas Barth would encounter in his early education and continue to wrestle with throughout his career.

Phase One: The Revival Decade of the 1860s

On February 27, 1855, a statue of Kant was unveiled in Königsberg, and celebrated natural scientist and Kant devotee Hermann von Helmholtz (1821–94) was invited to deliver a lecture for the occasion. His presentation, *Über das Sehen des Menschen*, played a prophetic role in the decades to come. Hegelian idealism had suffered severe attacks in the 1830s and 1840s, and by the end of the 1840s would be thoroughly criticized both from outside (primarily by Adolf Trendelenburg's *Logische Untersuchungen* and Hermann Lotze's *Metaphysik*) and within (by Ludwig Feuerbach's *Grundsätze der Philosophie der Zunkunft*).[34] This was a problem, as Helmholtz saw it, because Kant's legacy had been closely tied to Fichte, Schelling, and Hegel; if that tradition was on the wane, there was an inherent risk that Kant would go out with it. Helmholtz therefore argued for Kant to be distinguished from the Hegelian tradition and for the relevance of his philosophy for the decades ahead.

The major figures involved in Kant's revival in the 1860s, including but not limited to Kuno Fischer (1824–1907), Otto Liebmann (1840–1912), and Friedrich Albert Lange (1828–75), would share Helmholtz's sensibilities. While they each had their own interpretations of Kant, they all advocated a psychological interpretation of his epistemology in the tradition of Fries, Herbart, and Beneke rather than that of the speculative idealism of Fichte, Schelling, and Hegel. "All these thinkers saw Kant's epistemology essentially as psychology, as an investigation into the basic mental activities behind human cognition," Beiser notes, "a first-order account of the *causes* of human cognition rather than a second-order evaluation of the *reasons* for it" (*GN-K*, 209). They agreed that Kant's epistemology, in other words, should be understood as a *mode of investigation* rather than an *object of scrutiny itself*; they were interested in how it was *used* rather than how it functioned in the abstract.

The main challenge to mid-century neo-Kantianism was no longer the speculative idealism of Fichte, Schelling, and Hegel, however, but rather a new development: the rise of the empirical sciences—a related but extraordinarily different challenge to any epistemology, Kantian or otherwise. It was a related challenge because the central issue once again, as was the case with speculative idealism, was whether Kant's epistemology should be read *descriptively* or *prescriptively*: that is, does his critical philosophy primarily *describe* how the mind *in fact* works, or does it *prescribe* how the mind *should* work? It was an extraordinarily different challenge, however, because the methods of the empirical sciences demanded rigorous standards of

34. Trendelenburg, *Logische Untersuchungen*; Lotze, *Metaphysik*; Feuerbach, *Grundsätze der Philosophie der Zukunft*. Trendelenburg's and Lotze's works, according to Beiser, "broke utterly with the Hegelian heritage and . . . pushed metaphysics in a new direction" (Beiser, *After Hegel*, 1). Trendelenburg took aim in particular at Hegel's dialectical reasoning, while Lotze criticized and exposed weaknesses in Hegel's logic. Beiser examines both of these works in further detail in *Late German*, 28–68, 153–64. See also Toews, *Hegelianism*, 95–140. Beiser further suggests that Hegelian idealism not only suffered severe criticisms but actually *collapsed* entirely by the end of the 1840s both as a result of these criticisms and because of the collapse of the Prussian Reform Movement (*GN-K*, 5). This strikes me as an overstatement, particularly given how influential Karl Marx and Søren Kierkegaard would prove to be, but it is important to note that Hegel's position was severely weakened by the end of the 1840s, and he would not exercise the same influence, comparatively, that Kant would.

verification that the abstract idealism of Fichte, Schelling, and Hegel never did. Beiser rightly observes, therefore, that there was "extraordinary pressure to bring epistemology in line with the empirical sciences, which had set the intellectual standards of the nineteenth century after the decline of speculative idealism" (*GN-K*, 210).

The question of whether epistemology should be an empirical science among other empirical sciences, or whether it should be an autonomous philosophical discipline in its own right with its own standards and procedures, was a major fault line in mid-nineteenth-century philosophy in general but was particularly important for neo-Kantianism in the 1860s. At the center of the dispute was the status of the relationship between philosophy and *psychology*, which increasingly adopted empirical methods as the century progressed:

> It was not clear [in the 1860s] whether psychology was a unique kind of science having its own methods, or whether it was just another empirical science with methods like those of physiology and biology. The more psychology progressed in the later half of the century, however, the more it seemed to be just another empirical science, reaching its results through observation and experiment, and having as its goal the formulation of general causal laws. *If this were so, then the identification of philosophy with empirical psychology meant surrendering philosophy's claim to autonomy.* (*GN-K*, 210; emphasis added)

At the time of Kant's revival in the 1860s, therefore, the very nature of epistemology, philosophy, and psychology *qua* disciplines was in question. This was tenuous ground indeed for Kant to re-enter conversations about precisely these topics, and this had profound implications for one of the central and ongoing disputes of neo-Kantianism: knowledge of things-in-themselves. The neo-Kantians of the 1860s were in a precarious situation indeed in this respect. Beiser notes,

> None of the neo-Kantians were willing to accept a complete Fichtean idealism, which derives all the content of experience from the knowing subject; they insisted that, to some extent, the matter of experience, the content of sensation, is given. . . . If, however, we accept a given content to experience, and if we insist that all objects of knowledge are conditioned or determined by the activities by which we know them, it becomes impossible to avoid the unknowable thing-in-itself. (*GN-K*, 211)

As Kantians, they acknowledged that knowing subjects actively contribute to knowledge, and they also recognized that things-in-themselves were non-negotiable in Kant's system. In one sense, this is the central dilemma of any attempts to understand Kant's epistemology, but the environment in which the neo-Kantians of the 1860s were active posed unique challenges.

The Fischer-Trendelenburg Dispute

One major fault line that arose in the 1860s was between Kuno Fischer and Adolf Trendelenburg, who was introduced earlier as one of Hegel's leading critics. Their dispute has become infamous for its intensity, and it produced dozens of publications, articles, and books.[35] The debate was complex and involved granular details of Kant's epistemology, but the crux of the matter was a dispute over Kant's Transcendental Aesthetic in the first Critique and the role of the pure intuitions (space and time) in Kant's epistemology. As discussed in chapter 2, the pure intuitions, for Kant, provide the *context* for the operations of pure theoretical reason. At stake in the Fischer-Trendelenburg dispute, however, was a question of *application*: do the intuitions apply only to *appearances of* things-in-themselves, or do they apply *actually* to things-in-themselves?

Trendelenburg's argument was that Kant left open the possibility that the intuitions could apply to things-in-themselves *as well as* their subjective appearances. Trendelenburg does not suggest that Kant argued this directly; rather, he suggests that Kant's *logic* in the Transcendental Aesthetic merely renders it *not impossible*, or that it fails to exclude it. Fischer rejects this possibility first by arguing that Kant *does* exclude the possibility of space and time being properties of things-in-themselves because that would render our knowledge of things-in-themselves *entirely* subjective. Beiser states,

> Trendelenburg adamantly affirmed a transcendental realism according to which these forms give knowledge of nature only if they are true of things-in-themselves, that is, for reality independent of how we perceive it.... Fischer, however, passionately defended transcendental idealism, insisting that transcendental realism is unnecessary for an objective knowledge of nature. All that is necessary, and indeed possible, for objective knowledge of nature, Fischer contended, is a Kantian *empirical realism*, according to which objectivity is possible *within* the realm of appearances ... the conformity of representations with universal and necessary forms of consciousness. (*GN-K*, 214)

His second and related objection is that an entirely subjective interpretation of Kant's epistemology leaves the door open for skepticism, for there is no

---

35. Vaihinger, *Kommentar zu Kants Kritik der reinen Vernuft*, 2:545–48.

way to establish a correspondence between our subjective impressions and things-in-themselves.

Otto Liebmann (1840–1912)

These were not necessarily new issues, but Kant was now officially exhumed and at the forefront of a new generation of Kant interpreters. "If the Trendelenburg-Fischer dispute showed anything," Beiser notes, "it was how important Kant become to German philosophy. It was not only that Kant interpretation could be seen to arouse intense passions and heated controversy; it was also that so much seemed to depend upon it philosophically. Whether personally or philosophically, Kant mattered; he was now at the center of attention" (*GN-K*, 214). This was certainly true for Otto Liebmann, whose *Kant und die Epigonen* of 1865 is, as I have noted above, often mischaracterized as "the" beginning of neo-Kantianism, which is in turn mischaracterized as a development that belongs to the last third of the nineteenth century. Of the disorienting landscape Kant interpreters inherited, Liebmann summarized:

> We have only to recall with what enthusiasm the oracular pronouncements of Schelling were once listened to, which Herbart afterwards declared to be "metaphysical nonsense"; with what astonishment Hegel's dialectic, embracing the whole world in its never-extinguished germinal power, was gazed at, though Arthur Schopenhauer . . . knows not how to treat it with sufficient hatred and contempt. When in addition we take into account Fries's polemic against Fichte, Schelling and Hegel, Herbart's against the last two, and Schopenhauer's against all of them, not to speak of the squabbling and wrangling indulged in among themselves and with others by their adherents and semi-adherents, there extends before our eyes so inextricable a chaos of opinions, a terrain so overgrown with briers, the more distant observer might think it a quite impossible task to make his way through it, let alone orientate himself within it.[36]

---

36. Liebmann, *Kant und die Epigonen*, 5. Of the many historically significant figures I have had to omit in my analysis, Arthur Schopenhauer is a significant one in the development of neo-Kantianism. According to Ludwig Noack, Schopenhauer believed Kant had been "romantically patched up and plastered with old, colorful cloths" by previous generations of his interpreters: "So war allmählich, nachdem es im Reiche der Philosophie gar viele Male Morgen und Abend geworden war, Kants kräftige Geisteschat romantisch verquidt und mit alten bunten Lappen aufgeputzt worden" (Noack, *Immanuel Kant's Auferstehung aus dem Grabe*, 12).

Despite his stature as one of neo-Kantianism's chief architects, Liebmann took extraordinary liberties with both Kant and his interpreters. One of his most striking claims, particularly for the purposes of this chapter, is that the Kantian thing-in-itself, an obviously central element of any interpretation of Kant, was nothing more than a "dogmatic chimera" (*dogmatisches Hirngespinnst*) and a "transcendent scarecrow" (*transcendente Vogelscheuche*)—not only for Kant's interpreters but even for Kant himself—that should be completely done away with.[37] It is difficult to imagine how a book that makes such a brazen conjecture could survive as the defining work of neo-Kantianism, but it would continue to stand for the dawn of a new era of Kant interpretation at least in form if not in content.

Friedrich Albert Lange (1828–75)

Friedrich Albert Lange would close out the 1860s as one of the decade's most towering figures, particularly his work *Geschichte des Materialismus*, about which Beiser states, "No other work did more to revive Kant's reputation, to place him at the center of German philosophy in the middle of the nineteenth century. Its influence overshadows Fischer's and Zeller's 1860 lectures and Liebmann's *Kant und die Epigonen*" (*GN-K*, 356). Köhnke likewise notes, "After the appearance of the first edition in 1866 it was in a few years to become one of the most important and above all the most read of all the writings of neo-Kantianism: through this book Lange became the most significant of all the early neo-Kantians."[38]

Like so many of the neo-Kantians of his era, Lange had a unique disdain for Hegel's speculative rationalism, and his interest in Kant follows the general outlines of the "lost" psychological tradition of Fries, Herbart, and Beneke, which emphasized the description of the mind's operations. But Lange's interest in Kant also coincided with the ongoing so-called "materialism controversy"—whether modern empirical science leads necessarily to scientific naturalism, or materialism—and he saw in Kant an ally in splitting the difference between the two sides of this bitter dispute.[39] Kant, for Lange, is an ally of both natural science and idealism. As Beiser notes,

---

37. "Das 'Ding an Sich' spukte in den Köpfen aller Epigonen ... in der That endlich ist es ein dogmatisches Hirngespinnst, welches nicht einmal ein Scheindasein im Worte zu führen berechtigt ist. Von Kant war es ursprünglich als transcendente Vogelscheuche benutzt worden.... Also weg!" (Liebmann, *Kant und die Epigonen*, 205).

38. Köhnke, *Rise of Neo-Kantianism*, 151.

39. For a succinct overview of the materialism controversy in Germany in the nineteenth century, see Beiser, *After Hegel*, 53–96.

> If materialism stands for the triumph of a complete mechanism and naturalism, which undermines moral and religious ideals, speculative idealism represents a revival of metaphysical rationalism, which save these ideals but only by going beyond the limits of reason. Kant's philosophy offers a middle path between these extremes, because it saves the autonomy of our moral and religious ideals without metaphysics, and because it upholds the principles of mechanism and naturalism without jeopardizing morality and religion. (GN-K, 366)

Like so many other interpreters of his time, Lange had difficulty accounting for Kant's thing-in-itself, and he explicitly changes his views on the subject over the course of two editions of *Geschichte des Materialismus*. In the first edition, he maintains its existence and necessity for Kant's system, but in the second edition, he argues that "the 'thing-in-itself' is a mere idea of limit . . . beyond [the whole realm of experience] lies a sphere which to our knowledge is absolutely inaccessible. . . . We do not, then, really know whether a thing-in-itself exists. . . . The more the 'thing-in-itself' refines itself away to a mere representation, the more the word *phenomena* gains in reality."[40] Kant's thing-in-itself gradually recedes in significance as the psychologist tradition takes root.

Phase Two: The Neo-Kantian Schools of 1870–1914

Lange's affirmation of the psychologist tradition, his attempt to respond to the materialism controversy, and his ambivalence about Kant's thing-in-itself was a fitting conclusion to the revival decade of the 1860s, and his concerns pave the way for the second phase of the "golden era" of neo-Kantianism: its dissemination into distinct schools of thought, which would be where Barth would eventually encounter Kant during his early career. Most accounts of this period will introduce two distinct schools: the Marburg school and the Southwestern or Baden (or less commonly, Heidelberg) school. While it is true that these two dominated the landscape, a third school, the Göttingen or neo-Friesian, was active as well. For the purposes of this chapter, the most important observation to be made is that beginning in the 1870s, the default Kantian orthodoxy began to shift from the psychologist tradition of Fries, Herbart, and Beneke—from the *causes* and *conditions* of knowledge, in other words—to a new alternative that was more consistent with the rise of the empirical sciences: the *validity* of knowledge itself. "The emphasis of

---

40. Lange, *History of Materialism*, 2:216–17. Lange notes his change of mind at 2:216n35.

Kant interpretation had shifted, therefore, away from the *quid facti?*—'What are the origins and causes of knowledge'—to the *quid juris?*—'What makes judgments true and reasoning valid?'" (*GN-K*, 460).

Göttingen: Neo-Friesian Neo-Kantiansim

Dedicated accounts of the neo-Friesian school are lacking. The most recent and focused history is Erna Blencke's "Zur Geschichte der neuen Fries'schen Schule und der Jakob Friedrich-Fries Gesellschaft"; prior to that was Arthur Kronfeld's "Geleitworte zum zehnjährigen Bestehen der neue Friesischen Schule" from 1913.[41] The "neo" in "neo-Friesian" refers to a previous and short-lived attempt by followers of Fries to establish a distinct interpretive school in the 1840s following his death. The chief figure associated with the later neo-Friesian school is Leonard Nelson (1882–1927), who re-established the journal *Abhandlungen der Fries'schen Schule, Neue Folge*, in 1904 and published it until 1937. (The original edition, published by Ernst Friedrich Alpert in the years following Fries's death in 1843, lasted only two years, from 1847 to 1849.)

True to the original concerns of Fries, Nelson would come to advocate a primarily psychological interpretation of Kant, but with an additional concern for its compatibility with the scientific method.[42] Unsurprisingly, like Fries, Nelson was opposed to both Hegelianism and romanticism, but he went further and suggested that both traditions represented a period of philosophical *regress* rather than progress—an assertion that cut to the very roots of Hegelian progress in history.[43] Nelson reiterated what I have identified in this chapter as a deep divide in neo-Kantianism: whether Kant's project is *descriptive* or *prescriptive*. Nelson strongly affirmed the former and, like Fries, saw Kant's first Critique primarily as a descriptive attempt to identify the limits of human reason rather than a constructive, programmatic method of its deployment.[44]

---

41. Blencke, "Zur Geschichte der neuen Fries'schen Schule," 199–208; Kronfeld, "Geleitworte zum zehnjährigen Bestehen," 46–65.

42. Nelson, preface to *Abhandlungen der Fries'schen Schule, Neue Folge*, 1:viii. This will become a major point of contention between Nelson and Hermann Cohen, who will be discussed below.

43. Nelson, *Fortschritte und Rückschritte der Philosophie*, translated as *Progress and Regress in Philosophy*. Sedgwick also notes "a diversity of opinion with regard to the question whether the transformation of idealism from Kant to Hegel counts as an instance of philosophical progress" ("Idealism from Kant to Hegel," 1).

44. Nelson, "Die kritische Methode und das Verhältnis der Psychologie zur Philosophie," 1–88, translated as Nelson, "Critical Method and the Relation of Psychology to Philosophy," 105–54.

For the purposes of theology, which will become increasingly important as this chapter's narrative approaches Barth, it is important to note that one of the other figures associated with the neo-Friesian tradition is Rudolf Otto (1869–1937). Otto is best known for his work *Das Heilige*, but prior to this work, he also published a significant treatise on how the neo-Friesian interpretation of Kant applies to theology titled *Kantische-Fries'sche Religionsphilosophie*.[45] Both works emphasize (1) a *subjective* application of Kant's epistemology for theology and religion specifically that still meets (2) the demands of modern scientific method. Note, for instance, how Otto summarizes his project in *Kantische-Fries'sche Religionsphilosphie*: "The old theology was a metaphysic about God, man, world, and their relations, drawn from reason and revelation. Religion itself would prefer a narration of the deeds of God. Modern theology proposes, as a task that can be performed, something less than the latter, something different from the former. Modern theology is a science of religion; Christian theology, a science of the Christian religion."[46]

Baden and Heidelberg: Southwestern Neo-Kantianism

Like the neo-Friesian school, there is no equivalent, dedicated history of the Southwestern school. It was no less significant, however, in the development of neo-Kantianism and early twentieth-century philosophy and theology generally. Martin Heidegger, for instance, studied and completed his habilitation under Heinrich Rickert (1863–1936), one of the leading thinkers of the Baden school, and Ernst Troeltsch would favor the Baden Kant over that of Marburg.[47]

The most significant figure in Baden neo-Kantianism is Wilhelm Windelband (1848–1915), Rickert's teacher. Initially, Windelband and Hermann Cohen (1842–1918), one of the founders of the Marburg school I will address below, were aligned in their criticism of the association of epistemology with psychology, that is, *quid facti* rather than *quid juris*. Entailed in

---

45. Otto, *Das Heilige*, translated as *Idea of the Holy*; Otto, *Kantisch-Fries'sche Religionsphilosophie und ihre Anwendung auf die Theologie*, esp. 87–103, translated as *Philosophy of Religion Based on Kant and Fries*.

46. Otto, *Philosophy of Religion*, 222. ("Die alte Theologie war eine angeblich aus Vernuft und Offenbarung geschöpfte Metaphysik über Gott, Mensch, und Welt und ihre Beziehungen. . . . Die moderne Theologie . . . ist Religionswissenschaft, und die christliche Theologie christliche Religionswissenschaft." Otto, *Kantisch-Fries'sche Religionsphilosophie*, 192.)

47. On the influence of Baden neo-Kantianism on Troeltsch's intellectual development, see Dietrich, *Cohen and Troeltsch*, 56.

this shift, for both Windelband and Cohen, was a shift of focus away from any transcendent reference for epistemology and toward the immanent apparatus of the knowing subject. "Cohen and Windelband understood Kant's philosophy as a 'critical idealism,'" Beiser states, "that is, as a strictly immanent analysis of the conditions of experience which involves *no transcendent dimension*, whether that of the thing-in-itself or Platonic forms. Because of their leading roles in the neo-Kantian movement, Windelband's and Cohen's views on these issues became the new orthodoxy of the 1880s and 1890s" (*GN-K*, 492; emphasis added).

This would be one of the only points of substantive agreement between the two. Windelband's primary contribution to neo-Kantianism would be to conceive of philosophy, based on his reading of Kant, as a *normative* discipline based on the autonomy of reason, which he addresses in an 1881 lecture on Kant's philosophy and secularism.[48] The central issue for Kant—and the central issue of philosophy—Windelband argues, is not the correspondence of human knowledge with things in themselves, or even the correspondence of *concepts* with things in themselves, but rather with the *concepts themselves*, which Windelband refers to as "rules" (*Regel*) or "norms."[49] If this is the case, philosophy's primary concern should be precisely these rules and norms; truth itself, Windelband suggests, depends on normativity of thought.[50] "Philosophy was for him essentially a science of norms. The task of philosophy is to determine the basic norms that bestow value upon all human activity, whether thinking, willing, or feeling." The consequence of this shift, according to Beiser, is that "Windelband issues an embargo against . . . speculation, insisting upon the strictly immanent status of Kant's philosophy, whose intent is to stay firmly within the limits of experience" (*GN-K*, 496).

Marburg Neo-Kantianism

The Marburg neo-Kantians, for their part, are easily the most well-documented of the three major schools, even in theological accounts of the era,[51] and it would be the branch of neo-Kantianism that both would initially influence Barth's intellectual formation but also be the specific interpretation

48. Windelband, "Immanuel Kant," 111–46.
49. Windelband, "Immanuel Kant," 138.
50. Windelband, "Immanuel Kant," 138.
51. Sieg, *Aufstieg und Niedergang des Marburger Neokantianismus*; Krijnen and Noras, *Marburg versus Südwestdeutschland*; Luft, "Philosophy of the Marburg School," 221–39.

of Kant he would depart from. The beginning of a distinct Marburg interpretive tradition can be traced to Hermann Cohen (1842–1918), particularly his 1871 book, *Kants Theorie der Erfahrung*. I mention above that Cohen and Windelband were initially of similar mind in emphasizing the non-transcendental dimensions of Kant's epistemology, and Cohen's early work follows this trend. He is fond of emphasizing, that is, the subjective conditions that make knowledge possible rather than questions surrounding correspondence between subjective knowledge and things-in-themselves per se. "The dualism between the subject and object now falls *within* the formal conditions of experience, *inside* the transcendental perspective itself" (*GN-K*, 484).

The second edition of *Kants Theorie der Erfahrung*, published in 1885, is an expanded and more programmatic approach to Kant's critical philosophy that also addresses the role of modern science. It would also set the precedent for a distinct Marburg school of interpretation.[52] The most important development between the two editions for the purposes of this chapter is Cohen's evolving opinion on the matter of things-in-themselves. Cohen continues to place an emphasis on the role of subjective experience in knowledge, and there are two important distinctions: the *content* of subjective experience is provided by *science*, and subjective experience *is itself* a thing-in-itself. According to Geert Edel, "Critique of reason now means: *critique of objectified reason in science*."[53] And as Andrea Poma summarizes, "Experience itself becomes the thing-in-itself that was being sought."[54] Cohen accepts, in other words, the conceptual starting point of knowledge—subjective experience—but unlike either Windelband or the neo-Friesian school, he focuses on its employment in science in particular. The consequence of this development, according to Poma, is that it enabled Cohen to *surpass* Kant on Kant's own terms and also bring Kant into conversation with modern science.[55]

The Marburg School was not limited to Hermann Cohen. Its other founder, Paul Natorp (1854–1918), would codify the Marburg approach in his 1912 article, "Kant und die Marburger Schule,"[56] which emphasized not just the scientific relevance of Kant's critical philosophy but also the outsized

52. Andre Poma emphasizes that while the second edition of *Kants Theorie der Erfahrung* marks a significant development from the first edition and sets the stage for original philosophical constructions, it still does not represent Cohen's final, mature thought. Poma, *Critical Philosophy of Hermann Cohen*, 38.

53. Edel, Introduction to *Kants Theorie der Erfahrung*, 1:23.

54. Cohen, *Kants Theorie der Erfahrung*, 641.

55. Poma, *Critical Philosophy of Hermann Cohen*, 48.

56. Natorp, "Kant und die Marburger Schule," 193–221.

and active role human cognition plays in the process: "There is no object by virtue of reference to it through cognition.... The much-discussed Kantian forms of intuition and thought are . . . processes, acts of forming and shaping, acts of intuitive perception, of thought, that is of beholding, of *creating the objects in thought*. The objects originate as the contents of intuitive perceptions, as thought-contents."[57] The notion of the subjective *production* of objects would become the hallmark of the Marburg school. As Köhnke states, "The basic principle of all Marburg neo-Kantianism [is] that objects are not 'given' but 'produced' or 'constructed' by a priori subjectivity."[58]

Conclusion

While it is accurate to identify the decade of the 1860s as the "golden age" of neo-Kantianism, it is less accurate to suggest, as the standard account of neo-Kantianism does, that it *began* in the 1860s with, for instance, Otto Liebmann's *Kant und die Epigonen*. There were significant developments in Kant interpretation well before the revival decade of the 1860s, and the rise of speculative idealism that "culminated" with Hegel is not the only one. To the contrary, as Köhnke demonstrates, there was a robust prehistory to 1860 that made the emergence of a clearly definable neo-Kantianism in the 1860s possible in the first place. More significant, perhaps, is Beiser's argument that neo-Kantianism not only has a *prehistory* prior to 1860 but *its own history* that began in the late eighteenth century. Contrary to many accounts, Fries, Herbart, and Beneke were not ancillary characters; they initiated a defense of Kantian themes that persisted through Helmholtz, appeared again in the debates of the 1860s, and continued in the emergence of the schools in the later nineteenth century.

As I have demonstrated, neo-Kantianism was a powerful and even necessary movement given the rise of scientific materialism and anxieties over philosophy's role as a discipline. "Neo-Kantianism was not only a powerful bulwark against materialism," Beiser states, "but it also had the best account available about the role of philosophy in the modern scientific age. The thesis that philosophy should be first and foremost epistemology, the examination of the logic of the sciences, seemed to ensure the survival of philosophy. It not only gave philosophy a distinctive vocation, so that it could not be rendered obsolete by the sciences, but it also made it a valuable adjunct to the sciences" (*GN-K*, 455).

---

57. Natorp, "Kant und die Marburger Schule," 186; emphasis added.
58. Köhnke, *Rise of Neo-Kantianism*, 178.

All accounts agree that the narrative of neo-Kantianism itself drew to a close in 1914, but not before Karl Barth would be immersed in Hermann Cohen's and Paul Natorp's version of it at Marburg. Barth would ultimately break from that interpretation of Kant in favor of a different reading, but this break was precisely that: a break with an *interpretation of* Kant, not Kant himself. To the contrary, as I will demonstrate in the next chapter, Kantian themes—such the relationship between realism and idealism, our knowledge of objects, belief in God, and the normativity of science—would not only persist well into his later work in the *Church Dogmatics* but even play a central role in his theological strategy.

4

Ad Fontes
Kant and Barth's Early Theology

IT IS WIDELY RECOGNIZED in Barth scholarship that Barth's debt to Kant runs deep, but how and to what extent this is the case remains an open question.[1] Barth's immersion in Herrmann Cohen's and Paul Natorp's version of neo-Kantianism through his teacher Wilhelm Herrmann at Marburg was extraordinarily influential for his intellectual development.[2] Barth would ultimately break from that interpretation of Kant in favor of a different reading, but this break was precisely that: a break with an *interpretation of* Kant, not Kant himself. To the contrary, Kantian themes would not only persist well into his later work in the *Church Dogmatics* but even play a central role in his theological strategy.

"The first book which really moved me as a student," Barth recalls, "was Kant's *Critique of Practical Reason*."[3] But Barth's interest in Kant was not limited to his student years or to his early period; he continued to wrestle with and understand Kant deeply, such that Heinz Cassirer would inquire, "Why is it that this Swiss theologian understands Kant far better than any philosopher I have come across?"[4] The answer to that question, Colin Gunton suggests, is that "Barth identified that after Kant, theology

---

1. Beyond the relevant sections in the standard introductions to Barth's theology by Hunsinger, Torrance, Balthasar, Busch, Webster, and others, important resources for Barth's theological method include McCormack, *Karl Barth's Critically Realistic Dialectical Theology*; Pugh, *Anselmic Shift*; Fisher, *Revelatory Positivism?*; Sykes, *Karl Barth*; La Montagne, *Barth and Rationality*; Rumscheidt, *Revelation and Theology*; Gunton, *Barth Lectures*; McFarlane, "Human Person as an Epistemic Agent,"; Oakes, *Karl Barth on Theology and Philosophy*; Diller, *Theology's Epistemological Dilemma*.

2. In addition to McCormack's *Karl Barth's Critically Realistic Dialectical Theology*, important resources for understanding Barth's reception of Kant include Fisher, *Revelatory Positivism?*; Lyden, "Karl Barth's View on the Knowledge of God"; Adriaanse, "Kant-Rezeption in der Theologie," 74–90; Stanley, "Barth after Kant?," 423–45; Beintker, "Grenzbewusstsein," 19–30; Lohmann, *Karl Barth und der Neukantianismus*.

3. Busch, *Karl Barth*, 34.

4. Letter from Ronald Weitzman, March 20, 2001, as reported in Gunton, introduction to Barth, *Protestant Theology in the Nineteenth Century*, xvi.

(and for that matter, philosophy) could never be the same. Any theologian had to come to terms with Kant, to follow in his tracks, or branch out in some way from what he established."[5]

These observations raise the question of *how* exactly Barth incorporated Kant's ideas into his own theological epistemology. Bruce McCormack suggests, "To the extent that Barth concerned himself with philosophical epistemology at all, he was an idealist (and more specifically, a Kantian)" and also that "all of his efforts in theology may be considered, from one point of view, as an attempt to overcome Kant by means of Kant, not retreating behind him and attempting to go around him, but going through him."[6] D. Paul La Montagne has proposed more recently that "Barth uses a foundationalist epistemology, Kant's, in a postfoundational way because he finds it necessary if he is to remain faithful to the object of his discourse."[7] Colin Gunton, on the other hand, views Barth's strategy for using Kant as one of reversal: "My view is that on the whole Barth is trying to outdo Kant, so to speak. But as ever when you try to outdo someone else they continue to shape your thought. . . . Barth changes the Kantian pattern because he wants to say not that the mind shapes the object but that God shapes the mind."[8]

Over the course of this chapter, I will be working my way toward emphasizing the fact that for both Kant and Barth, God's existence is a presupposition of theological epistemology, not something that can be achieved through proofs or procedure; God's existence is not a concept that is subject to external argument or demonstration but rather one that must be already incorporated into one's epistemological framework. For Kant, God was incorporated into epistemology morally; Barth does not restrict theological epistemology to morality, but for both Kant and Barth, questions surrounding God's existence and epistemology proper were intimately related, even inseparable, and one cannot sufficiently explain one without eventually referencing the other. Neither of their theological epistemologies, in other words, happen to have certain incidental theological features but rather are necessarily theological by definition.

Barth's Initial Reception of Kant

In order to do this, I will begin with Barth's initial encounter with Kant via Marburg neo-Kantianism. I will then proceed to trace how this continued

---

5. Gunton, *Barth Lectures*, 13.
6. McCormack, *Karl Barth's Critically Realistic Dialectical Theology*, 465–66.
7. La Montagne, *Barth and Rationality*, 12.
8. Gunton, *Barth Lectures*, 135.

to develop thematically in his early career, but this requires some nuance. To this end, I recruit the insights of Eberhard Busch, Simon Fisher, Bruce McCormack, and Christophe Chalamet. This will give way to a brief discussion of the additional, related issue of Barth's alleged break with "liberalism," which will clear the way for a straightforward textual consideration of Kantian themes in Barth's early corpus.

Eberhard Busch

Barth began his studies in theology in Bern in 1904. His initial interest in the subject was moderate: "[My Berne professors] were incapable of interesting me more deeply and to any lasting extent," he recounts (*KB*, 34). Two things, however, left a lasting impression on him, which he would carry with him into his further education at Marburg: criticism of orthodoxy and the importance of Kant for theology: "I was earnestly told, and I learnt, all that can be said against 'the old orthodoxy' . . . and that all God's ways begin with Kant and, if possible, must also end there" (*KB*, 34). From this early point in Barth's education, Kant would begin to stand out as a uniquely important influence. I note above that Kant's second Critique in particular was one of the first books that struck his imagination as a student, but reading Kant's *Metaphysics of Morals* led him to a "great discovery" that "the gospel was simple, that the divine truth was not a complicated, difficult construction with hundreds of different hypotheses, but a simple, clear knowledge, accessible to any child" (*KB*, 35).

After Bern, Barth was interested in studying in Marburg but matriculated at Berlin as a compromise with his father. In addition to studying with von Harnack in Berlin and reading Schleiermacher extensively, Barth was introduced to the work of Wilhelm Herrmann, a major figure in the Marburg neo-Kantian school along with Paul Natorp and Herrmann Cohen. Barth eventually made his way to Marburg in 1908 after a stop in Tübingen, and significantly for my purposes, he records that he "worked through the whole of Kant before I made my pilgrimage to Marburg! That is really where I came from: first I studied Kant's *Critique of Practical Reason*, and then I went twice through the *Critique of Pure Reason* almost with a toothcomb. At that time we thought that it was the way one had to begin with theology" (*KB*, 45). During an editorship at *Christliche Welt* under Martin Rade in 1909, Barth would describe his own position as "somewhere between Kant and the young Schleiermacher," and those two figures would continue to comprise the heart of his personal research during this period (*KB*, 49, 57).

Marburg is where Barth's exposure to neo-Kantianism reached its peak, and there is a uniform consensus in Barth scholarship that the most influential neo-Kantian on Barth was Wilhelm Herrmann. This influence was both positive and negative: Herrmann was one of Barth's greatest original intellectual inspirations, but he also came to represent what Barth would reject. This comes to us not only from the secondary literature—Chalamet, McCormack, and Fisher—but from Barth himself. Barth notes, "I can remember the day when I . . . first read his *Ethics* as though it were yesterday. . . . If I had the temperament of Klaus Harms, I could speak of Herrmann as he does of Scheiermacher, or say what Stilling says of Herder: 'This book started me off in perpetual motion.' With more restraint, but no less gratefully, I would prefer to say: 'I think that my own personal interest in theology began on that day'" (*KB*, 40–41). Herrmann, according to Barth, was "*the* theological teacher of my student years. . . . I soaked Herrmann in through all my pores" (*KB*, 44, 45).

Within Marburg neo-Kantianism, Herrmann played a unique role. While he would advocate both Kant and Schleiermacher, he also maintained that theology as a discipline was capable of standing on its own two feet; its claims were not required to pass through the tribunal of critical reason first: "[Herrmann] showed us that theology could have its own professional fervor, not merely as a parasite on the fourth faculty, but in its own right. . . . The decisive thing for him was the christocentric impulse, and I learnt that from him" (*KB*, 45). And yet Herrmann's theology was simultaneously iconoclastic in rejecting old dogmatic authorities, both philosophical and theological. Christian faith, for Herrmann and for Barth at this time, was primarily an inward experience that was expressed outwardly in the moral life (*KB*, 46).

Simon Fisher

One of the first monographs to analyze Barth's reception of Marburg neo-Kantianism specifically was Simon Fisher's *Revelatory Positivism?* Fisher's modest aim in this text is to trace the influence of Marburg idealism on Barth's earliest theology—*how* it influenced him, not just the fact *that* it did—and to demonstrate that for Barth in particular (but also, by implication, theological method in general), the academic question of method in theology cannot be separated from the practice of theology—that is, the actual act of knowing God: "in relation to method a simple dichotomy between means and ends will not do."[9] In order to do this, Fischer has to

---

9. Fisher, *Revelatory Positivism?*, 5.

navigate the issue of Barth's break with liberalism. I will address this in the next section, but at this point note that on one hand, F.-W. Marquardt has suggested a deep continuity between Barth's early and late theology and called for a reassessment of the notion of a "break" with liberalism at all: Barth created a framework during his early period, Marquardt argues, that "was to govern his entire theological work to come."[10] On the other hand, Fisher also must avoid the tendency to characterize Barth's earliest theology, common in Anglo scholarship, as "a brief half-hearted flirtation with a liberalism which means very little."[11] Fisher stops short of making both claims and instead seeks to understand Barth's earliest period on its own terms.

Fisher begins his narrative with Hermann Cohen, who, he states, played an outsized influence in the development of one of Marburg neo-Kantianism's key distinctives: "a totally different approach [to the relationship between science and idealism] which, being both scientific and critical, would demonstrate the absolute validity of the foundations from which all knowledge derives."[12] This leads Fisher to Wilhelm Herrmann, perhaps the most significant figure in Barth's early theological development. According to Fisher, Herrmann's neo-Kantianism displays several distinct characteristics: an assumption of Kant's tripartite division of knowledge into epistemology, morality, and aesthetics; a strong distinction between myth and science; and, most significant, a discomfort with the Ritschlian demand for a "sound epistemology [as] an essential prelude to any systematic theology."[13]

Herrmann's relationship to Marburg neo-Kantianism was complex; he operated within it, but his views were unique and nuanced. His *Dogmatik*, for example, opens with a preamble on methodological *Religionswissenschaft* and emphasizes the obligation of Christian religious communities to demonstrate their validity to intellectual culture as the "first task of a Christian systematic theology."[14] Like other Marburg neo-Kantians, Herrmann placed a strong emphasis on human experience as a starting point in theology. But Herrmann then proceeds to discuss religious experience, revelation, and belief—even religion's *basis* in the experience of revelation. Indeed, Herrmann would come to suggest that the reality of the Christian faith is given (*gegeben*) through revelation and not something that is achieved through the processes of reason through *Religionsphilosophie*. The reality of God, for

---

10. Marquardt, "Socialism in the Theology of Karl Barth," 70.
11. Fisher, *Revelatory Positivism?*, 173.
12. Fisher, *Revelatory Positivism?*, 19.
13. Fisher, *Revelatory Positivism?*, 125.
14. Herrmann, *Systematic Theology*, 15.

Herrmann, by definition "eludes the grasp of any philosophical thought."[15] He only arrives at this conclusion, however, after clearing the ground in a way that would retain the attention of other Marburg neo-Kantians.[16] Unlike some of the other neo-Kantians, therefore, he did not agree with epistemology as a starting point in theology, and he also emphasized the importance of revelation in religious experience. Religious experience and revelation, for Herrmann, were precursors to epistemology.

This does not mean that epistemology is irrelevant for Herrmann, however; it is simply not primary. Among the many ways in which Barth was influenced by Herrmann, according to Fisher, the most significant for my purposes is epistemological. "When referring to the epistemology he had embraced," Fisher states, "Barth was often at pains to stress the importance of autonomy for the cognitive enterprise."[17] Barth, at this point, rejected the notion that reason was obligated to assent to truths based solely on outside authority, but he also believed that an autonomous subject was required for both philosophy and theology: "The transcendental method must accept the thought of personality as a limitative concept, but only as a limitative concept, as a thought which cannot be executed, but which nevertheless cannot be dispensed with."[18] This was important for both Barth and Herrmann because it created space within a Kantian framework for divine revelation; "[Barth] spotted," Fisher states, "an *Ich*-shaped lacuna in Marburg philosophy which afforded an entrance for 'religious individualism.'"[19] For Herrmann and the early Barth, individuals experience revelation directly. Herrmann defines *revelation* specifically as "the experiences out of which man acquires the power of real life or becomes religious. . . . Here lies for us the way to God."[20] This experience involves "the realization on the part of any religious man that he has encountered a spiritual power in contact with which he has felt utterly humbled."[21] This is an important step for the direction Barth would eventually go, but it also had one important corollary: religious individualism, for the early Barth, takes precedence over theological doctrine.[22]

---

15. Fisher, *Revelatory Positivism?*, 134.
16. Herrmann, *Systematic Theology*, 34–36.
17. Fisher, *Revelatory Positivism?*, 134.
18. Barth, "Der Glaube an den persönlichen Gott," 25.
19. Fisher, *Revelatory Positivism?*, 193.
20. Herrmann, *Systematic Theology*, 34.
21. Herrmann, *Systematic Theology*, 36.
22. Fisher, *Revelatory Positivism?*, 247.

> Barth aspired to convert neo-Kantianism to Christ by transferring his benefits into the operative center of Marburg philosophy. Thought no longer actualized its possibilities by virtue of its innate dynamism; the revealed actuality of God rather actualized the subject, who then received power to construct a cultural order in which truth, goodness, and beauty would continuously become incarnate.[23]

Theology, for the early Marburg Barth, does not *produce* knowledge of God but rather *receives* it.[24]

Bruce McCormack

Another resource for understanding Barth's relationship to Marburg neo-Kantianism, Bruce McCormack's *Karl Barth's Critically Realistic Dialectical Theology*, has a more ambitious aim than that of Fisher's. McCormack's narration of Barth's intellectual development, including but not limited to Marburg, argues that Barth's alleged "break" with liberalism—and subsequent break from dialectical theology in favor of analogical thought—has been incorrectly characterized. I will return to this particular part of McCormack's argument in the following sections and focus here on his account of Barth's relationship with Herrmann in particular.

On McCormack's account, Wilhelm Herrmann's theology was forged in the crucible of two influences: philosophically, by Hermann Cohen and Paul Natorp, and theologically by Albrecht Ritschl and Ernst Troeltsch. Although he was an early sympathizer of Ritschl, Herrmann was dissatisfied with the limitations of both influences and sought to forge a third way in theology within the confines of Marburg neo-Kantianism. Even in his earliest work, McCormack notes, Herrmann was concerned to "distinguish faith from knowledge and to oppose every attempt to ground the former in the latter."[25] This distinction between faith and knowledge—or in the preferred locutions of the neo-Kantians, metaphysics and science (*Metaphysik* and *Wissenschaft*)—is a subtle one, for it can be taken to mean many different things. It can be found in Ritschl, for instance, but Ritchsl would prioritize *Wissenschaft* over *Metaphysik*, or more precisely, sought to establish scientific boundaries for theological procedure. Herrmann also accepts the distinction but insists that "the methodological knowing of the real in science absolutely does not reach to the reality of God. . . . We can only come to God

---

23. Fisher, *Revelatory Positivism?*, 324.
24. Fisher, *Revelatory Positivism?*, 334.
25. McCormack, *Karl Barth's Critically Realistic Dialectical Theology*, 50.

because he has come to us in history."²⁶ How exactly Herrmann would apply this distinction between knowledge and faith in his constructive theology in his later writings would not only be one of his unique contributions to the Marburg neo-Kantian school but also what would influence Barth's own thinking.

Herrmann's sharp distinction between faith and reason led him to conclude not that one should be privileged over the other but rather that religious and theological reason is simply distinct from other sorts of knowledge. McCormack notes that for Herrmann, "religious knowing—the knowledge of faith—is a special kind of knowing which is independent of all other forms of cognition and therefore cannot be reduced to any branch of scientific knowledge that was acknowledged by the neo-Kantians. The reason for this," McCormack continues, "lies first of all in the fact that the reality known by faith (i.e., God) lies beyond the reality to which science has access. God, for Herrmann, was a unique, transcendent, supramundane being, not to be confused with the world which science knows."²⁷ One of the end results of Herrmann's insistence upon the unique operations of the knowledge of faith is that it allowed for the possibility of revelation: "Faith is made to stand on its own two feet," McCormack notes, "when religion lives from revelation alone."²⁸ Subjecting faith to the rigors of scientific reason, one of the hallmarks of Marburg neo-Kantianism, renders faith irrelevant. Faith, for Herrmann, was rather rooted in an *encounter with* God in which "a Reality is experienced to which science has no access but whose existence cannot be doubted."²⁹ The end result of Herrmann's distinction, according to McCormack, is that "he has used the neo-Kantian epistemology . . . to create a space for religion at a point lying outside those limits, thereby overcoming the neo-Kantian treatment of religion from within."³⁰ Herrmann's emphases are unusual for Marburg neo-Kantianism, but he still operates within its general confines.

Christophe Chalamet

More recently, Christophe Chalamet has built on McCormack's correctives in his *Dialectical Theologians*, but he also suggests that McCormack does not go far enough in examining the depth of Barth's indebtedness to Herrmann.

26. Herrmann, "Zur theologischen Darstellung der christlichen Erfahrung," 245.
27. McCormack, *Karl Barth's Critically Realistic Dialectical Theology*, 55.
28. McCormack, *Karl Barth's Critically Realistic Dialectical Theology*, 55.
29. McCormack, *Karl Barth's Critically Realistic Dialectical Theology*, 59.
30. McCormack, *Karl Barth's Critically Realistic Dialectical Theology*, 60.

"It is not sufficient," he states, "to show the limits of von Balthasar's thesis [more on which in the next section] if we want to understand how Barth's theology changed over time."[31] A complete understanding of how Barth's theology changed, Chalamet suggests, requires a more extensive examination of Barth's neo-Kantian roots as well as the ways in which his later thought demonstrates consistency with his early thought.

Chalamet's account of Herrmann's role in Marburg neo-Kantianism emphasizes the contrast between Herrmann's approach to theology and that of Ernst Troeltsch. Indeed, "to be a disciple of Herrmann meant to be opposed to the other major figure of Protestant theology at that time, Ernst Troeltsch. Between Marburg and Heidelberg, where Troeltsch taught, one had to decide."[32] Like Ritschl's interest in an epistemology that precedes theology, mentioned above in Fisher's account of Herrmann, Troeltsch was interested in defending the "scientific character of theology," but this was opposed to Herrmann's emphases on the personal experience of revelation and the sharp distinction between God and world.[33] This God-world distinction was central to Herrmann's theological outlook, such that, according to Chalamet, "God is either totally transcendent or not at all. He is wholly other or an idol, an object of the world."[34] God, for Herrmann, is a reality that is encountered, not an object that is reasoned toward through a well-organized epistemological procedure that is consistent with the scientific method.

> If God were an object of the world, his reality could eventually be demonstrated by science, he could be reached by our theoretical and ethical efforts. But God is beyond what we can know from ourselves, he is beyond our scientific efforts and our will. Our natural reason cannot know God. . . . God is beyond the world. Nobody can prove his existence: "a God which can be proven is a god of the world, and a god of the world is an idol." God is totally other, and he remains so at the moment when he encounters us. He remains transcendent in his action toward us. His action takes place in the world, yet it is never "of" the world.

---

31. Chalamet, *Dialectical Theologians*, 17.
32. Chalamet, *Dialectical Theologians*, 26.
33. Chalamet, *Dialectical Theologians*, 26. McCormack notes that "these two elements—religious individualism and historical relativism—constitute the content of the satchel which a student of modern theology takes with him from the university" (*Karl Barth's Critically Realistic Dialectical Theology*, 69).
34. Chalamet, *Dialectical Theologians*, 26.

Its origin is beyond the world. Therefore God's action can never be explained by natural sciences.[35]

These twin commitments of Herrmann's—the transcendence of God and the limits of knowledge—simultaneously separated him from the rest of the Marburg neo-Kantians and also had an enduring influence on Barth's theology. Twin commitments such as these, furthermore, were grist for the dialectical mill, which was Herrmann's preferred method of procedure and one that Barth would inherit. One example of Barth's early enthusiasm not just for dialectics in general but for the specific dialectical tension between finite human subjects and the transcendence of God can be found in his 1912 review of Karl Heim's *Das Gewißheitsproblem in der systematischen Theologie bis zu Schleiermacher* (*The Problem of Certainty in Systematic Theology up to Schleiermacher*), in which, Chalamet states, Barth found an ally with Herrmann. Specifically—and importantly for Barth's future trajectory—both Heim and Herrmann helped him articulate one of the central dialectical tensions that would persist throughout his career: "the direct trend of realism together with the indirect trend of critical thought. . . . not to be either realistic or critically idealist (or employ a mix of the two) but to be fully realistic and critical, in other words to present God's revelation and hiddenness, or God's 'givenness' and non-'givenness,' as well as God's love and freedom, in all their radicality."[36]

Approaches to Barth's Alleged Break with Liberalism

Barth's earliest exposure to Kant came from reading him directly during his student years, and Wilhelm Herrmann would determine how Barth would interpret Kant's importance for theology. Two important commitments emerge during this period: (1) a commitment to theology's integrity as a discipline and (2) a commitment to methodological dialectics. Dialectical method in theology refers to the belief that for every theological affirmation, there must be a corresponding theological denial; in contrast to rhetoric, persuasion, or analogy, which aim toward theological affirmation and certainty, dialectical method emphasizes comparison, contrast, paradox, and limitation. "Dialectical theology," Robert Scharlemann notes, "had as its fundamental contention that every theological position had to be denied because it was not, and could not be, authentically theological."[37] The

---

35. Chalamet, *Dialectical Theologians*, 39.
36. Chalamet, *Dialectical Theologians*, 73.
37. Scharlemann, "The No to Nothing and the Nothing to Know," 61.

commitment to dialectics in theology is not an arbitrary choice for either Herrmann or Barth; to the contrary, the method arises from the subject matter itself. "The presence of dialectics in theology is not the consequence of a personal preference for a dualist or indirect thought but the consequence of the paradox lodged in the subject matter itself."[38]

The next major phase in Barth's intellectual development involves a break with Hermann and the tradition of Marburg neo-Kantian "liberalism" he assumed in his early career.[39] This break is well-known, but questions of continuity and discontinuity have been raised in recent years following Bruce McCormack's *Karl Barth's Critically Realistic Dialectical Theology*. How clean was this alleged break? That is, did Barth abandon his early commitments wholesale, or did he retain some of his early methodological sensibilities throughout his career? Answers to these questions have significant consequences not only for Barth studies in general but also for the purposes of my arguments specifically: if Barth had an early interest in Kant but abandoned that interest after his break with liberalism, my suspicions about a continuity with Kant even in Barth's later writings will be weakened considerably; if, however, Barth had an early interest in Kant that persisted during and even beyond the break with liberalism, then my suspicions about continuity are defensible. The issue I will investigate in this section, then, is the extent of the break in general, but I will also be paying particular attention to Barth's interest in Kant and neo-Kantianism throughout this time.

Biographical Considerations

Barth's career trajectory began to change in 1911 when he began to serve as a pastor in Safenwil, a traditionally agricultural community of less than 1,700 that was in a period of transition to industrialization. "It was during my time in Safenwil," Barth states, "that I changed my mind decisively in a way which also affected the outward form of my future career" (*KB*, 60–61). In addition to weekly sermon preparation, Barth took particular pride in

---

38. Chalamet, *Dialectical Theologians*, 74.

39. I use the term *liberalism* descriptively to refer to the Protestant theological tradition that arose primarily in late-eighteenth and early nineteenth century Germany and persisted through Barth's time at Marburg. Its distinguishing feature is the priority given, in varying degrees, to individual human reason and experience over received theological tradition. How and to what extent Kant's philosophy is amenable to this outlook was central to its ongoing development. The beginnings of the movement are commonly attributed to F. D. E. Schleiermacher—particularly his *Über de Religion* (1799)—Friedrich Schelling, and G. W. F. Hegel, but important philosophical precursors to them include Jean-Jacques Rousseau and Gotthold Ephraim Lessing.

his confirmation course, the first part of which ("The Way to Jesus") makes explicit use of Kant:

> By nature man should be distinguished by his *reason*, that is, by the fact that he thinks, wills and feels according to certain laws which he bears within himself. He fulfills his destiny by *applying* his reason or *striving* for what is true, good and beautiful. And this destiny is man's destiny with *God*, for God is eternal truth, goodness and beauty. To *seek* God means to *find* God (Plato). And therefore: this divine destiny for man is expressed most clearly in the inner law of the *will*. Each man should act as he believes *everyone* should act. Such a will is a good will (I. Kant). (*KB*, 64–65)

Barth served in Safenwil for twelve years, and the research trajectory begun at Marburg would give way to the demands of parish ministry.

The outbreak of the first World War would prove to be a watershed moment for Barth both personally and theologically. He was devastated at the German intellectual community's support of Kaiser Wilhelm II leading up to the first World War—the very community that forged his early theological preoccupations and interest in neo-Kantiansim. Indeed, among the supporters of Wilhelm II's policies were not only Adolf von Harnack but also Wilhelm Herrmann himself. Barth's intellectual foundations were shaken to the core: "To me they seemed to have been hopelessly compromised by what I regarded as their failure in the face of the ideology of war. . . . Their exegetical and dogmatic presuppositions could not be in order. . . . A whole world of exegesis, ethics, dogmatics and preaching, which I had hitherto held to be trustworthy, was shaken to the foundations, and with it, all the other writings of the German theologians" (*KB*, 81). The war began on August 1, 1914, and by 1915, Barth decided it was time to move in a new direction (*KB*, 91).

Discontinuity Theses

It is clear that Barth's new direction in 1915 would chart the course for the remainder of his life's work, and this would commence with the first edition of his Romans commentary in 1919. The precise character of that new direction, and the extent to which that new direction demonstrates continuity or discontinuity with his previous commitments, is a matter of some dispute in secondary literature. One option, advanced in different ways by Hans Urs von Balthasar and T. F. Torrance, emphasizes the differences between the interests of the early and post-1915 Barth. In his *The Theology of Karl Barth*, von Balthasar suggests that the break between the early and later Barth can be characterized primarily by a fundamental methodological shift from dialectics to analogy.[40] The early turn away from liberalism, for von Balthasar, was an initial step in this direction, and a full methodological break—"his final emancipation from the shackles of philosophy, enabling him finally to arrive at a genuine, self-authenticating theology"—occurred around 1930. Barth gradually moves beyond dialectics and arrives at a mature theology based on analogy—*analogia entis* and *analogia fidei*—particularly in the third and fourth volumes of the *Church Dogmatics*: "Indeed," von Balthasar states, "so victorious does it become that by the time of the later volumes on creation, Incarnation and providence (1945, 1948, and 1950), it has become the central theme of his theology."[41]

Thomas Torrance's claims about the early and later Barth are more ambitious. While von Balthasar suggests that Barth abandoned one method for another, Torrance suggests that Barth abandoned an inherently liberal theological procedure—dialectics—for "dogmatic thinking." The turning point, for Torrance, came with the second edition of the Romans commentary, which was the result, above all else, of "listening to the mighty voice of Paul, which had been so new to him when he first went to Safenwil." Torrance summarizes the significance of this moment at length:

> Barth . . . had to abjure entirely the exegetical method of men like Jülicher and Lietzmann who in their different ways brought to the text a prior understanding in terms of which they distinguished in the raw material of the Bible what they approved from what they rejected, and so instead of wrestling with the difficult and scandalous passages, set them aside as "Jewish" or "popular Christian" or "Hellenistic" or some other kind of material of no concern to modern men. Barth rejected that as a flight from the given realities, as an avoidance of the hard work of genuine interpretation, and as a failure to apply the rigorous methods of exact science. *True interpretation involves the determination to face up to what the text is actually saying whether we like it or not, and whether it agrees with our presuppositions or not, and especially a struggle with it at the uncomfortable points until we let it yield what it really has to say to us* without any

---

40. Balthasar, *Theology of Karl Barth*, 93.

41. Balthasar, *Theology of Karl Barth*, 107. Von Balthasar does not suggest that Barth ever resolves the tension between the analogy of being and the analogy of faith but rather that it, rather than dialectical method itself, becomes Barth's focus in his later work. Since von Balthasar's text was originally published, the literature on Barth, analogy, and particularly Erich Pryzwara has increased; see, for instance, Johnson, *Karl Barth and the "Analogia Entis"*; White, *Analogy of Being*; Spencer, *Analogy of Faith*; Gonzales, *Reimagining the "Analogia Entis."*

attempt on our part to chop it down or to foreclose the dialogue before we have gone through with it to the end. As a matter of fact, Barth confessed—and this is what had such an impact on him—he found that it was in his wrestling with those elements in the Epistle which were "scandals to modern thought" that he really broke through to the characteristic and veritable discernment of St. Paul. Faithful exegesis entailed a ruthless, radical self-criticism, but that was the very thing the older and contemporary commentators avoided. For Barth it meant the shaking and shattering of his own frame of reference, the tearing down of his own scaffolding, in fact, a radical repentance.[42]

Barth's break with his previous assumptions, for Torrance, was thoroughgoing and involved not just an abstract change in method but a complete reorientation of thought and outright rejection of his prior theological foundations—neo-Kantianism included.[43]

Modified Discontinuity Theses

Bruce McCormack does not deny a significant shift (or shifts) in Barth's thinking, but he does argue that both von Balthasar and Torrance overstate their cases. Von Balthasar's thesis in particular cast a "massive shadow" over accounts of Barth's intellectual development.[44] Torrance's arguments are derived from von Balthasar's and, according to McCormack, add an additional layer of complication, particularly in Anglo scholarship, by introducing Barth's *Anselm* book as the major turning point in Barth's theology.[45] Rather than a methodological break from dialectic to analogy (von Balthasar) or an ideological break from dialectic to dogmatics (Torrance), McCormack suggests that the shift in Barth's thinking was more nuanced. Instead of abandoning dialectical thinking wholesale, Barth rather exchanged one sort of dialectical method for another. More specifically, McCormack suggests, Barth retained a methodological interest in dialectic but relocated the source of theology in God's initiative rather than in the human subject. One significant frustration Barth encountered with Herrmann's emphasis on personal religious experience, for instance, was that it yielded inconsistent results. "If religious experience could give rise to such divergent and even contradictory conclusions," McCormack states, "perhaps it could no

---

42. Torrance, *Karl Barth*, 48–49; emphasis added.
43. Torrance, *Karl Barth*, 56–57.
44. McCormack, *Karl Barth's Critically Realistic Dialectical Theology*, 1.
45. McCormack, *Karl Barth's Critically Realistic Dialectical Theology*, 5.

longer be relied upon to provide an adequate ground and starting-point for theology."[46] This does not mean that Barth needed to abandon dialectical method entirely; rather, Barth had reached the epistemological limits of what human knowledge could produce *about* God on its own terms and instead shifted focus to how knowledge of God is received *by* human knowing. "Barth's *break* with his early theology," McCormack suggests, "lies here: in the abandonment of the liberal axiom of a 'God in us' in favor of a new conception of the speaking of God which was better calculated to protect the sovereign freedom of the divine Subject in the process of revelation."[47] These emphases were of course already present in Herrmann, but Barth is now rearranging and reprioritizing them in his own way.

Once Barth makes this shift, which McCormack suggests begins with the first Romans commentary, the result is not a new method but rather a modified dialectical procedure based on critical realism, a species of Kantian idealism that acknowledges *both* the mind-independent reality of God *and* the conceptual apparatus that knowing human subjects bring to the process of knowing God. Indeed, Barth states in his *Ethics* that while idealism cannot *produce* knowledge of God, "the idealistic view can give to theology, which moves in the same sphere as itself, a most important tool in the presentation of Christian truth. . . . When it is a matter of *thinking* the thought of God . . . we constantly follow the idealistic track."[48] McCormack summarizes this central part of his argument at length as follows:

> When Barth's break with Herrmannian theology would finally come, the focal point would be the latter's idealism. The idealistic theology of Barth's youth would be replaced by . . . a "critical realism." . . . Barth never simply abandoned his idealistic inheritance. Idealism would prove to be a valuable ally in establishing the limits of human knowing. Barth would continue to acknowledge the validity of the idealistic point of view where the knowledge of the "given" was concerned. The "given" (or what we customarily think of as the "real") is the product of the knowing activity of the human subject. . . . "Realism" is meant to suggest, however, that after the break Barth would always insist that the divine being was real, whole, and complete in itself apart from the knowing activity of the human subject; indeed, the reality of God precedes all human knowing. The result would be a completely new framework for theological thinking. Barth would seek to ground theological reflection

---

46. McCormack, *Karl Barth's Critically Realistic Dialectical Theology*, 113.
47. McCormack, *Karl Barth's Critically Realistic Dialectical Theology*, 107.
48. Barth, *Ethics*, 308.

in the objectively real "self-presupposing divine subjectivity" in revelation; i.e., to start from the reality of God. All the other differences between Barth and Herrmann would flow from this difference in starting-point.[49]

A different starting point, however, does not necessarily entail a different method, and a different framework does not necessarily entail different concerns. These are rather different ways of approaching the same work. If this is the case, McCormack, argues, we can continue discern thematic continuities with the neo-Kantianism Barth inherited from Herrmann throughout Barth's corpus, even in the later volumes of the *Church Dogmatics*. "Virtually all of the themes and tendencies which we have seen in Herrmann (the definition of revelation as *Self*-revelation and the insistence on its self-authenticating character, the opposition to natural theology, apologetics, etc.)," McCormack argues, "would survive Barth's break with the theology of his teacher and would remain enduring elements in his dialectical theology as well. And yet all of these themes and tendencies would be brought into the service of a very different theological programme."[50]

McCormack is not alone in emphasizing elements of continuity between Barth's early and late theology while also acknowledging that Barth's thinking did indeed undergo a major shift. Johann Friedrich Lohmann's *Karl Barth und der Neukantianismus*, for instance, is the first monograph since Fisher to trace the influence on Marburg neo-Kantianism not just on Barth's early theology (as Fisher did) but also his later writings as well. Lohmann identifies three Marburg neo-Kantian preoccupations and traces them throughout Barth's career: antisubjectivism (*Die anti-subjektivistische Erkenntnistheorie*), a persistent interest in *Ursprung* ("origin") philosophy, and an opposition to positivism.[51] Lohmann suggests that while Barth loses interest in the second two, the first, antisubjectivism, persists throughout Barth's early and late work alike.[52]

Christophe Chalamet takes matters a step further and suggests not only thematic continuity between Barth's early and late periods but also methodological consistency during his transition away from liberalism. Specifically, Chalamet argues not for an *abandonment* of the concerns he

49. McCormack, *Karl Barth's Critically Realistic Dialectical Theology*, 67.

50. McCormack, *Karl Barth's Critically Realistic Dialectical Theology*, 68.

51. For a helpful overview of these themes in Marburg neo-Kantianism, see Fisher, *Revelatory Positivism?*, 34–55.

52. Lohmann, *Karl Barth und der Neukantianismus*, 377–88. In a review of Lohmann's work, McCormack suggests that the third emphasis can be discerned throughout Barth's career as well. See McCormack, Review of *Karl Barth*, 129–30.

inherited from Herrmann but rather an *intensification of them*. Regarding Barth's reaction against his teachers' explicitly theological support of German nationalism, Chalamet notes that Barth was led to ask, "Is this God really God? Is he not a human projection, an idol? *Precisely as a Herrmannian theologian,*" Chalamet concludes, "trained to preserve God's transcendence and otherness, Barth was obliged to raise these questions."[53] If this is the case, then Barth not only retained interest in some select Kantian and neo-Kantian themes in his later work but applied them in different ways. Indeed, Chalamet suggests that it is more accurate to speak of a "reorientation" in Barth's theology rather than a "break": "Strictly speaking," he states, "Barth did not need to find other bases for his theology. His pre-war theology had the one true basis: God's revelation in Jesus Christ. The problem was in the understanding of the revelation, as the encounter with the power of Jesus' 'inner life' in our experience. So *there was no 'break.'* The idea of a break would imply a radical discontinuity with the past and a new understanding of revelation and theology."[54]

Barth's reorientation, according to Chalamet, specifically involved a gradual move away from Herrmann's preoccupation with the *experience* of God and instead toward the possibility of *knowledge* of God.[55] Beginning in 1915, therefore, faith does not revolve around religious experience but rather a decision—"a risk, a leap"—to acknowledge God's reality. And like McCormack, Chalamet argues that dialectic still plays a central role in Barth's reorientation; now, however, the method is employed in service of knowledge of God rather than in the interpretation of religious experience. "Barth has not ceased to be a dialectical theologian, but there has been a crucial modification: the dialectic is no longer located simply in our experience of revelation. Barth is orienting his theology toward 'God and his kingdom.' . . . He wishes to ground his theology differently, in God alone and not in our religious experience."[56] The end result, for Chalamet, is that Barth has shifted his dialectical concerns from one side to the other: from our religious experience and the knowledge of God it produces to "God and God alone."[57]

---

53. Chalamet, *Dialectical Theologians*, 86; emphasis added.
54. Chalamet, *Dialectical Theologians*, 90; emphasis added.
55. Chalamet, *Dialectical Theologians*, 93. See also Spieckermann, *Gotteserkenntnis*, 18–19, 69–70.
56. Chalamet, *Dialectical Theologians*, 94.
57. Chalamet, *Dialectical Theologians*, 94.

Kantian Themes in the Romans Commentaries and *Anselm*

Neo-Kantianism's influence on Barth's early thought is well attested, but Barth's alleged break with liberalism poses a challenge and places my argument in a potentially precarious position; the neo-Kantianism I have been describing as being so thoroughly influential for Barth was, according to the discontinuity theses described above, ultimately what he would come to *reject*. Is this not possibly at cross-purposes with what I ultimately want to demonstrate, that is, that Kant still continued to influence Barth not only in his earliest work but even in his mature thought as well? According to Fisher, McCormack, and Chalamet, discontinuity theses are less defensible than von Balthasar and Torrance might lead us to believe. Barth did not abandon dialectical method, for example, after 1915 but rather simply shifted—or in Chalamet's terms, "reoriented"—his concern away from religious experience as a reliable resource for faith toward the reality of God.

How and to what extent God can be known from the standpoint of this new orientation would be Barth's abiding concern for the remainder of his career. As McCormack notes, "Knowledge of God . . . would be *the* central question in Karl Barth's new theology."[58] Both the first and second editions of the Romans commentary as well as *Anselm* support this suggestion, and I will address each text in the remainder of the chapter. I suggest that while a discontinuity with *Marburg* neo-Kantianism is accurate, Barth's new orientation retains some key Kantian themes. The liberalism he rejected did not have a monopoly on Kant or neo-Kantianism; as the previous chapter demonstrated, the Marburg school was one of many open interpretive avenues, and Barth's new direction did not abandon Kant altogether in his rejection of neo-Kantianism but rather shifted interpretive strategies while retaining an appreciation of Kant specifically.[59]

58. McCormack, *Karl Barth's Critically Realistic Dialectical Theology*, 125.

59. Marburg neo-Kantianism continued to exercise great influence on Kant interpretation into the first decades of the twentieth century, with a brief period of revival in the 1920s that came to an end in 1929 in Davos with a famed public dispute between Ersnt Cassirer and Martin Heidegger. Part of a series of public meetings held in Davos, Cassirer and Heidegger's dispute involved whether Kant's significance for the contemporary world was primarily practical (Cassirer) or ontological (Heidegger). For both of them, the stakes were high: these abstract philosophical issues held great significance not only for how human beings were defined but for culture and society at large. See Gordon, *Continental Divide*, 5–11. While Barth engages with aspects of Heidegger's existentialism in the *Church Dogmatics*, he makes no references to Heidegger's ongoing involvement in Marburg neo-Kantianism, and he does not re-engage with any of the other figures of the Marburg school regarding Kant interpretation. Barth makes no mention, for instance, of the neo-Kantians of the early twentieth century such as Ernst

Romans I

Barth and Eduard Thurneysen "decided that the time had come to rethink the foundations of the theology they had inherited from their teachers in a more systematic fashion than they had heretofore."[60] Significantly for my purposes, after Scripture, the first place Barth turns for guidance in this pursuit is Kant, which he follows in short order with a direct engagement with the book of Romans.[61] The result? The first edition of his Romans commentary in 1919. In this commentary we see Barth begin to wrestle with what he comes to identify as the proper *subject* of theology: God, not human experience *of* God. "It is no longer possible for Barth to speak 'on the basis of experience' from which 'we have God,' as he did in 1913," Chalamet suggests. "We do not know God, we do not 'have' him. But God 'has' us and speaks to us in Scripture. There, and not in our knowledge or experience, God's new world can be known."[62] Barth gestures toward this at the outset of *R I*, and we also see how he uses Kant to make this point in the following passage:

> Our thinking has become empty—"Concepts without intuitions are empty" (Kant)—after God's own thinking can no longer fill our opinions and beliefs with spirit and substance and reality. It has become a subjective refinement, which is always and in every detail right, and yet, in the whole, always wrong with the best intentions; an aphoristic flash or a constructive cunning, both of which are condemned to the same infertility, because they run away from the fullness and dynamism of the divine word from the outset. And our feelings are darkened, blind— 'Intuitions without concepts are blind' (Kant)." (*R I*, 31)

Cassirer, Georg Lukáks, Rudolf Carnap, or Max Horkheimer in the *Church Dogmatics*. He mentions Paul Natorp and Edmund Husserl only once, and he refers to even Wilhelm Herrmann only in passing in occasional excurses. Barth's focus in the years ahead, as I will demonstrate in what follows, was on Kant, not on neo-Kantianism. In retrospect, it is possible Barth could have found some common ground with Max Wundt, for instance, who would suggest that "the revelation of God in the world was the actual content of Kant's philosophy" (Wundt, *Kant als Metaphysiker*, 496), but Barth's focus was elsewhere.

60. McCormack, *Karl Barth's Critically Realistic Dialectical Theology*, 135–36.

61. McCormack, *Karl Barth's Critically Realistic Dialectical Theology*, 136. The first Romans commentary of 1919 has not been translated into English, and little secondary literature on it currently exists. See, however, Burnett, *Karl Barth's Theological Exegesis*; Brazier, "Barth's First Commentary on Romans (1919)," 387–403; Peterson, *Early Karl Barth*, 141–68.

62. Chalamet, *Dialectical Theologians*, 105.

Barth uses Kant to both demonstrate the limits of human knowledge and gesture toward the necessity of divine revelation. The significance of this for the remainder of Barth's career cannot be overestimated. The source of theological knowledge, for Barth, is now God himself, not human efforts to cognize God, and the first commentary on Romans is where Barth begins to stake this claim. Chalamet states,

> This new theological understanding of the source of our knowledge of God is crucial. In it, one can understand a great deal of what Barth will say theologically until the end of his life. . . . We are not able to speak God's Word, but God can grasp our words and transform them into his own Word. . . . Barth's commentary is the expression of his new theological orientation as it developed around 1915–1917, namely as he was moving toward the "objective knowledge" of God and not toward "experience" and its "confusions between God and the world." . . . God's objective reality is the only possible ground for theology and the Christian life, whereas the "inner life" and the subjective reality inevitably falter.[63]

While the idealism of Marburg neo-Kantianism emphasized—or *overemphasized*, as Barth now begins to suggest—the contributions the knowing subject in theological epistemology, Barth now begins to take into consideration the other half of the knowledge equation—God as he reveals himself, not just the effects God in his revelation might have on the knowing subject. "He wanted to place faith beyond the reach of psychological investigation," McCormack states. Barth emphasizes the significance of this shift for theological epistemology as follows:

> By making this happen by "raising himself," by making himself visible in the world and distinguishing himself from the world as its Creator, and thus making the world visible and distinguishing it as His creation . . . knowledge of the only one becomes possible and true. Whatever the world as a whole and whatever an individual in the world might be (as if it were its own final reasons and principles!), it is not creative as God is creative, not free as God is free, not Lord as he is the Lord—because it exists through God and not as God in himself, what he is. A singular God! This is the description of the knowledge of him who becomes recognizable in this distinction he makes for himself. Our knowledge will only be able to follow this distinction. Arise God! By following this "ascent," our thinking comes

---

63. Chalamet, *Dialectical Theologians*, 106, 108–9.

to this knowledge of God and can only come to this knowledge of God. [Do we come] to knowledge of God partially? No, quite understood, this is precisely the whole of all true knowledge of God and precisely for this very purpose that this very statement may rightly be at the forefront of confession. (*R I*, 52)

For Marburg neo-Kantians, Herrmann included, knowing subject must first sift through their *experience of God* before having claimed to arrive at *knowledge of* God. For Barth, knowledge of God now originates completely with God himself. This move, according to McCormack, is the single most important source of departure from his early theology: "Nowhere is the distance separating the theology of *Romans* I from Barth's pre-war theology more apparent than in his treatment of the knowledge of God. In Barth's liberal period . . . knowledge had been restricted to the 'objects' generated by the laws governing each of the branches of cognitive activity. . . . In *Romans* I, however, a dramatic shift was registered. Barth's concern now was precisely 'knowledge of God in the strictest sense.'"[64]

This reorientation is significant for at least two reasons. First, it provides interpreters of Barth with a clear point of departure from Wilhelm Herrmann. "By relocating revelation not in experience but rather in the events as they are witnessed by Scripture, by speaking about the knowledge of God as an acknowledgment, he breaks with Hermann and reintroduces an element of assent in faith. . . . As a student of Hermann, Barth had begun to see how theological method must be determined by the subject matter, and not by something else."[65] Second, and perhaps more important, it demonstrates that although Barth went in a new direction, he did not leave Kant behind but rather intensified his interest in Kant and returned *ad fontes*. As McCormack notes, "Barth's tendency at this time is to leave the neo-Kantian epistemology largely unchallenged. The affirmation that God lays hold of the human cognitive apparatus and reorients it introduced an element of realism which would eventually drive Barth away from Cohen's conception back in the direction of a more classically Kantian epistemology."[66] Barth's move away from the neo-Kantianisms he inherited do not imply a move away from *Kant*; to the contrary, as I will continue to show, Kantian themes continued to provide a support structure for his theology from this point forward.

---

64. McCormack, *Karl Barth's Critically Realistic Dialectical Theology*, 159.
65. Chalamet, *Dialectical Theologians*, 109–10.
66. McCormack, *Karl Barth's Critically Realistic Dialectical Theology*, 162.

Romans II

I just noted that McCormack suggests that Barth moves "back in the direction of a more classically Kantian epistemology" in the *Romans* commentary. What exactly it means for Barth to utilize a more "classically Kantian epistemology" will be an important consideration for this section, because the theological achievements of the second edition of the Romans commentary will persist into the *Church Dogmatics*. "The gains made in *Romans II*," as McCormack suggests, "are everywhere presupposed throughout the *Church Dogmatics*."[67]

At this juncture I would like to introduce a major component of my overall argument, and that is that three major themes in particular emerge in the second Romans commentary that both qualify as "classical Kantianism" and continue to emerge throughout the remainder of Barth's career: (1) God as a presupposition in theological epistemology; (2) the strategic significance of boundaries and limits in human cognition; and (3) the strategic priority of the division of cognition into theoretical and practical domains. I will begin to refer to these elements in this section and continue to refer to them throughout the remainder of my argument.

It is also important to note at this juncture *how* exactly Barth makes use of Kant, because if we are expecting Barth to make a straightforward, unambiguous declaration of where his philosophical allegiances lie prior to articulating theological claims, we will be disappointed. It is important to recall that one of the tendencies Barth is attempting to steer *away from* during this phase of his career is precisely the Marburg neo-Kantian tendency to articulate a clear philosophical procedure as a necessary precursor to theology, so we should not expect to encounter anything of this sort. "At no point during this phase," McCormack notes, "did he give himself over to the task of a sustained and rigorous *philosophical* reflection upon problems of epistemology. The shift which occurred in his philosophical *point of view*— it was never more than that—was the consequence of his concentration on the *theological* problem of the knowledge of God."[68] Barth's focus was on theology, and philosophical commitments were subordinated to that primary commitment; his philosophical sympathies, therefore, are not always explicit but rather implicit.

First, however a word about the relationship between the first and second editions of the commentary are in order. In Anglo scholarship in particular, it has been assumed that the primary philosophical influence on

---

67. McCormack, *Karl Barth's Critically Realistic Dialectical Theology*, 244.
68. McCormack, *Karl Barth's Critically Realistic Dialectical Theology*, 207.

Barth between the first and second editions was Kierkegaard, but recent scholarship has rightly noted that even Kierkegaard's influence was a derivative of Barth's forays into Kant.[69] My own opinion is that as a result of this shift from the extreme realism of Romans I—which was an important first step for Barth to pass through before arriving to a more mature position—to a more critically idealist position in Romans II, Barth's Kantian sensibilities emerge more clearly. Chalamet corroborates this position when he notes that "the influence of the two Blumhardts, which was so evident in the first edition, was replaced by references to critical thinkers such as Kant."[70] This is consistent with what Barth notes in the preface, where he suggests that after (1) continued study of Paul and (2) accounting for criticisms of Franz Overbeck, the next most important influence in his decision to revise the commentary was "closer acquaintance with Plato and Kant" (*ER*, 4) or more accurately, "a better understanding about the actual orientation of the thought of Plato and Kant" (*die bessere Belehrung über die eigentliche Orientierung der Gedanken Platos und Kants*; R II, 7).

God as a Presupposition of Knowledge

One possible direction Barth could go in distancing himself from the idealism of Marburg neo-Kantianism would be to overemphasize epistemological *realism*. His ongoing appreciation of Kant, however, prevents him from this sort of overcorrection. And like Kant, furthermore, Barth is interested in steering a middle course between both dogmatism and enthusiasm (his preferred terms are between *tote Rechtgläubigkeit* ["dead orthodoxy"] and *lebendige Flattergeistigkeit* ["lively, flighty spirit"]; *A*, 35), and a drastic course correction in the direction of realism would run the risk of the dogmatism he seeks to avoid. With this in mind, Barth acknowledges that "there is no objective observation of the Truth; for its objectivity is that by which we are

---

69. McCormack, *Karl Barth's Critically Realistic Dialectical Theology*, 216-17; Spieckermann, *Gotteserkenntnis*, 109; Beintker, *Die Dialektik in der 'dialektischen Theologie' Karl Barths*, 231. Relevant recent literature on the second Romans commentary includes Bakker, *In der Krisis der Offenbarung Karl Barths Hermeneutik*; Ruschke, *Entstehung und Ausführung*; Webster, "Karl Barth"; Link, "Karl Barths Römerbrief (1921) als theologisches Signal," 135-52; Mauer, "Theologische Weichenstellungen in Karl Barths Römerbriefauslegung von 1922," 209-18; Grube, "Reconstructing the Dialectics in Karl Barth's 'Epistle to the Romans,'" 127-46; Peters, "Das Skandalon Gottes," 136-38; Oakes, *Reading Karl Barth*; Haas, "Karl Barths 'Römerbrief' von 1922," 120-32; Stegemann, "'Kritischer müssen mir die Historisch-Kritischen sein!,'" 3-17; Thurneysen, *Das Römerbriefmansuskript habe ich Gelesen*.

70. Chalamet, *Dialectical Theologians*, 130; Chalamet also notes the importance of Cohen, Dostoevsky, and Kierkegaard.

observed before ever we have observed anything at all" (*ER*, 278). Recall that Kant likewise states in his *Lectures on Philosophical Theology* that "God is independent benevolence. He is not limited by any subjective ground, because he himself has no needs" (*LPT*, 114). For both Barth and Kant, God is distinct from our experience. But rather than overemphasize epistemological realism, Barth reverses the foundational neo-Kantian assumption that humans are the subjects who know God the object through sophisticated epistemological strategies. Knowledge of God—theological epistemology—according to Barth runs the opposite direction: God, assumed to be objective, communicates *to* knowing human subjects, and this is an inextricable component of knowledge itself. "Truth is that primal objectivity by which the observing subject is itself constituted," he continues. "Truth cannot therefore depend upon my observation: that is to say, it cannot be 'subjectivized.' Truth is that redeeming subjectivity which secretly confronts every 'I' and 'Thou' and 'He,' critically and immanently dissolving them by the objectivity which everywhere accompanies them" (*ER*, 278). Chalamet further concurs that Barth did not abandon Kantian themes but rather reworked them in service of his new outlook. "The theme of objectivity, which was so important to Barth in the first edition, has not disappeared, but it has been re-interpreted in the light of the dialectic of God as hidden and revealed. God is never 'objectively,' directly present to us, he is always hidden in his action. The theme of objectivity has thus retreated to the background of Barth's theology yet remains active *as a presupposition*."[71]

Boundaries and Limits in Human Cognition

Closely related to Barth's subtle shift away from Wilhelm Herrmann's focus on the human subject's experience *of* God is a revised emphasis on the function of boundaries and limitations in theological epistemology. The acknowledgment of limitations in epistemology is a Kantian theme that Herrmann emphasized as well, and Barth did not abandon the notion altogether. Rather, Barth shifted the center of gravity away from the human subject to the reality of God. Epistemological boundaries, for Barth, are not something that knowing human subjects establish for themselves; they are revealed by God as a necessary precondition of knowledge itself. "It is evident that no man can of himself utter the humiliating fact that he is—a man," Barth states.

> It must have been said, the answer must have been given, before he has cried out. Clearly, he has not sought it out, thought it

---

71. Chalamet, *Dialectical Theologians*, 136; emphasis added.

out, worked it out, willed it of himself; for it is in itself the presupposition of all searching and thinking and working and willing. The point from which the circle is seen to be closed cannot be situated within the circle. The possibility of comprehending human possibility to be, as such, limited, is manifestly an altogether unheard of, new possibility; especially so, if, in agreement with Kant, we deny ourselves every prospect beyond that by which we are limited. (*ER*, 271)

McCormack likewise notes that this emphasis on the limitations of human knowing—a necessary epistemological step in order for God to reveal himself on his own terms—is "an important deviation from neo-Kantian epistemology" and "a turn in the direction of a more classically Kantian view."[72]

If the center of gravity in the establishment of cognitive boundaries is shifted away from constructive knowing subjects toward God first, knowers are, ironically, liberated from the labor of attempting to search for those limits themselves. The givenness of epistemological limitations, furthermore, serves a preventative function against idolatry for Barth, or what Kant refers to as "metaphysical mischief" in the second Critique (2.2.3). "When, therefore, the will of God is displayed, it must manifest itself in radical criticism of what we possess and do and shall do, both individually and socially. It can never be manifested as sanctioning and justifying us, or even as a thing which contradicts and opposes us: 'The idea of freedom lies beyond our investigation, for it bars the way to every positive representation' (Kant). Therefore we must not fail to observe the hand uplifted against the totality of human capacity" (*ER*, 294).

Receiving epistemological limits in revelation also involves confronting the reality of mortality, which further reinforces God as a necessary presupposition of knowledge. "Set under complete corruption and mortality, words and deeds and movements bear witness to life out of their ambiguity. *Only when men take up their position within this insecurity can they perceive the witness which it bears*," Barth states (emphasis added). And Barth recruits Kant specifically to support this observation: "The flesh is mortified by its relation to the Spirit and by this alone, precisely in order that it may be thrust by this death into the light of hope and of life: 'This pure, soul-exalting, merely negative representation of moral behaviour' (Kant) is the ultimate position—which is no position—to which we are led when we encounter and accept the pre-eminent Truth. (*ER*, 294–95). Knowing subjects must reach their epistemological inadequacies in order to appreciate the need for revelation.

72. McCormack, *Karl Barth's Critically Realistic Dialectical Theology*, 207n1.

Theoretical and Practical Knowledge in Theological Epistemology

The third explicitly classically Kantian theme that can be discerned in Romans II is the strategic epistemological distinction between theoretical and practical knowledge. Barth describes the application of Kant's division to his own project as follows:

> All human conjunctions and adjustments and presuppositions—however transcendentally conceived of—are there confronted by the sovereignty of God. For very good reason and with admirable acuteness Kant did not set out upon a critique—that is to say, an establishing—of the pure reasoning of piety. From the human side we are able to take account only of the freedom of God: that is to say, we are concerned only with obedience. And here Kant was possessed of far greater insight than his—religious!—opponents. But obedience means . . . to be accessible to the one-sided, passionate, and exclusive claim which God makes upon men. (*ER*, 386)

Barth continues to distance himself from Marburg neo-Kantian constructivism in theological epistemology, but now he explicitly recruits Kant in support of his case. In both the Canon of Pure Reason and in the Second Critique, Kant *presupposes* rather than *demonstrates* the existence of God; Barth proceeds along similar lines here, and this paves the way for the apprehension of revelation.

But true to classical Kantianism, Barth does not stop with theoretical knowledge alone; to the contrary, theoretical knowledge and practical knowledge—specifically, morality—are inseparable. In a well-known, if curious, passage of Romans II, Barth states that "the problem of 'ethics' is . . . identical to the problem of 'dogmatics': Soli deo gloria!" In Barth's new direction, practical theological knowledge—ethics—and "pure" theological knowledge—dogmatics—don't *lead to* God but rather both *begin with* the presupposition of God's existence. In the same way that constructivism does not precede pure theological knowledge, likewise "there is no such thing as the 'building up' by men of an adequate ethical life, not even if the quality of their moral behavior were so sublime that it might be claimed that the will of God had been united with the human will" (*ER*, 431). Rather, "It is grace alone that is competent to provide men with a truly ethical disturbance" (*ER*, 430). Barth's appreciation of Kant, furthermore, at this important juncture in the development of his thought continues to be explicit:

Pure ethics require—and here we are in complete agreement with Kant—that there should be no mixing of heaven and earth in the sphere of morals. Pure ethical behavior depends upon its primal origin, an origin which needs to be protected by a determination on our part to call God God and man man, however much we may be tempted to stray into romanticism. . . . Once again we have affinities with the ethics of Kant. (*ER*, 432, 468-69)

Just as knowledge of God cannot be achieved by epistemological systems, so moral perfection cannot be achieved by effort. Both require the input of revelation.

Anselm

Bruce McCormack confirms that "Barth's theological epistemology in *Romans* II stands everywhere in the long shadow cast by Immanuel Kant. . . . He took for granted the validity of Kant's epistemology as set forth in the First Critique, as well as the success of his attack on metaphysics."[73] Barth has started to chart his new course, and the next relevant text is *Anselm: Fides Quaerens Intellectum*, where readers encounter much more developed philosophical language that not only clarifies Barth's new line of thought but also reinforces Kant's ongoing influence.[74]

At the beginning of *Anselm*, Barth refers to the "danger on the one hand of a dead orthodoxy and on the other of a flightiness that is only too much alive" (*A*, 35), a sensibility that would have been familiar to him from Kant's objective to avoid dogmatism, skepticism, and enthusiasm. And in the preface to the second edition, he gestures toward the importance of this book for the consistency of his larger project: "in this book on Anselm I am working with a vital key, if not the key, to an understanding of that whole process of thought that has impressed me more and more in my *Church Dogmatics* as the only one proper to theology" (*A*, 11). From the other end of his career, he states in *CD* II/1 that he "learned the fundamental attitude

---

73. McCormack, *Karl Barth's Critically Realistic Dialectical Theology*, 245.

74. See Josuttis, *Die Gegenständlichkeit der Offenbarung*; Vignaux, "Saint Anselme, Barth et au-delà," 83-95; Shofner, *Anselm Revisited*; Watson, "Karl Barth and St. Anselm's Theological Programme," 31-45; McKenzie, "Barth's Anselm and the Object of Theological Knowledge," 272-75; Oesterle, "Karl Barths These über den Gottesbeweis des Anselm von Canterbury," 91-107; Watson, "Study in St. Anselm's Soteriology and Karl Barth's Theological Method," 493-512; Pugh, *Anselmic Shift*; Sheveland, "Tears of Dependence," 181-86; Stanley, "Returning Barth to Anselm," 413-37; Jones, "Barth and Anselm," 257-82.

to the problem of the knowledge and existence of God . . . at the feet of Anselm of Canterbury, and in particular from his proofs of God set out in *Prosl.* 2–4" (*CD* II/1, 4).

One of the most important distinctions Barth makes in this text, particularly for the purposes of my argument, is between *probare* ("proof") and *intelligere* ("understanding"). According to Barth, Anselm is concerned not primarily with proofs but rather understanding: "In point of fact [Anselm's] own particular description of what he is doing is not *probare* at all but *intelligere*. As *intelligere* is achieved it issues in *probare*" (*A*, 14). Theological epistemology, for Barth, most properly seeks first to *understand* God, not *prove* God's existence. This is consistent with the Romans commentary, which suggests that knowledge of God is *presupposed* rather than *achieved*.

The linchpin connecting presupposition and *intelligere*, for Barth, is *fides*. *Intelligere* is preceded by faith, not the other way around. Barth discerns an important order of operations in Anselm that runs as follows: faith seeks understanding, and only after this can one begin to discuss matters of proof. "To 'prove' means to investigate the meaning of a particular article of faith x given that articles a, b, c, d and so on are assumed to be true."[75] This is significant for the purposes of my argument because I take Barth to now be formalizing his departure from the school of neo-Kantianism that argued for a clearly defined epistemological method *prior* to making theological claims. Against that background, Barth's new position is most striking: "The reality of the Word of God must precede and ground every attempt to think correctly about it. . . . To 'prove,' to 'demonstrate rationally,' means simply to *explicate* the meaning of the object of faith as it is given to us in the incarnation."[76] Christian truth, for Barth, "is derived from no external necessity" (*A*, 28).

Barth employs more specifically Kantian language to support his position in 1.3.3 when he insists on the necessary discrepancies between our theological statements *about* God and God in himself: "Every theological statement is an inadequate expression of its object. . . . Every attempt on our part, even the highest and best, to reproduce that Word in thought or in speech is inadequate. . . . All that we have are conceptions of objects, none of which is identical with God. . . . Every one of the categories known to us by which we attempt to conceive him is, in the last analysis, not really one of his categories at all" (*A*, 29). Barth is now trafficking in the language of Kant's second Critique, where Kant finally completes the circuit between theoretical and practical reason, but he adds his own unique twist to the matter. Like

---

75. McCormack, *Karl Barth's Critically Realistic Dialectical Theology*, 433.
76. McCormack, *Karl Barth's Critically Realistic Dialectical Theology*, 425.

Kant, Barth acknowledges that human knowers bring native concepts to the process of knowing God, but ultimately, God comes *to* us externally in revelation. For Barth as for Kant, the concepts of theoretical reason can only take us so far in knowledge of God. The existence of God is an idea, and it is ultimately dependent on practical reason for its refinement. For Kant, this takes place morally; for Barth, it takes place in God's self-revelation. "Concepts which are inadequate in themselves for giving expression to God," as McCormack states, "can be given a relative adequacy by God's grace."[77]

This being the case, Barth has now cleared the ground for God's revelation to be apprehended: "God himself comes within this system as the object of his thinking, that he 'shows' himself to the thinker and in so doing modifies 'correct' thinking to an *intelligere esse in re*. Only thus does the grace of Christian knowledge become complete" (*A*, 24). Note in particular that in the event of revelation, human thinking about God is *modified* through God's self-revelation, and only then can it be considered "complete." Furthermore, for Barth as for Kant, this theological-epistemological cycle plays a *defensive* role as well: "God must stand in encounter with him if his *intelligere* is not to be delusion and if he himself is not to be a mere *insipiens*" (*A*, 39). Here again Kant's caution against "metaphysical mischief" comes to mind.

One of the most important strategic themes of *Anselm*, in my estimation, is that of *presupposition*. I gestured at this in the opening paragraph of this section, but some additional explanation is necessary, particularly as my argument begins to give way to the *Church Dogmatics* in the next chapter. "The knowledge, the *intellectus*, with which Anselm is concerned is the *intellectus fidei*," Barth states. "It cannot establish this object of faith as such but rather has to understand it in its very incomprehensibility" (*A*, 39–40). Knowledge of God is not something that human knowers *achieve*; it is a presupposition that knowers must bring to the table *in order to* acquire the understanding they seek. "The conformity of *ratio* to truth depends neither upon the object nor the subject but on that same revealing power of God which illumines faith and which faith encounters as authority.... *Man first attains faith and then on the basis of that faith attains knowledge*" (*A*, 48; emphasis added). "Truth," for Barth, "disposes of all *rationes* and not *vice versa*" (*A*, 48).

Where do human knowers begin in theological epistemology? "Should he therefore have begun *quaerens intellectum* with nothing," Barth asks rhetorically, "that is with the rules of an autonomous human reason and with the data of general human experience, and therefore of his own accord?" (*A*,

---

77. McCormack, *Karl Barth's Critically Realistic Dialectical Theology*, 433.

54). The answer that now emerges is clearly "No." It is not the job of human knowers to make determinations about where to begin on their own terms:

> Throughout all Anselm's investigations the origin of the *rationes necessariae* is to be found somewhere other than where it ought to be found in a philosopher who deduces the *Credo a priori*—namely, on the same level as that on which the question to be answered is raised, within the *Credo* itself.... The Articles of faith ... are assumed to be known. The inquiring theologian, with his capacity for forming concepts and making judgments, is never assigned the function of determining the fixed point or fixed points from which the argument is to proceed.... And so—not mastering the object but being mastered by it—he achieves true noetic *ratio*, a real comprehension of the ontic *ratio* of the object of faith; he attains the *intellectus fidei*. (*A*, 55)

Theological epistemology, according to Barth's reading of Anselm, rather begins with *Credo*: "I believe." *Credo* is not a conclusion that human knowers reach after an epistemological search but rather where the journey begins, "at no point the subject of discussion but on the contrary ... the self-evident basis of discussion" (*A*, 60). Anselm first *accepts* the existence of God in faith as a presupposition and only then begins to consider the possibility of *probare*: "Anselm speaks about God while speaking to him. The knowledge which the proof seeks to expound and impart is the knowledge that is peculiar to faith, knowledge of what is believed from what is believed" (*A*, 101-2). Anselm's "proof," ultimately, is an arrival, not a journey. "It is a question of theology. It is a question of the proof of faith by faith which was already established in itself without proof. And both—faith that is proved and faith that proves—Anselm expressly understands not as presuppositions that can be achieved by man but as presuppositions that have been achieved by God" (*A*, 170). As McCormack states, "It is not in mastering the object but in being mastered by it that the interpreter achieves a true comprehension of the ontic *ratio* of the object of faith, and the *intellectus* that is sought takes place."[78]

Conclusion

Barth's journey with Kant began in Marburg with Wilhelm Hermann, a neo-Kantian who both mediated Cohen and Natorp's interpretations of Kant but also introduced Barth to a dissatisfaction with the Ritschlian demand for a "sound epistemology [as] an essential prelude to any systematic

78. McCormack, *Karl Barth's Critically Realistic Dialectical Theology*, 430.

theology."⁷⁹ Rather, for Herrmann, faith is given (*gegeben*) through revelation, not achieved. The reality of God, for Herrmann, by definition "eludes the grasp of any philosophical thought."⁸⁰ As Barth's career progressed, even Herrmann's departure from other Marburg neo-Kantians became insufficient for the new direction he wanted to go, even as it provided him with the conceptual apparatus to do just that.

That new direction, however, involved a break with certain *interpretations of* Kant, not Kant himself. To the contrary, Kantian themes not only persist but increase in both intensity and sophistication beginning with the first Romans commentary, continuing in the second edition, and coming into maturity with *Anselm*. We begin to discern a "movement away from the thoroughgoing constructivist epistemology of the neo-Kantians," McCormack states. "And that meant that the theological category of revelation set forth in *Romans* II was more Kantian than it was neo-Kantian."⁸¹

Colin Gunton suggested that "Barth identified that after Kant, theology (and for that matter, philosophy) could never be the same. Any theologian had to come to terms with Kant, to follow in his tracks, or branch out in some way from what he established."⁸² I suggest that what we see in Barth's new direction is that he does all three things: he comes to terms with Kant theologically by working within Kant's general epistemological architecture, following him in some cases, and also branching out in his own direction when needed. Indeed, as McCormack suggests, "all of [Barth's] efforts in theology may be considered, from one point of view, as an attempt to overcome Kant by means of Kant, not retreating behind him and attempting to go around him, but going through him."⁸³

That this is the case is commonly accepted in the Barth guild, and yet the question of *how* exactly this works out in practice has remained unclear. In this chapter I have identified three particular themes that I argue are explicitly Kantian and also appear with increasing frequency and sophistication in the major works of Barth's early period: the two Romans commentaries and *Anselm*. Those three themes are (1) God as a presupposition in theological epistemology; (2) the strategic significance of boundaries and limits in human cognition; and (3) the strategic priority of the division of cognition into theoretical and practical domains. For both Kant and Barth, God's existence is not a concept that is subject to external argument

---

79. Fisher, *Revelatory Positivism?*, 125.
80. Fisher, *Revelatory Positivism?*, 134.
81. McCormack, *Karl Barth's Critically Realistic Dialectical Theology*, 226.
82. Gunton, *Barth Lectures*, 13.
83. McCormack, *Karl Barth's Critically Realistic Dialectical Theology*, 465–66.

or demonstration but rather one that is already part of how knowledge works in the first place. Theism and epistemology are inseparable; this is a foundational premise of Kant's critical philosophy, and it becomes *the* central theme of Barth's work as it matures. "Knowledge of God," McCormack affirms, "would be *the* central question in Karl Barth's new theology."[84] It is possible for Kant, therefore, to be an asset to theology rather than the liability it is often taken to be. Barth's theology, I suggest, is one of the better examples of this in practice, and this will continue to be the case throughout his most mature statement: the *Church Dogmatics*.

---

84. McCormack, *Karl Barth's Critically Realistic Dialectical Theology*, 125.

5

Presupposing God
Kantian Themes in the Church Dogmatics

IN THE PREVIOUS CHAPTER I suggested that Kantian, rather than neo-Kantian, themes begin to emerge in the first Romans commentary and not only persist but increase in intensity and sophistication in *Romans II* and *Anselm*. I also suggested that Barth comes to terms with Kant theologically by working within Kant's general epistemological architecture rather than against it, following him in some cases and also branching out in his own direction when needed. Three specific Kantian themes, I suggest, begin to emerge in the early period: (1) God as a presupposition in theological epistemology; (2) the strategic significance of boundaries and limits in human cognition; and (3) the strategic priority of the division of cognition into theoretical and practical domains.

In this chapter I will extend the same line of enquiry into Barth's mature theology as reflected in the *Church Dogmatics*, where Barth picks up where he left off in *Anselm*. As Martin Westerholm notes, "The movement of thought that that emerges from Barth's engagement with Paul and Anselm . . . is then characteristic of the *Church Dogmatics* quite generally."[1] Theism and epistemology in *CD* remain inseparable, as they were for Kant. Barth continues to use the language of presupposition, but this is just the beginning. I will be suggesting that the intensification and sophistication of Kantianism continue to increase throughout the *CD* well beyond this first theme, and that Barth also expands on the other two themes in explicitly Kantian terms. Through a close primary reading of relevant sections of the *CD*, I will demonstrate how Barth employs distinctively Kantian themes such as the relationship between theoretical and practical reason, postulation, and conceptualism in service of his own specifically christological purposes.

---

1. Westerholm, *Ordering of the Christian Mind*, 11.

Method in Theology

Kevin Diller observes that "the key move in any theory of knowing is the first move, or the logically primary move. How does an epistemology get off the ground, or what primal glue holds it together?"[2] I have shown that Barth's dissatisfaction with epistemological constructivism in theology becomes apparent with *Romans II* in particular, and it persists in *Anselm*. This continues in *CD*, but it also poses a unique challenge: my argument requires comments on Barth's theological epistemology in the *CD*, but ironically Barth intentionally does not leave behind a clearly delineated epistemology as Diller defines it or a theological method in the modern sense. As I will demonstrate, he is actually opposed to doing so. He states in *CD* II/1, for instance, that "our starting point is not in any sense epistemological. However man's capacity for knowledge may be described, whether more narrowly or more broadly, yet the conclusion that God is known only through God (we speak of the God who has revealed Himself in His Word) does not have either its basis or origin in any understanding of the human capacity for knowledge" (II/1, 44). In order to gain clarity on his strategy and procedure in theology, therefore, I will first examine how Barth introduces the subject of theology in the first place and then highlight epistemological themes relevant to my argument.[3]

Strategy in Theological Epistemology: Presupposition

"The church confesses God as it talks about God," Barth states at the outset of the *CD* (I/1, 3). Already Barth's primary concern is not proof, defense, or method per se but rather confession. The very act of speaking about God itself already assumes, or presumes, belief in God. Speaking about God in human terms, however, is an endeavor that must open itself up to correction and refinement: "In so doing it recognizes and takes up as an active church the further human task of criticizing and revising its speech about God" (I/1, 3). But how is this done? Against what standard is human speech about God measured?

---

2. Diller, *Theology's Epistemological Dilemma*, 44–45.

3. Resources on the matter of knowledge in *CD* specifically include Müller, "Credo, ut intelligam," 167–76; Wolf, *Karl Barth*; Bouillard, *Karl Barth*; Spieckermann, *Gotteserkenntnis*; Hunsinger, *How to Read Karl Barth*, 27–66; Chia, *Revelation and Theology*; Gunton, *Barth Lectures*, 64–75; Webster, *Barth*, 49–93; McFarlane, "Human Person as an Epistemic Agent"; La Montagne, *Barth and Rationality*, 113–51; Leman, "Reason after Revelation," 92–115.

Some Marburg neo-Kantians would suggest that human speech about God is measured according to the standards of the scientific method or by appeals to epistemological standards that precede theological speech. Barth, however, has been steadily working away from this approach, and *CD*, particularly I and II, is where we observe the fruits of this labor. "Theology," he continues, "follows the talk of the Church to the extent that in its question as to the correctness of its utterance it does not measure it by an alien standard but by its own source and object" (I/1, 4). That source and object, as he reiterates throughout the *CD*, is God's self-disclosure in Jesus Christ; God himself is the standard by which human thinking and speaking about God is to be judged. "What is required," Barth states, "is its criticism and correction in the light of the being of the Church, of Jesus Christ as its basis, goal and content" (I/1, 6).

Barth is aware that he is breaking rank in sidestepping modern Protestant theology's preoccupation with method and instead presuming to speak about God prior to establishing how this is possible in human terms. But if the alternative is judging God's existence and character by standards that we construct ourselves, Barth sees little alternative:

> Even though we cannot show that this is in accordance with any necessity of principle, even those historians, pedagogues, etc., and especially philosophers who kindly take this aspect into account always miss the real problem by setting it within the sphere of their own sciences, judging the utterance of the Church about God in accordance with alien principles rather than its own principle, and thus increasing rather than decreasing the mischief which makes critical science necessary for the Church. (I/1, 6)

The definition of science was contested in the early twentieth century. In rejecting the need to construct an epistemological architecture *prior to* speaking about God, Barth runs the risk of transgressing the boundaries of science.[4] His answer to this conundrum is to first suggest that theology simply has no obligation to operate according to an alien standard, science or otherwise. "If theology allows itself to be called, or calls itself, a science, it cannot in so doing accept the obligation of submission to standards valid for other sciences" (I/1, 10). It is its own discipline that operates according to its own rules. This does not mean that theology is *unscientific*; it simply means that the standards of establishing, say, the predictability of a chemical reaction are not the most fitting standards for speaking about God. "In Barth's view," Kevin Diller notes, "there are no first principles to establish

---

4. See Zachhuber, *Theology as Science in Nineteenth-Century Germany*, 287–89.

or appeal to. God has taken the initiating action.... We cannot ground the actual knowledge of God in a theoretical epistemological account. There is no other source that we can appeal to other than the actual knowledge of God."[5]

The criteria for what qualifies as science, for Barth, is not the extent to which a branch of knowledge adheres to this or that abstract scientific standard but rather the extent to which is adheres to the standard most fitting to its own object of inquiry. And theology's standard, for Barth, is given by the object of knowledge itself: "The only way which theology has of proving its scientific character is to devote itself to the task of knowledge as determined by its actual theme and thus to show what it means by true science. *No science has any manorial rights to the title, nor does any theory of science have absolute power either to grant or withhold the title*" (I/1, 10; emphasis added). As Christophe Chalamet states, "Conformity with the subject matter, much more than theological method, is the decisive criterion for the scientific character of theology. The subject matter is a living reality, not a dead one.... The theologian does not choose his subject matter, and he is called upon to give a faithful account of it."[6]

Speaking about God, for Barth, is *theology*. A related concept, *dogmatics*, involves speaking about human speech about God. The latter assumes the former: "Dogmatics as an enquiry presupposes that the true content of Christian talk about God can be known by man. It makes this assumption as in and with the Church it believes in Jesus Christ as the revealing and reconciling address of God to man.... Hence *it does not have to begin by finding or inventing the standard by which it measures*. It sees and recognises that this is given with the Church" (I/1, 12). Here Barth introduces one of the central themes of my argument, which proceeds from the Romans commentaries, *Anselm*, and from Kant's Canon of Pure Reason: *presupposition*.

> Dogmatics *presupposes* [*Dogmatik setzt voraus*] that, as God in Jesus Christ is the essence of the Church, having promised Himself to it, so He is the truth, not merely in Himself, but also for us as we know Him solely by faith in Jesus Christ. To the extent that dogmatics *receives* this standard by which it measures talk about God in Jesus Christ, in the event of the divine action corresponding to the promise given to the Church, it is possible for it to be knowledge of the truth. (I/1, 12; emphasis added)

The significance of the word *receives* in this passage cannot be overstated. According to Ritschl and others, dogmatics does not receive its content

---

5. Diller, *Theology's Epistemological Dilemma*, 46.
6. Chalamet, *Dialectical Theologians*, 74.

but rather *constructs* it. The reception, however, relates only to the standard by which our knowledge is judged, not necessarily the content of that knowledge. Knowledge of God from the human side still involves ambiguity, mystery, and effort; because the object of knowledge has been *disclosed*, however, we can be assured that our epistemological labors are not in vain. "In, with and under the human question dogmatics speaks of the divine answer," Barth states. "It knows even as it seeks. It teaches even as it learns. In human uncertainty like any other science, it establishes the most certain truth ever known. In relation to its subject, every statement in dogmatics, as a statement of faith, must be ventured with the assurance of speaking divine and not just human truth" (I/1, 12).

The consistencies with *Anselm* are apparent: knowledge of God does not begin with *probare* but rather *fides* (which leads to *intelligere*, which issues in *probare*); faith involves *presupposing* God, not demonstrating it prior to assent, and it is always a process of seeking and achieving varying levels of insight:

> Dogmatics . . . has to be enquiry. It knows the light which is intrinsically perfect and reveals everything in a flash. Yet it knows it only in the prism of this act, which, however radically or existentially it may be understood, is still a human act, which in itself is no kind of surety for the correctness of the appropriation in question, which is by nature fallible and therefore stands in need of criticism, of correction, of critical amendment and repetition. For this reason the creaturely form which the revealing action of God assumes in dogmatics is never that of knowledge attained in a flash, which it would have to be to correspond to the divine gift, but a *laborious movement from one partial human insight to another* with the intention though with no guarantee of advance. (I/1, 14; emphasis added)

One would rightly expect a twentieth-century systematic theology text such as the *CD* to open with some explicit comments about prolegomena: the method by which its conclusions will be established, or "the attempt to give an explicit account of the particular way of knowledge taken in dogmatics, or, as we might also say, of the particular point from which we are to look, think and judge in dogmatics" (I/1, 25). Barth seems to be indicating little interest in this, however. Rather he seems to be proceeding in the opposite direction: the conclusion of theology establishes the method, not the other way around.

> Even its question of knowledge cannot, then, be put as follows: How is human knowledge of revelation possible?—as though

there were doubt whether revelation is known, or as though insight into the possibility of knowledge of divine revelation were to be expected from investigation of human knowledge. It can only take this form: What is true human knowledge of divine revelation?—on the assumption that revelation itself creates of itself the necessary point of contact in man. . . . *Prolegomena to dogmatics do not so much lead up to the real work of dogmatics as lead away from it.* (I/1, 29; emphasis added)

"You'll notice I didn't say anything about prolegomena in the opening pages of this project," Barth seems to be saying. He now indicates that this is intentional, and that prolegomena—deciding how to speak of God before doing so—is actually potentially counterproductive to both theology and dogmatics because it runs the risk of restricting theological thinking before the process even starts:

> Theological thinking which by the grace of God is truly responsible and relevant . . . will even to-day show itself to be such by not allowing itself to be drawn into discussion of its basis, of the question of the existence of God or of revelation. On the contrary, it will refrain from attempted self-vindication as its theme demands, and thus show its responsibility and relevance by simply fulfilling itself as thinking on this basis, and therefore by simply existing as the witness of faith against unbelief. . . . Theology goes its own way sincerely and with no pretence. (I/1, 29–31)

Diller corroborates the significance of this move of Barth's as well as its difficulty in modern epistemological debates:

> It is common for commentators well-versed in the philosophical debates in epistemology to struggle to grasp this theo-foundationalism in Barth. In order to make sense of Barth, often an expedition is launched to unearth a basic principle that is motivating his thought—the *real* foundation or source. Barth insists, however, that his theological reflections . . . are not the basis of his view of revelation but really are reflections based on the revelation given. What may seem confusing is that *at no point does Barth offer an argument to ground this supposition.* He urges instead that all theology should be done as an attempt to think correctly from this a priori.[7]

---

7. Diller, *Theology's Epistemological Dilemma*, 46–47. For further discussion of the term "theo-foundationalism" and its detractors, see 66–93. See also Oakes, *Karl Barth on Theology and Philosophy*, 245.

The only caveat Barth allows with respect to the usefulness of prolegomena is that is it rightly understood simply as what comes *first* in theology, not what comes *before it*: "The prefix *pro* in prolegomena is to be understood loosely to signify the first part of dogmatics rather than that which is prior to it" (I/1, 42). Barth continues to emphasize that theology and dogmatics cannot be constrained to a procedure of our own making. "It can only venture to embark on its way," Barth states,

> and then on this way, admittedly perhaps as its first task, yet genuinely on this way, concern itself with the knowledge of the correctness of this way. It knows that there can be no entering the self-enclosed circle of this concern from without, whether from a general human possibility or an ecclesiastical reality. It realises that all its knowledge, even its knowledge of the correctness of its knowledge, can only be an event, and cannot therefore be guaranteed as correct knowledge from any place apart from or above this event. In no circumstances, therefore, can it understand the account which is to be rendered in prolegomena as an attempt to secure such a guarantee. This account can be given only within, even if at the beginning of, the dogmatic work which is not guaranteed from that point apart or above. (I/1, 42)

With Kant, Barth recognizes that knowledge of God falls short of the level of apodictic certainty required by other sciences, but for neither of them does that mean that knowledge of God is impossible, nor is it a lesser form of knowledge; rather it is a unique form of knowledge whose outcome is determined by its object.

Knowledge and Acknowledgment

Note carefully Barth's use of the phrase "self-enclosed circle," because this provides a clue not just to how Barth conceives of the moment that the human subject encounters the object of divine revelation—or better, the moment that divine revelation in its objectivity encounters the knowing human subject—but also insight into his use of Kant for his mature work. Recall Kant's description of the "circuit" (*Umschweif*) between pure theoretical reason and practical reason in the second Critique: pure theoretical reason encounters reality outside itself with native concepts, but those concepts require the input of practical reason for their refinement and completion (*CPrR*, pref.). I suggest that now that Barth has established that theology best proceeds through *presupposition* rather than *demonstration*—something that Kant also held—he now continues to proceed along Kantian lines in characterizing the shape of theological knowledge itself as an encounter in which the knower, unable to generate knowledge on his or her own terms, requires contact with external information in order for the circuit of knowledge to be complete. Barth states,

> By the knowledge of an object by men we understand confirmation of their acquaintance with its reality in respect of its existence and its nature.... Their acquaintance with it, instead of being a contingent and outward determination of their own existence, now becomes a necessary and inward determination. Knowing, they are affected by the object known. They no longer exist without it, but with it.... Whatever else and however else they may think of it, they must begin by thinking of the truth of its reality. Face to face with this truth they can no longer withdraw into themselves in order to affirm, question or deny it thence. Its truth has come home to them, has become their own. And in the process they themselves have become the truth's. *This event, this confirmation, in contrast to mere cognizance, we call knowledge.* (I/1, 188; emphasis added)

Barth has now reached an important definition in his account of theological epistemology: *knowledge* is defined by an encounter with an external reality, not by subjective processes of knowing alone. Subjective processes of knowing are always active—as Kant describes in detail in the first Critique—but they are incomplete in themselves—as Kant describes in the second Critique. "When we ask about the possibility of knowledge of the Word of God," Barth states, "we are presupposing that the concept of knowledge is known. But ... *the possibility is left open of correction, restriction or reversal in the light of the object concerned*" (I/1, 190; emphasis added).

This specific fissure in the process of knowing—the capacity of the knowing subject to be *active* but not *in complete control of the outcome*—is one that Barth traces specifically to misunderstandings of Kant at the beginning of the twentieth century. These interpretations took Kant to mean that because the knowing subject is *active* in the process of knowing, therefore the knowing subject *determines the outcome* of knowledge, "a capability or property grounded in man as such and as the corresponding freedom of control" (I/1, 193). While Barth has been suggesting that God is a *presupposition* of knowledge on the part of the knowing subject, he realizes in doing so that he exposes himself to the risk of collapsing or reducing knowledge of God to the presupposition of the knowing human subject.

Barth wants to emphasize both that the knowing human subject *contributes* to knowledge through presupposition—idealism—and that the process of knowledge is not complete until an external object of knowledge enters into its view and completes the circuit. The Word of God specifically, as an object of knowledge, retains its own integrity *apart from* its knowability by human subjects. "The fact of God's Word does not receive its dignity and validity in any respect or even to the slightest degree from a presupposition that we bring to it," Barth states.

> Its truth for us, like its truth in itself, is grounded absolutely in itself. The procedure in theology, then, is to establish self-certainty on the certainty of God, to measure it by the certainty of God, and thus to begin with the certainty of God without waiting for the validating of this beginning by self-certainty. When that beginning is made, but only when it is made, it is then, but only subsequently, incidentally and relatively validated by the necessary self-certainty. In other words, in the real knowledge of God's Word, in which alone that beginning is made, there also lies the event that it is possible, that that beginning can be made. (I/1, 196)

Theological knowledge occurs when knowing subjects, who presuppose God, are encountered by the Word of God, and Barth insists that God cannot be known any other way, for instance, as "an onlooker who is interested in the event but only from outside. . . . But the external onlooker with this interest fails to see . . . that the co-existence of God and man as it occurs in the experience of God's Word is not a co-existence on the same level, so that it is completely impossible to see it from a higher vantage point and to view it in its possibility" (I/1, 199–200).

A potential problem arises at this juncture, however, because in addition to describing how theological knowledge occurs, Barth has now ruled out both (1) any other method of obtaining theological knowledge and also (2) any attempt to validate or verify the accuracy of theological knowledge by external means. But there does not appear to be any other way if the alternative is to judge the accuracy of theological knowledge by some prior epistemological method, which we know Barth does not allow for. The answer, for Barth, is not to stop for verification but rather proceed to investigate how theological knowledge works from within.

We now arrive at another important distinction in Barth's theological epistemology: if God is presupposed, and God becomes known through disclosure or revelation, the particular shape that theological knowledge takes is not knowledge in general (*Erkenntnis*) but rather *acknowledgment* or *recognition* (*Anerkennung*). Acknowledgment specifically, rather than knowledge in general, has nine features:

1. It is distinct from knowledge but assumes it;
2. it is personal, not factual;
3. it is modified according to the object of knowledge;
4. it defers to the priority of the object of knowledge;
5. it is controlled by the object of knowledge in the process of knowledge;
6. it implies that the object of knowledge is free to disclose itself or not;
7. it is derived from the object, not the subject;
8. it still implies some initiative on the part of the knowing subject; and
9. the knowing subject yields to the object of knowledge. (I/1, 205–8)

Barth later describes acknowledging, or recognizing, God as "a halting before the mystery . . . a basing of man's whole life on this mystery that is beyond himself" (I/1, 219). Human knowledge is involved in the process, but only up to a certain point; past that point, God's self-disclosure must be acknowledged in order to be known—and acknowledgement is not an achievement because "the possibility of knowledge of God's Word lies in God's Word and nowhere else. . . . We cannot produce this event" (I/1, 222, 228). As Diller notes, "The initiating move in Barth's theological epistemology . . . is not a claim we make but a claim made on us. The initial move is made by God himself."[8]

This brings Barth, finally, to one final definition: *faith*. So far Barth has discussed presupposition, knowledge, and acknowledgment, but faith in theological epistemology retains some unique characteristics. Faith, Barth suggests, "is the making possible of knowledge of God's Word that takes place in actual knowledge of it" (I/1, 228), and in it "the knowability of the Word of God . . . comes into view" (I/1, 229). Barth is faced with a familiar complication, because faith could potentially involve an intellectual movement on the part of the knowing subject that the knowing subject could lay claim to having initiated or achieved; however, it has become clear that Barth does not allow for this, so he continues to insist against this in a manner consistent with his previous caveats about theological epistemology:

> The knowability of the Word of God given in the event of faith
> that it is not a possibility which man for his part brings to real
> knowledge, nor is it a possibility which in real knowledge accrues

---

8. Diller, *Theology's Epistemological Dilemma*, 45.

> to man from some source as an enrichment of his existence. But as faith has its absolute and unconditional beginning in God's Word independently of the inborn or acquired characteristics and possibilities of man.... We cannot establish it if, as it were, we turn our backs on God's Word and contemplate ourselves, finding in ourselves an openness, a positive or at least a negative point of contact for God's Word. We can establish it only as we stand fast in faith and its knowledge, i.e., as we turn away from ourselves and turn our eyes or rather our ears to the Word of God. (I/1, 236-37)

Furthermore, faith not only *originates* with God but is *given to* knowing human subjects for use in the process of knowing God. "Faith is not one of the various capacities of man," Barth states, "whether native or acquired. Capacity for the Word of God is not among these. The possibility of faith as it is given to man in the reality of faith can be understood only as one that is loaned to man by God, and loaned exclusively for use" (I/1, 238). If it were otherwise, knowledge of God would be something knowing human subjects could claim to have achieved on their own terms. Here Barth aligns himself with a broadly Augustinian view of the origin of faith, which emphasizes the necessity of divine grace even in the movement of the will toward God. As Augustine argues in *De gratia et libero arbitrio*, "God works in human hearts to incline their wills to whatever He wills, either to good due to His mercy or to evil due to their deserts. Of course, this happens through His judgment, which is sometimes clear and sometimes hidden. Yet it is always just."[9] Similarly, Barth states, "He has not created his own faith; the Word has created it. He has not come to faith; faith has come to him through the Word. He has not adopted faith; faith has been granted to him through the Word. As a believer he cannot see himself as the acting subject of the work done here" (I/1, 244). Knowledge of God is given by God; it is not something knowing subjects can claim to have produced.

So far Barth has been discussing the *form* that knowledge of God takes and summarizes it by suggesting, "All that we have said thus far implies only a turning around and placing ourselves in the direction in which we must look" (I/1, 248). What about the *content* of theology? For Barth, these issues are not unrelated; in fact, form and content in theology are inseparable (I/1, 248-49). Barth begins working toward the content of theology by clarifying what he means by the term *dogmatics*: "The task of dogmatics is the examination of Church proclamation in respect of its agreement with the Word of God, its congruity with what it is trying to proclaim" (I/1, 250). This is

---

9. Augustine, *On Grace and Free Choice*, 180-81.

a deceptively simple definition, and it is important to note what Barth is denying with this affirmation: the task of dogmatics is *not* the church's attempts to understand God or construct its own knowledge of God or prove God's existence. Rather its task is to proclaim theological statements and then examine whether those statements are congruous and consistent with what God has disclosed to us. Dogmatics segregates our own speech about God and God's own speech about himself, and measures the accuracy of its own speech according to the standard that God has disclosed: "the Church holds apart God's Word and its own and questions the latter in the light of the former" (I/1, 250). If that is dogma*tics*, dog*ma* is what results when our speech proves to be consistent with God's self-disclosure: "Dogma is the agreement of Church proclamation with the revelation attested in Holy Scripture" (I/1, 265).

Barth has come a long way from his initial discussions of the scientific character of theology, but we now observe how relevant those definitions were. "It does not recognise the need to understand and legitimate itself as a science at all. Nor does it recognise as normative for itself the general concept of science that is authoritative to-day. Nor does it recognise any obligation to oppose to this another concept which will include and therefore justify itself" (I/1, 275). Theology's accuracy is not measured by an external norm but by its own norm; this does not mean it is unscientific but rather that it is simply scientific by a standard of measure that is consistent with its unique content.

Revelation

The next step in theological epistemology, for Barth, after we have acknowledged that the content of theology—God's self-disclosure—dictates the form theology takes, is to continue to follow the path that God's self-disclosure has paved (I/1, 275). What does that path consist of? The short answer is *God's Word* in its threefold form of proclamation, Scripture, and revelation. "As the Word of God reveals itself, the Bible and proclamation are the Word of God. Hence it is the concept of revelation which must give us the key to an understanding of the relations between the two and from which we must also take the very questions with which we approach the two" (I/1, 290).[10]

It is impossible to overestimate the importance of revelation in the *Church Dogmatics*. In this section I will focus specifically on his descriptions

---

10. On the matter of the Word of God in its threefold form in Barth's *CD*, see Runia, *Barth's Doctrine of Holy Scripture*, 18–56, 116–36; Clark, *Karl Barth's Theological Method*; Currie, *Only Sacrament Left to Us*, 9–29.

in §17, "The Revelation of God as the Abolishment of Religion." This section provides insight not only into Barth's positive doctrine of revelation but also how it is distinct from competing conceptions. Addressing the issue of revelation and religion is both difficult and necessary for Barth because in the world of Marburg neo-Kantianism, *religion* connoted the constructivist approach to theology that Barth has been arguing against. Herrmann attempted to retain a unique place for revelation within constructivist religion, but this did not go far enough for the later Barth. The challenge Barth now faces with his emphasis on revelation rather than religion is to account for how religion is still possible.

Barth starts by re-emphasizing that while human cognition necessarily *participates* in theological epistemology, knowledge of God does not *originate* in human cognition; rather, the source of knowledge of God originates in the event of God's self-disclosure. Note the repetition of "circle" language:

> As we tried to be faithful to Holy Scripture as the only valid testimony to revelation, we saw that we were committed to the statement that as an event which encounters man, this event represents a self-enclosed circle. Not only the objective but also the subjective element in revelation, not only its actuality but also its potentiality, is the being and action of the self-revealing God alone. (I/2, 280)

Yet even though the event of God's self-disclosure both initiates and fulfills the process of theological knowledge, Barth acknowledges that it still retains certain elements of standard human cognition in general: "We have to recognise that it has at least the aspect and character of a human phenomenon. It is something which may be grasped historically and psychologically. We can inquire into its nature and structure and value as we can in the case of all others" (I/2, 280). This admission is where Barth locates religion in his account of theological epistemology: the residual elements of human cognition that participate in the encounter between self and God's self-disclosure: "The problem of religion is simply a pointed expression of the problem of man in his encounter and communion with God" (I/2, 283).

A potential hazard in this admission, however, is losing sight of the fact that the encounter originates with God: "it is, therefore, a chance to fall into temptation. Theology and the Church and faith are invited to abandon their theme and object and to become hollow and empty, mere shadows of themselves" (I/2, 283). This, Barth suggests, is where modern Protestant liberalism went awry; it lost sight of where theological knowledge *originates from* and instead focused on the psychological and social *effects* of it (I/2, 284). Traditionally, Barth suggests, revelation is the norm by which religion is assessed, not the other way around, but modern Protestant liberalism proceeds in exactly the opposite direction. According to this tradition, "religion has not to be understood in the light of revelation, but revelation in the light of religion.... Anything that we say later, within this systematic framework, about the necessity and actuality of revelation, can never be more than the melancholy reminder of a war which was lost at the very outset. It can never be more than an actual veiling of the real message and content" (I/2, 291, 294). Revelation begins where human attempts to know God end; it provides theological information that cannot be obtained by any other means: "Man's attempts to know God from his own standpoint are wholly and entirely futile.... In revelation God tells man that He is God, and that as such He is his Lord. In telling him this, revelation tells him something utterly new, something which apart from revelation he does not know and cannot tell either himself or others" (I/2, 301). Knowledge of God is not achieved through demonstration but through presupposition and revelation. And to continue to make this case in more detail, Barth's reliance on Kant increases rather than decreases.

Theology and Practical Reason

In the previous section I posed the question of what the *content* of theological epistemology is for Barth given how he establishes its *form*, but Barth only takes preliminary steps toward this end in the first volume of *CD* by demonstrating the inseparability of form and content. In the second volume of *CD*, Barth is now in a position to make positive theological claims, in other words, to describe not just *how* God is known but *who* God is according to God's self-disclosure. In this section I will describe how Barth begins to use the epistemological principles I introduced in the previous section in service of theology, and I will also begin to indicate how he uses Kantian themes specifically to accomplish this. Specifically, I will discuss the relationship between theoretical and practical reason, the inseparability of theology and epistemology, limits and boundaries in theological epistemology, and conceptualism.

The Fulfillment of Theological Epistemology

Barth is aware that he cannot assume a consensus on what is meant by the term *God*. "In the doctrine of God," he therefore notes, "we have to learn what we are saying when we say 'God.' In the doctrine of God we have to learn to say 'God' in the correct sense. If we do not speak rightly of this

Subject, how can we speak rightly of His predicates?" (II/1, 3). How is "the correct sense" (*rechten Sinne*) determined? So far Barth has been insisting that this is not something we can achieve; it is rather something we *receive*. Barth now adds an additional, practical condition to this initial requirement: Christ's church is the *location* where knowledge of God is received. "God is known in the Church of Jesus Christ; that is to say, that this Subject is objectively present to the speakers and hearers, so that man in the Church really stands before God. . . . But if the life of the Church is not just a semblance, the knowledge of God is realised in it. This is the presupposition which we have first of all to explain in the doctrine of God" (II/1, 3).[11] Presupposing God is a general requirement for theological epistemology, and now presupposing the church as the location of theological epistemology is a more specific requirement of God's particular self-disclosure in Jesus Christ.[12]

Presupposing the church as the proper location of theological epistemology will be unsatisfactory to knowing subjects who would seek to confirm this claim before assenting to it for the same reason that presupposing God as a condition of theological epistemology in general is unsatisfactory: they are not claims that are subject to outside verification or validation *prior to* making them. John Webster acknowledges,

> Modern scholarly prose has, by and large, become the standardized expression of a certain understanding of intellectual inquiry in which the implied reader is appealed to by the author as an impartial tribunal, hearing the case which the book makes, weighing the evidence it brings forward and then reaching a judgment. When Barth broke with the liberal historicist scholarship of his teachers, one of the things which was jettisoned was this ideal of disinterested inquiry and its embodiment in the literary form of the scholarly treatise.[13]

---

11. Barth emphasizes the continuity between his train of thought here and *Anselm* as follows: "I learned the fundamental attitude to the problem of the knowledge and existence of God which is adopted in this section—and indeed in the whole chapter—at the feet of Anselm of Canterbury, and in particular from his proofs of God set out in *Prosl.* 2–4. May I therefore ask the reader to keep that text in mind, and to allow me to refer to my book *Fides quaerens intellectum: Anselms Beweis der Existenz Gottes* (1931), for an understanding of it" (II/1, 4).

12. Barth notes that Kant also "takes a quite strikingly systematic interest in the notion of the Church. It is here for the first time that something becomes visible on the borders of the conception of the problem peculiar to him." Barth, *Protestant Theology in the Nineteenth Century*, 275.

13. Webster, *Barth*, 49–50.

Barth holds, by contrast, that knowledge of God does not proceed by these rules. Knowledge of God is not a matter that can be articulated and evaluated in the abstract because no Archimedean point outside the process of human knowledge of God exists from which to validate its conclusions. "The question cannot be then posed *in abstracto* but only *in concreto*; not *a priori* but only *a posteriori*. The *in abstracto* and *a priori* question of the possibility of the knowledge of God obviously presupposes the existence of a place outside the knowledge of God itself from which this knowledge can be judged" (II/1, 5). There is no such place outside the knowledge of God, for Barth; knowledge of God occurs from within. "The possibility of the knowledge of God and therefore the knowability of God," Barth states, "cannot be questioned *in vacuo*, or by means of a general criterion of knowledge delimiting the knowledge of God from without, but only from within this real knowledge itself" (II/1, 5).

Knowledge of God, in other words, takes place not only in abstraction but tangibly—not only *theoretically*, but *practically*. These are familiar terms, and the scheme that Barth is now establishing, I suggest, is similar in *form* to Kant's scheme in the first two Critiques, although not necessarily identical in *content*. For Kant, the existence of God is a theoretical idea that we are obligated to believe in order to understand the moral law we encounter through practical reason and which provides content for theoretical reason; for Barth, the existence of God is an idea that we are obligated to believe as a presupposition but is ultimately only clarified through God's tangible self-revelation in Christ.

One might suggest that this is a stretch, and if the foregoing passages were all that was available to draw this parallel, the suspicion would be warranted. At this juncture, however, Barth presses the language of Kantianism even further in support of his characterizations of theological epistemology, beginning with a characteristically Kantian posture: "The only legitimate and meaningful questions in this context are: how far is God known? and how far is God knowable?" (II/1, 5). Kant, similarly, summarily suggested in *LPT*, "It is one of the worthiest of inquiries to see how far our reason can go in the knowledge of God" (*LPT*, intro.)

Like Kant, Barth has been characterizing his epistemology so far in both idealist and realist terms; the knowing subject *contributes to* the product of knowledge, but the final product of knowledge is circumscribed by and ultimately anchored in the reality of the external object of knowledge. "The knowledge of God with which we are here concerned takes place," Barth states, "not in a free choice, but with a very definite constraint. It stands or falls with its one definite object. . . . The knowledge of God with which we are here concerned is bound to the God who in His Word gives

Himself to the Church to be known as God. Bound in this way it is the true knowledge of the true God" (II/1, 7). Similarly, Barth furthermore distinguishes his position from strong forms of idealism, which reduce the object of knowledge to the cognitive activity of the knowing subject: "We therefore separate ourselves from all those ideas of the knowledge of God which understand it as the union of man with God, and which do not regard it as an objective knowledge but leave out the distinction between the knower and the known. It is not as if we can arrive at the real knowledge of God on this view" (II/1, 9–10).

The appearance of objects in the view of knowing subjects was a significant building block of Kant's first Critique, particularly in the Transcendental Aesthetic (A 42/B 59). Similarly, Barth states, "Biblical faith lives upon the objectivity of God. In one way or another, God *comes into the picture, the sphere, the field of man's consideration and conception in exactly the same way that objects do*, uniting Himself to man, distinguishing Himself from him, evoking by His existence and nature man's love, trust and obedience" (II/1, 13; emphasis added). Kant would not suggest that *God* appears as an object of appearance, but Barth does, and he does so in Kantian language. God as an object of knowledge is both *distinct from* the knowing subject's conceptual apparatus *and also* joined with it in the process of knowledge; theological knowledge, for Barth as for Kant, is simultaneously both realist and idealist. But God is not an object among objects; God as an object of knowledge is different from other objects of knowledge not in *degree* but entirely in *kind*: "[God as object] is not an object that can give itself to be known and will be known just like any other object; not an object which awakens love, trust and obedience in the same way as other objects. Its objectivity is the particular and utterly unique objectivity of God. And that is tantamount to saying that this knowledge is the particular and utterly unique knowledge of faith" (II/1, 14).

To reiterate, Barth's theological epistemology retains the *form* of Kantian critical knowledge if not the precise *content*, but Kant left his epistemological form intentionally open to variations in content. Barth, I suggest, is taking tactical advantage of Kant's open architecture and simply describing what happens when we presuppose God's self-disclosure specifically. The result is that "this knowledge becomes and is a special knowledge, distinct from the knowledge of all other objects, *outstanding in the range of all knowledge*. What our consideration and conception mean in this context cannot be determined from a general understanding of man's consideration and conception, but only in particular from God as its particular object" (II/1, 15; emphasis added). Importantly, Barth does *not* suggest that "man's consideration and conception" must be *abandoned*—fideism—in light of the fact that it cannot produce knowledge of God; rather, it simply requires supplementation through practical reason. Barth continues, "As knowledge of faith the knowledge of God is just like any other knowledge in that it also has an object. We have seen that thereby the primary objectivity of God is to be *distinguished—but not separated—*from the secondary. But He and none other is the object of the knowledge of faith" (II/1, 21). Finally, Barth clarifies and summarizes the theoretical-practical process of theological knowledge as follows:

> The will of God offers itself as good will towards men and is met by faith. Man with his will yields and becomes submissive to the will of God. Faith becomes the determination of his existence and therefore obedience. And in this way the knowledge of God takes place. According to the Bible there is no knowledge of God outside this cycle.... In love we are set on the circular course in which there is no break, in which we can and shall only go further—from faith to faith, from knowledge to knowledge—never beginning with ourselves (and that means, with our own ability for faith and knowledge) but therefore also never ending with ourselves (and that means, with our own inability for faith and knowledge). (II/1, 29, 37–38)

The way in which knowledge of God operates for Barth, I suggest, is Kantian in form if not exactly in content. Barth has different objectives than Kant, but that does not mean he cannot use Kant's apparatus for his purposes. Kant's theological epistemology is moral in character, but it is part of a much larger architecture that Barth freely uses.

God's Knowability

How is knowledge of God possible? This question, Barth suggests, can only be answered *after* presupposing that God is knowable and encountering God's self-disclosure in Christ, not before. "We cannot ask: 'Is God knowable?' For God is actually known and therefore God is obviously knowable. We cannot ask about an abstract possibility of the knowledge of God. We can ask only about its concrete possibility as definitely present already in its actual fulfilment" (II/1, 63–64), Barth states. But Barth is still not done weaving Kantian themes into his theological epistemology. He continues to describe his architecture specifically in terms of *postulates* in a manner similar to Kant, but Barth fills it with his own theological content. In reviewing the ground he has covered thus far, he states,

> Making a *postulate*, we tried to see how the readiness of man must be constituted as included in the readiness of God. We described it as the openness and therefore the neediness, knowledge, and willingness of man in relationship to grace. Making a further *postulate*, we also gave to it reality; i.e., we understood this open man expressly as man in the Church, as man placed by the Word of God under judgment, but also under grace. But we saw that even in this man we cannot really discern the man who is opened for the grace of God and therefore the knowability of God. It is not in his reality as such that we find the human readiness enclosed in the readiness of God. (II/1, 142; emphasis added)

The postulate of finding the fulfillment of theological knowledge within the knowing subject's conceptual apparatus yields a dead end for Barth as it does for Kant in the Canon of Pure Reason. But this hardly means that theological knowledge is impossible; the relationship between concepts and postulates is dialectical and exploratory by design and requires ongoing refinement. This particular postulate, in other words, does not render theological knowledge impossible but rather simply exposes the limitations of the knowing subject's conceptual apparatus to achieve it on its own terms. Barth therefore asks rhetorically, "Does this conclusion mean that our main question is to be answered negatively? Is there simply no readiness of man for the knowledge of God? Is the enmity of man against grace, and therefore his closedness against God, the last thing to be said of him?"

No. According to Kant, the circuit of knowledge is only completed by external objects of knowledge. So too with Barth. "If in face of this position we look round for a positive answer to our question, we certainly cannot make any further use of *anthropological* postulates. . . . The knowability of God is not, therefore, to be made intelligible as the predicate of man as such" (II/1, 144–45; emphasis added). If we continue to search for knowledge of God in the knowing subject's conceptual apparatus, we will only find limitations, not fulfillment; we will perpetually be "treading on air" if this is the presupposition we begin with (*Man tritt in die Luft*; II/1, 145). The circuit of knowledge—the nexus of human attempts to know God and the fulfillment of those attempts—is rather completed only through God's self-disclosure in the person of Christ: "The only aspect of man under which the picture we have already drawn is actually altered, and the decision investigated (i.e., the readiness of man included in the readiness of God and therefore God's real knowability) is actually disclosed, is the christological. . . . No anthropological or ecclesiological assertion is true in itself and as such. Its truth subsists in the assertions of Christology, or rather in the reality of Jesus Christ alone"

(II/1, 148–49). God's self-disclosure in Christ perfectly completes the circuit of postulation. This is both consistent with Kant's description of the circuit of theoretical and practical reason and also provides an original and specifically theological resolution to it. Barth freely uses Kant's epistemological architecture in order to achieve his theological objectives.

Limits in Theological Epistemology: Concepts

Barth has worked presupposition, the theoretical-practical circuit, and postulation into his theological epistemology, but readers of Kant's first two critiques will notice an omission: conceptualism. While Barth alludes to the role of concepts in postulation, so far he has neglected to directly incorporate this central piece of Kant's puzzle into this own schematic. In §27, "The Limits of the Knowledge of God," Barth now addresses this lacuna. "Human cognition," he states descriptively, "is fulfilled in [intuitions] and concepts [*Anschauungen und Begriffen*]. [Intuitions] are the images [*Bilder*] in which we perceive objects as such. Concepts are the counterimages with which we make these images of perception our own by thinking them, i.e., arranging them" (II/1, 181). Barth continues to walk a fine line between human *capacity* for knowledge of God, which he acknowledges and affirms, and its *completion* and *fulfillment*, which he maintains humans are incapable of. Only with that in mind is Barth able to describe in further detail the concept of God that is native to our conceptual apparatus. "[Images] and their corresponding objects are capable of being expressed by us. If men can speak of God in human words—and this is the presupposition which we have to examine—it is obvious that they can first view and conceive (i.e., perceive and think) God" (II/1, 181). Humans *are* capable of *conceiving of* God, Barth now suggests, but the fact that he is pursuing this line of thought at the *end* of his theological epistemology rather than the beginning suggests the importance of establishing the *incapacity* of human knowledge to attain full knowledge of God first. "Our attempt to answer God's revelation with our views and concepts is an attempt undertaken with insufficient means, the work of unprofitable servants, so that we cannot possibly ascribe the success of this attempt and therefore the truth of our knowledge of God to ourselves, i.e., to the capacity of our views and concepts" (II/1, 183). The fulfillment of the knowledge of God has only just begun where the limitations of our conceptual apparatus ends: "The *terminus a quo* of the knowledge of God is not, therefore, identical with the *terminus ad quem* which we can reach when we discern the inability—i.e., the limitation—of our perception and discursive thinking. When we reach this insight, which perhaps forms the end of self-knowledge, we have not even begun to know God" (II/1, 184).

We have a native concept of God, but that is only the beginning of theological knowledge. "We confess that, knowing God, we do not comprehend how we come to know Him, that we do not ascribe to our cognition as such the capacity for this knowledge, but that we can only trace it back to God" (II/1, 184). God, Barth asserts, is actually *hidden* from our concepts, but God *must* be hidden from our concepts in order to reveal himself as something distinct from them. "God's hiddenness (which includes God's invisibility, incomprehensibility and ineffability) tells us that God does not belong to the objects which we can always subjugate to the process of our viewing, conceiving and expressing and therefore our spiritual oversight and control" (II/1, 187). God's self-disclosure in Christ is just consistent enough with our native concept of God to get our attention, but it is sufficiently distinct from our native concept of God for us to know that it is not something we produce on our own terms. "The possibility of the personal and cognitive revelation of God," Diller states, "is, next to all other acts of human knowing, unreservedly sui generis."[14] Knowledge of God must come from somewhere else, and we can acknowledge that the circle of theological knowledge is complete: "Moving in our *circulus veritatis Dei*, we are in the sphere of Jesus Christ, where that which in an earlier context we called the veiling and unveiling of God, the way from the one to the other, forms the household rule from which we cannot except ourselves. Faith is nothing but the acknowledgment of this rule" (II/1, 254).

Reconciling Theological Knowledge

Barth has been insisting that the form of theological epistemology is inseparable from its content. On a purely technical level, this means that a prior epistemological method can only produce so much; the knowing subject is ultimately dependent on the object of knowledge for knowledge's final product. Kant has been useful in getting Barth started in this direction. If theological knowledge is going to be fulfilled, according to Barth, God must take the initiative to do. And that is exactly what God has done in Jesus Christ: God has postulated himself into the problem of human knowledge and closed the circuit. But this isn't simply a resolution to an abstract epistemological problem. As God closes the circuit of knowledge in the disclosure of Jesus Christ and the fellowship of the Holy Spirit, redemption itself takes place. "He Himself is the reconciliation of the world to God which He

---

14. Diller, *Theology's Epistemological Dilemma*, 57.

declares. As He declares this and therefore Himself (ἐγώ εἰμι), as in the discharge of His prophetic office *He mediates and establishes knowledge of Himself*, He encounters man, approaching and confronting him, setting Himself over against him as the One who is for him but is not known" (IV/3.1, 183; emphasis added).

Kant did not go this far, but Barth did not need him to; Kant provided the architecture that Barth freely uses. Barth agrees that we have a native, theoretical concept of God, but that concept requires an appearance from outside the knowing subject's conceptual apparatus in order to be fulfilled. "This is how it is with the knowledge of God," Barth states specifically. "The 'knowledge of the Holy One' according to Prov. 9 is *practical understanding*. That is, the willing and doing of the Holy One, as it is known, *creates for itself a counterpart in the history of the one who knows*. If man knows God, this includes and primarily implies the fact that God acts towards man as the One who knows" (IV/3.1, 184; emphasis added).

Barth takes matters one step further, however, in considering the specific *content* of theological epistemology. In encountering God's self-disclosure in Christ, knowing human subjects do not come to know God in general, and they don't simply come to know God specifically in God's particular self-disclosure; knowing subjects, in other words, don't only come to know *information about* God or come to know God in impersonal, technical, rational terms. Rather, as God closes the circuit of knowledge in the self-disclosure of Christ as redeemer specifically, redemption itself occurs: "Nothing less or other than reconciliation itself is made present and takes place wherever and whenever it establishes, awakens and fashions knowledge of itself and therefore Christian knowledge" (IV/3.1, 212). The seemingly laborious and labyrinthine process of knowing God is not just a journey but a destination; in the very process of reaching the limits of theological knowledge itself and having them breached by God's self-disclosure in Christ, the knowing human subject experiences redemption, justification, and sanctification. "As the divine work of justification and sanctification, it achieves its own real presence in the world and among men by revealing itself in the totality of its occurrence and establishing Christian knowledge. Or, to put it the other way round, the real presence of reconciliation, i.e., of the living Lord Jesus, is the theme and basis and content of Christian knowledge" (IV/3.1, 212). God's self-disclosure—God's revelation in Christ—is necessarily epistemological, but this is just the beginning. Revelation and its acknowledgement by knowing human subjects is the means by which God establishes salvation itself.

> In and in virtue of His revelation, it becomes the object, basis and content of human knowledge. It makes itself present in this. As the event of salvation it thus takes place, not just primarily there and then in Him, but also secondarily and no less really in the knowledge of salvation created by Him. *It is thus the case that the one who participates in this knowledge participates in the event of salvation itself.* (IV/3.1, 217; emphasis added)

Theological epistemology, for Barth, has consequences. It is genuinely unique among other types of knowledge, that is, other sciences. The knowledge that results from theological inquiry that proceeds as Barth has been describing and salvific knowledge of God in Christ are indistinguishable. "Just as the way of knowing God is fundamentally different from the way we know other objects of knowledge," Diller notes, "so too is the nature of the knowing itself unlike any other knowledge."[15] That, according to Barth, is as it should be: "The knowledge of God is unlike all other knowledge in that its object is the living Lord of the knowing man: his Creator, from whom he comes even before he knows Him; his Reconciler, who through Jesus Christ in the Holy Ghost makes knowledge of Himself real and possible; his Redeemer, who is Himself the future truth of all present knowledge of Himself" (II/1, 21). Theological epistemology, in other words, is not just *knowledge of* God's reconciling work in Christ, but it *is itself* reconciliation; it is the process by which God achieves reconciliation with knowing human subjects. "For theological knowledge to be possible, according to Barth, we must be drawn up, by the gift of the Spirit, to participate in the knowing by which God knows himself. In Barth's view, revelation is bound up with soteriology."[16]

Conclusion

Speech about God, for Barth, already assumes some sort of belief in God, and the accuracy of that speech is measured according to its own standard, not by one imposed on it. In this respect, it can be regarded as a science; it submits its hypotheses for correction and revision according to the information it receives from outside its initial assumptions. God, in Barth's theological epistemology, is a *presupposition* of this process, not a conclusion. "The doctrine of the knowledge of God," Barth states,

> does not form an independent prolegomenon to the actual doctrine of God. It is itself already a part of that doctrine, because it

---

15. Diller, *Theology's Epistemological Dilemma*, 60.
16. Diller, *Theology's Epistemological Dilemma*, 61.

> can consist only in a representation of the being and activity of God. ... For it is not only the basic reality to which all human speaking and hearing about God is related. As the basic reality, it is also a basis of knowledge from which all human speaking and hearing about God originates. (II/1, 32)

But this is just the beginning of a more complex circuit that requires input from outside the cognitive apparatus of the knowing subject. In order for knowledge to occur, an external object must come into view and make contact with that presupposition. A more accurate way to describe this moment, according to Barth, is *ac*-knowledgment, which recognizes that the human mind can only know so much on its own terms. Human knowledge *participates in* but does not *determine* the outcome of knowledge. As human knowledge participates in the knowledge of God, it does so in *faith*. This is the *form* that theological knowledge takes for Barth, but it only gestures at the *content* of faith. Before defining the content of theological knowledge more specifically, Barth must first re-emphasize, as he suggested in *Anselm*, that form and content in theological knowledge are inseparable. This is where Barth's definition of *dogmatics* comes into view: as a science, it seeks accuracy in theology by measuring itself against God's self-disclosure in Christ. The content determines the shape theological knowledge takes, but it does not render the original shape irrelevant; rather, it supplements, corrects, augments, and clarifies it.

Theology has a locative requirement according to Barth: God's self-disclosure occurs in the Word of God's threefold form in the church specifically. With this requirement in place, Barth is in a position to elaborate Kantian themes more explicitly. First, knowledge of God is not just theoretical but also practical; it is not abstract but also actual. While knowing subjects bring the presupposition of God to the knowing process, it is necessarily incomplete for the same reason pure theoretical reason is incomplete in Kant's critical philosophy; it requires the supplementation of practical reason for its fulfillment. God's self-disclosure comes into view, for Barth, and completes the circuit of knowledge. In this way, Barth's theological epistemology is both idealistic and realistic, as Kant's was. Barth retains the general architecture of Kant's critical philosophy but finishes the project with unique theological content. The primary point of contact between theoretical and practical reason, for Barth as for Kant, are *postulates*; in Barth's theological epistemology, the circuit of knowledge is both perfected and completed by God's disclosure of the reconciling Christ. And this, finally, entails not just an abstract *knowledge of* reconciliation, but the process of coming to acknowledge God's self-disclosure in Christ is itself redemptive.

Conclusion
A Case for Continuity

I SET OUT TO argue that there is a deep consistency between the theological epistemologies of Kant and Barth, so much so that Barth followed the contours of Kant's critical philosophy in order to develop what would eventually become the procedure of *Church Dogmatics*. It was the architecture that made Barth's theology possible, and it enabled him to say what he did in the particular way he said it. This was a strange claim to make for several reasons. First, until relatively recently, Kant scholarship has not been interested in arguing for positive religious or theistic emphases in Kant's corpus. Second, Kant's role in contemporary historical-theological narratives of modern Protestant theology has not necessarily been a favorable one; he is often dismissed as an agnostic or simply as a forerunner to Schleiermacher, Ritschl, and modern Protestant liberal tradition more generally. Third, and for this reason, Kant would seem like an unlikely conversation partner for someone such as Barth.

I supported this thesis in five stages. In chapter 2, my objective was to suggest that Kant's idealism retains some realist properties. Doing so required me to account for two of the major interpretive options in contemporary scholarship: the metaphysical readings of Pritchard, Strawson, Guyer, and Langton, which emphasize the discontinuity between our knowledge and things as they are in themselves, and the epistemological or deflationary readings of Bird, Pippin, and Allison, which allow for more continuity but also emphasize the subjective conditions of knowledge. A third way is possible, according to Lucy Allais, that accounts for *both* the metaphysical *and* epistemological aspects of Kant's system, both of which are present in the first Critique. This is consistent with Kant's own stated aims to steer a middle course between dogmatic metaphysics and the twin errors of skeptical epistemology and idealism. This was important for my argument because if purely idealist or antirealist readings of Kant's critical philosophy were accurate, it would be difficult to demonstrate why Barth would have a use for him as a theologian.

Establishing that Kant's idealism retains realist features was necessary for the argument of chapter 3, where I turned to Kant's positive account of theism specifically in his philosophical system. My first step was to demonstrate that God's existence is deeply engrained in the process of how knowledge itself works through the moral life. I furthermore suggested that according to Kant, we have a doxastic obligation to presuppose God (and freedom and immortality) in the process of our reasonings: "There is in us not merely the *warrant* but also the *necessity*, as a need connected with duty, to presuppose the possibility of this highest good, which, since it is possible only under the condition of the existence of God, connects the presupposition of the existence of God inseparably with duty; that is, *it is morally necessary to assume the existence of God*" (*CPrR* 1.2.5; emphasis added). We continue to see this principle employed in *Religion* and *LPT*, both of which, such that Allen Wood could suggest that Kant "remained quite sympathetic to traditional theology on many points."[1] If Kant was actually an agnostic or if his philosophical theology was nothing more than a reduction of religion to ethics, as some historical accounts suggest, this would pose a further difficulty for demonstrating his importance for Barth as a theologian.

The Kant that Barth encountered in his early education, however, was layered in and mediated by many decades of interpretive conflict and varying emphases. Therefore before moving directly to how Barth might have used Kant for his theology, it was necessary to account for some of the major ways Kant's philosophy was used and interpreted, which was the purpose of chapter 4. Neo-Kantianism in particular, Sebastian Luft suggests, was "the most broadly influential movement of European philosophy between approximately 1850 and 1918,"[2] but that doesn't even account for the nearly half century between Kant and neo-Kantianism, which involved the rise and decline of Hegel. The many conflicting histories and counterhistories suggest a much more complex picture than many of Kant's interpreters would lead us to believe. My aim was to narrate some of the major moments and developments during this period for clarity but also to destabilize any one school's claims to accuracy and also make clear which interpretive emphases Barth would have encountered at Marburg—and ultimately rejected.

Having cleared that ground, I was then prepared to begin to address Barth's initial reception of Kant during his education at Marburg in chapter 5. Barth indicated an interest in Kant from early in his student years, but it was not limited to an intellectual fascination. He continued to wrestle with Kant as Herrmann's student, and even after his break with the assumptions

1. Allen Wood, translator's introduction to *LPT*, 10.
2. Luft, *Neo-Kantian Reader*, xx.

of theological liberalism, he did not dispense with Kant but rather *returned* to Kant as a resource for his next phase, beginning with the first Romans commentary. Over the course of the two Romans commentaries and also in *Anselm*, three Kantian themes begin to emerge: (1) God as a presupposition in theological epistemology; (2) the strategic significance of boundaries and limits in human cognition; and (3) the strategic priority of the division of cognition into theoretical and practical domains.

The final stage of my argument in chapter 6 involved arguing that these Kantian themes not only persist in the *Church Dogmatics*, but Barth continues to utilize Kant in his mature statement with increased sophistication. In addition to insisting, like Kant, that God is a presupposition of knowledge, Barth elaborates the process of acquiring knowledge of God at length: as it does for Kant, it follows a circuit involving the input of practical reason through postulates to theoretical reason's concepts; unlike Kant, however, Barth fills this architecture with the unique content of God's self-disclosure in Christ.

A Case for Continuity

The objective of this project is to demonstrate continuity between the theological epistemologies of Kant and Barth. Having articulated the stages of my argument, I now suggest that this continuity is apparent in four different ways: *strategically, directly, thematically,* and *architecturally*. Kant's and Barth's theological epistemologies demonstrate *strategic continuity* because they both set out not to argue for one position over another per se but rather to articulate mediating positions between two extreme positions, and they do so in nearly identical language. At the outset of the first Critique, Kant states that he is interested in steering a middle course between dogmatism and skepticism (*CPR*, B xxxiv), and later, as his project progresses, between enthusiasm and skepticism (*CPR*, B 128). In *Anselm*, Barth likewise sets out to find a third way between orthodoxy and enthusiasm (*A*, 35). *Direct continuity* between their theological epistemologies is apparent when Barth engages with Kant outright, or directly. This occurs from Barth's earliest student days all the way through the *Church Dogmatics*. He indicates an early fascination with Kant, and he refers directly to Kant more than any other philosophical figure throughout his works by a wide margin.[3] He favored Kant's insights that "concepts without intuitions are empty; intuitions without concepts are blind" in the first Romans commentary (*R I*, 52), for

---

3. According to *The Digital Karl Barth Library*, Barth refers to Kant 769 times across all his works, followed in frequency by Heidegger, Hegel, Kierkegaard, and Nietzsche.

example, in order to demonstrate the limits of human knowledge and pave the way for the need of revelation, and he maintained this position in the second Romans commentary (*ER*, 271, 294–95). He also recruits Kant as he begins to advocate for the presupposition of God as well as distinguish how theoretical and practical reason work together in theological epistemology (*ER*, 432, 468–69), which continues with *Anselm*.

The best example of *thematic continuity* in Kant's and Barth's theological epistemologies is their mutual belief that God is a presupposition of knowledge, not something that can be demonstrated by proof. When it is observed that Kant was critical of the traditional proofs of God's existence, that does not mean that he did not believe in God's existence; he simply held that the proofs were not the best route to get there. It is telling that they shared an interest in Anselm for this reason, although they had different responses to him; whereas Kant dismissed Anselm, Barth made an effort to reinterpret him. Either way, their objective was similar: to find a way of accounting for God's existence that did not follow the route of the traditional proofs. They both believed that arguments for God's existence were unproductive, so the alternative for both of them is to presuppose God as part of the work of reason, not attempt to achieve knowledge of God as a result of reason. Once they establish this fact, the question for both of them then becomes not *whether* God exists but rather *to what extent* and *how far* God can be known.

Architectural continuity is more difficult to demonstrate, because intellectual architecture, like physical architecture, is by definition implicit rather than explicit. I suggest that architectural continuity can be discerned primarily in the *Church Dogmatics* through the strategy of presupposition, and then the employment of major Kantian themes such as postulation, conceptualism, and the theoretical-practical circuit. By the time we arrive at the *Church Dogmatics*, I suggest that Kant has already been established as a primary influence on Barth's project. Although Kant appears frequently throughout its pages, the cumulative force of the project does not come through direct engagements with Kant but rather the larger strategy and presuppositions. This implicit, architectural continuity combined with thematic, direct, and strategic continuity in other works, I suggest, reinforces the case for continuity between Kant's and Barth's theological epistemologies.

If my argument has been successful, it will have some consequences. First, I believe it will provide some additional insight as to why Barth's theology has been as influential as it has been: it was built around one of the most sophisticated epistemological architectures available. Second, there are some consequences for Barth interpretation. My intention with this project is not to provide a novel interpretation of Barth's theology but rather to explore in further detail what most Barth interpreters have been aware of: that Kant was a significant influence on Barth's theology. This influence is commonly accepted, but I have been interested in demonstrating how and to what extent this is the case. Third, it will have some implications for ongoing conversations in Kant scholarship regarding Kant's relationship to positive theological claims. Kant has not always been portrayed as an ally of such claims, but if Barth is any indication, he can be a useful resource for theology.

A Concluding Test Case

At the beginning of Nicholas Wolterstorff's article "Is It Possible and Desirable for Theologians to Recover from Kant?," Wolterstorff recalls the frustration of a student who stated, "What I find so frustrating about modern theologians is that they won't let me say the things about God I want to say about God—or won't let me say them until I've show that such things *can* be said about God."[4] This reflex to account for how to speak of God before actually speaking of God in some modern theology, Wolterstorff suggests, can be traced back specifically to Kant's use of the metaphor of boundaries between reality and our mental representations of it, between the phenomenal world and the noumenal world.[5] Knowledge operates through concepts, which interpret what we perceive through intuitions. But God is on the other side of the boundary of concepts and intuitions entirely, therefore we cannot really claim to have knowledge of God, so the argument goes.[6] Because God belongs to the noumenal rather than phenomenal realm, "Theology, on Kantian premises, looks impossible."[7] The only way forward for Kant, according to Wolterstorff—and according to the common theological reflex the student encountered to explain how to go about speaking of God *prior* to speaking about God his student encountered—is, "Before we think and speak about God, we must address the question of how such thinking and speaking are possible."[8]

In response to this potential conundrum, Wolterstorff suggests that we rethink how Kantian concepts and boundaries function. In perceiving an object, Wolterstorff suggests, instead of assuming that we are perceiving an awareness of a mental representation *of* the object, we could simply

4. Wolterstorff, "Is It Possible and Desirable?," 2.
5. Wolterstorff, "Is It Possible and Desirable?," 8.
6. Wolterstorff, "Is It Possible and Desirable?," 12.
7. Wolterstorff, "Is It Possible and Desirable?," 13.
8. Wolterstorff, "Is It Possible and Desirable?," 13.

assume that we are perceiving awareness of *the object*, even if there is not a one-to-one correspondence between our perception and the object as it is in itself. If we do this, concepts are *facilitators* of knowledge, not *barriers to it*. "Concepts are not barriers between mind and reality but links," Wolterstorff states.[9] And if *that* is the case, that reduces the obligation to sort out one's conceptual apparatus before actually beginning to use it to speak about God.

Wolterstorff's characterizations of Kant's theism in this article will seem somewhat foreign to my own reading of Kant. The suggestion that Kant's conceptualism is a *barrier* to knowledge is telling: this is a hallmark of metaphysical interpretations of Kant specifically, but as I have shown in chapter 2, metaphysical readings are not the only way of reading Kant. According to Prichard, for instance, the conditions of knowledge obscure rather than facilitate knowledge, but it is possible, at least according to Lucy Allais, to read Kant in a way that is both metaphysical and epistemological. If this is the case, knowledge of God becomes much less "agonizing" than Wolterstorff suggests. The question of whether it is possible and desirable for theologians to recover from Kant assumes that Kant is a problem to be solved. I have tried to suggest, by contrast, not only that Kant actually isn't a problem in the first place, but that he can furthermore be an asset that can be used in service of confessional theology. I think Barth would agree.

If Wolterstorff's characterization of Kant is accurate, instead of reconfiguring Kant's architecture to suit our theological needs, another option is to look for a different model altogether. Wolterstorff hints at Thomas Reid as an alternative to Kant. Wolterstorff does not go into detail about what this means in this article, but he does discuss Reid at length in *Thomas Reid and the Story of Epistemology*. The alternative picture we encounter there presumes that God is already involved in the processes of reasoning itself, and that the question of the discrepancy between objects and perception recedes in significance: "We perceive," Reid holds, "because God has given us the power of perceiving, and not because we have impressions from objects. We perceive nothing without those impressions, because our Maker has limited and circumscribed our powers of perception, by such laws of nature as to his wisdom seemed meet, and such as suited our rank in his creation."[10] We can trust, in other words, that our knowledge functions in the way that God intended it to, including but not limited to knowledge of God. We can trust our native dispositions to produce a reliable account of knowledge.

Are Kant's and Reid's outlooks really so different, however? The answer to this question turns on whether Kant's account of theological epistemology

---

9. Wolterstorff, "Is It Possible and Desirable?," 18.
10. Reid, *Essays on the Intellectual Powers of Man*, 2.iv.

is best described as dispositional or evidential. Wolterstorff seems to assume that Kant's theological epistemology, left intact, must lead to an evidential account, which leads to frustrations for theologians. Lee Hardy, however, suggests that Kant's account of religious belief is actually more dispositional in character, even if it is primarily moral rather than theoretical. Hardy states, "The rational cultivation of the *Beweisgründe* [ground of proof] in the development of the moral argument is best understood as an explication of the common human understanding."[11] The existence of God is a necessary postulate to make sense of our common moral experience. Kant admits that this falls short of apodictic certainty, but this is a much stronger starting point than what Wolterstorff's account assumes. "For Kant," Hardy insists, "the apprehension of the truth concerning God's existence is produced by a disposition embedded in sound common sense—specifically, by moral disposition."[12] Further, Martin Heidegger would go so far as to claim that "for Kant the question as to whether and how and within which limits the proposition 'God exists' is possible . . . is the secret thorn [*geheime Stachel*] that drives all thinking in the *Critique of Pure Reason* and subsequent works."[13] And if *that* is the case, we are back to my own suggestion that Kant's theological epistemology can actually be an asset to theology, not a liability.

For both Kant and Barth, God's existence is not a concept that was subject to external argument or demonstration but rather one that is built into the way knowledge functions. For both of them, questions surrounding God's existence and epistemology proper were intimately related, even inseparable, and one cannot sufficiently explain one without eventually referencing the other. Neither of their theological epistemologies, in other words, happen to have certain incidental theological features but rather are necessarily theological by definition. Theism and epistemology are inseparable. Recall that Colin Gunton notes, "Barth identified that after Kant, theology . . . could never be the same. Any theologian had to come to terms with Kant, to follow in his tracks, or branch out in some way from what he established."[14] Barth, I think, saw no need to make a choice. He did all three, and in doing so demonstrates that Kant's philosophy can be an asset to theology rather than the liability it is often taken to be.

---

11. Hardy, "Kant's Reidianism," 237–38.
12. Hardy, "Kant's Reidianism," 254.
13. Heidegger, "Kants These über das Sein," 455.
14. Gunton, *Barth Lectures*, 13.

Bibliography

Adams, Robert Merrihew. "Things in Themselves." *Philosophy and Phenomenological Research* 57 (1997) 801–25.
Adriaanse, Hendrik Johan. "Kant-Rezeption in der Theologie, insbesondere bei Karl Barth." *Zeitschrift für dialektische Theologie* 1 (1985) 74–90.
Allais, Lucy. *Manifest Reality: Kant's Idealism and His Realism*. Oxford: Oxford University Press, 2015.
Allison, Henry. *Kant's Transcendental Idealism: An Interpretation and Defense*. Rev. ed. New Haven: Yale University Press, 2004.
Alston, William. "The Deontological Concept of Epistemic Justification." *Philosophical Perspectives* 2 (1988) 257–99.
Ameriks, Karl. *Interpreting Kant's Critiques*. Oxford: Oxford University Press, 2003.
———. *Kant and the Fate of Autonomy*. Modern European Philosophy. Cambridge: Cambridge University Press, 2000.
———. "Kantian Idealism Today." *History of Philosophy Quarterly* 9 (1992) 329–42.
———. "Recent Work on Kant's Theoretical Philosophy." *Philosophical Quarterly* 19 (1982) 1–24.
Aquila, Richard E. *Matter in Mind: A Study of Kant's Transcendental Deduction*. Bloomington: Indiana University Press, 1989.
Asmuth, Christoph, et al., eds. *Schelling: Zwischen Fichte und Hegel*. Amsterdam: Grüner, 2000.
Augustine. *On Grace and Free Choice*. In *On the Free Choice of the Will, On Grace and Free Choice, and Other Writings*, edited and translated by Peter King, 141–84. Cambridge Texts in the History of Philosophy. Cambridge: Cambridge University Press, 2010.
Bader, R. M. "The Role of Kant's Refutation of Idealism." *Archiv für Geschichte der Philosophie* 94 (2012) 53–73.
Baier, Annette. *A Progress of Sentiments: Reflections on Hume's "Treatise."* Cambridge, MA: Harvard University Press, 1991.
Bakker, Nicolaas Tjepko. *In der Krisis der Offenbarung Karl Barths Hermeneutik, dargestellt an seiner Römerbrief-Auslegung*. Neukirchen-Vluyn: Neukirchener Verlag, 1974.
Balthasar, Hans Urs von. *The Theology of Karl Barth: Exposition and Interpretation*. Translated by Edward T. Oakes. San Francisco: Ignatius, 1992.
Barth, Karl. *Anselm: Fides Quaerens Intellectum: Anselm's Proof of God's Existence in the Context of His Theological Scheme*. Translated by Ian Robertson. London: SCM, 1960.
———. *The Epistle to the Romans*. Translated by Edwyn C. Hoskyns. Oxford: Oxford University Press, 1968.
———. *Ethics*. Edited by Dietrich Braun. Translated by Geoffrey Bromiley. Eugene, OR: Wipf & Stock, 2015.

———. "Der Glaube an den persönlichen Gott." *Zeitschrift für Theologie und Kirche* 24 (1909) 21–32.

———. *Protestant Theology in the Nineteenth Century: Its Background and History.* Translated by Brian Cozens and John Bowden. Rev. ed. Grand Rapids: Eerdmans, 2002.

———. *Der Römerbrief 1919*. Zürich: TVZ, 1985.

———. *Der Römerbrief 1922*. Zollikon–Zürich: Evangelischer Verlag, 1940.

Bausola, Adriano. *Metafisica e rivelazione nella filosofia positiva di Schelling*. Milano: Vita e Pensiero, 1965.

Beck, Lewis White. *Early German Philosophy: Kant and His Predecessors*. Cambridge, MA: Belknap, 1969.

———. *Essays on Kant and Hume*. New Haven: Yale University Press, 1978.

Becker, Wolfgang. *Selbstbewußtsein und Erfahrung: Zu Kants transzendentaler Deduktion und ihrer argumentativen Rekonstruktion*. Freiburg: Albert, 1984.

Beintker, Michael. *Die Dialektik in der 'dialektischen Theologie' Karl Barths: Studien zur Entwicklung der Barthschen Theologie und zur Vorgeschichte der 'Kirchlichen Dogmatik.'* Munich: Kaiser, 1987.

———. "Grenzbewusstsein: Eine Erinnerung an Karl Barths Kant-Deutung." *Zeitschrift für dialektische Theologie* 22 (2006) 19–30.

Beiser, Frederick C. *After Hegel: German Philosophy, 1840–1900*. Princeton: Princeton University Press, 2014.

———. *Genesis of Neo-Kantianism, 1796–1880*. Oxford: Oxford University Press, 2014.

———. *German Idealism: The Struggle against Subjectivism, 1781–1801*. Cambridge, MA: Harvard University Press, 2008.

———. *Late German Idealism*. Oxford: Oxford University Press, 2013.

———. *The Romantic Imperative: The Concept of Early German Romanticism*. Cambridge, MA: Harvard University Press, 2003.

Bird, Graham. *Kant's Theory of Knowledge: An Outline of One Central Argument in the "Critique of Pure Reason."* London: Routledge & Kegan Paul, 1962.

Blencke, Erna. "Zur Geschichte der neuen Fries'schen Schule und der Jakob Friedrich-Fries Gesellschaft." *Archiv für Geschichte der Philosophie* 60 (1978) 199–208.

Bouillard, Henri. *Karl Barth: Parole de Dieu et existence humaine*. Paris: Montaigne, 1957.

Brandt, Richard B. *The Philosophy of Schleiermacher*. New York: Harper & Brothers, 1941.

Brazier, Paul. "Barth's First Commentary on Romans (1919): An Exercise in Apophatic Theology?" *International Journal of Systematic Theology* 6 (2004) 387–403.

Breazeale, Daniel. *Thinking through the "Wissenschaftslehre": Themes from Fichte's Early Philosophy*. Oxford: Oxford University Press, 2013.

Burnett, Richard E. *Karl Barth's Theological Exegesis: The Hermeneutical Principles of the Römerbrief Period*. Grand Rapids: Eerdmans, 2004.

Busch, Eberhard. *Karl Barth: His Life from Letters and Autobiographical Texts*. Grand Rapids: Eerdmans, 1994.

Chalamet, Christophe. *Dialectical Theologians: Wilhelm Herrmann, Karl Barth, and Rudolf Bultmann*. Zurich: TVZ, 2005.

Chia, Roland. *Revelation and Theology: The Knowledge of God in Balthasar and Barth*. New York: Lang, 1999.

Chignell, Andrew. "Can't Kant Cognize His Empirical Self? Or, a Problem for (Almost) Every Interpretation of the Refutation of Idealism." In *Kant and the Philosophy of Mind: Perception, Reason, and the Self*, edited by Anil Gomes and Andrew Stephenson, 138–58. Oxford: Oxford University Press, 2017.

Chipman, Lauchlan. "Kant's Categories and their Schematism." *Kant-Studien* 63 (2009) 36–50.

Church, Ralph. *Hume's Theory of the Understanding*. Ithaca, NY: Cornell University Press, 1935.

Clark, Gordon Haddon. *Karl Barth's Theological Method*. Phillipsburg, NJ: P&R, 1963.

Cohen, Hermann. *Kants Theorie der Erfahrung*. Berlin: Ferdinand Dümmler, 1871.

———. *Kants Theorie der Erfahrung*. 2nd ed. Berlin: Dümmler, 1885.

Copleston, Frederick. *A History of Philosophy*. Vol. 7, *Modern Philosophy: From the Post-Kantian Idealists to Marx, Kierkegaard, and Nietzsche*. New York: Image, 1994.

Cupitt, Don. "Kant and Negative Theology." In *The Philosophical Frontiers of Christian Theology: Essays Presented to D. M. MacKinnon*, edited by Brian Hebblethwaite and Stewart Sutherland, 55–67. Cambridge: Cambridge University Press, 1982.

Currie, Thomas Christian. *The Only Sacrament Left to Us: The Threefold Word of God in the Theology and Ecclesiology of Karl Barth*. Cambridge: Clarke, 2016.

Danford, John W. *David Hume and the Problem of Reason: Recovering the Human Sciences*. New Haven: Yale University Press, 1990.

Davidovich, Adina. "Kant's Theological Constructivism." *Harvard Theological Review* 86 (1993) 325–40.

———. *Religion as a Province of Meaning: The Kantian Foundations of Modern Theology*. Minneapolis: Fortress, 1993.

Despland, Michael. *Kant on History and Religion*. Montreal: McGill-Queen's University Press, 1973.

Dicker, Georges. "Kant's Refutation of Idealism." *Noûs* 42 (2008) 80–108.

Dietrich, Wendell. *Cohen and Troeltsch: Ethical Monotheistic Religion and Theory of Culture*. Brown Judaic Studies 120. Atlanta: Scholars, 1986.

The Digital Karl Barth Library. https://search.alexanderstreet.com/bart.

Diller, Kevin. *Theology's Epistemological Dilemma: How Karl Barth and Alvin Plantinga Provide a Unified Response*. Downers Grove, IL: IVP Academic, 2014.

Dorrien, Gary. *Kantian Reason and Hegelian Spirit: The Idealistic Logic of Modern Theology*. Malden, MA: Wiley-Blackwell, 2012.

Dufour, Eric. *Les Néokantiens: Valeur et Verite*. Paris: Vrin, 2003.

Dyck, Corey W. "The Divorce of Reason and Experience: Kant's Paralogisms of Pure Reason in Context." *Journal of the History of Philosophy* 47 (2009) 249–75.

———. *Kant and Rational Psychology*. Oxford: Oxford University Press, 2014.

Edel, Geert. Introduction to *Kants Theorie der Erfahrung*. In Hermann Cohen, *Werke*. 3 vols. Hildesheim: Olms, 1987.

Estes, Yolanda, and Curtis Bowman. *J. G. Fichte and the Atheism Dispute, 1798–1800*. Burlington, VT: Ashgate, 2010.

Fackenheim, Emil. *The God Within: Kant, Schelling, and Historicity*. Edited by John Burbidge. Toronto: University of Toronto Press, 1996.

Feuerbach, Ludwig. *Grundsätze der Philosophie der Zukunft*. Winterthur: Fröbel, 1843.

Fichte, J. G. *Grundlage der gesamten Wissenschaftslehre*. Jena: Gabler, 1794.

———. *The Science of Knowledge*. Edited and translated by Peter Heath and John Lachs. Cambridge: Cambridge University Press, 1982.

Findlay, J. N. *Kant and the Transcendental Object*. Oxford: Clarendon, 1981.
Firestone, Chris L. *Kant and Theology at the Boundaries of Reason*. New York: Routledge, 2009.
———. "Rational Religious Faith and Kant's Transcendental Boundaries." In *Transcending Boundaries in Philosophy and Theology: Reason, Meaning, and Experience*, edited by Kevin Vanhoozer and Martin Warner, 77–90. Burlington, VT: Ashgate, 2007.
Firestone, Chris L., and Nathan Jacobs. *In Defense of Kant's "Religion."* Bloomington: Indiana University Press, 2008.
Firestone, Chris L., et al., eds. *Kant and the Question of Theology*. Cambridge: Cambridge University Press, 2017.
Fisher, Simon. *Revelatory Positivism? Barth's Earliest Theology and the Marburg School*. Oxford: Oxford University Press, 1988.
Flew, Antony. *Hume's Philosophy of Belief: A Study of His First "Inquiry."* London: Routledge & Kegan Paul, 1961.
Fogelin, Robert J. *Hume's Skepticism in the "Treatise of Human Nature."* London: Routledge & Kegan Paul, 1985.
Forum für Philosophie Bad Hamburg, et al., eds. *Kants transzendentale Deduktion und die Möglichkeit von Transzendentalphilosophie*. Frankfurt am Main: Suhrkamp, 1988.
Galbraith, Elizabeth C. *Kant and Theology: Was Kant a Closet Theologian?* San Francisco: International Scholars, 1996.
Gawlick, Günter, and Lothar Kreimendhal. *Hume in der deutschen Aufklärung. Umrisse einer Rezeptionsgeschichte*. Stuttgart-Bad Cannstatt: Frommann-Holzboog, 1987.
Gonzales, Philip John Paul. *Reimagining the "Analogia Entis": The Future of Erich Przywara's Christian Vision*. Grand Rapids: Eerdmans, 2019.
González, Justo. *A History of Christian Thought*. Vol. 3, *From the Protestant Reformation to the 20th Century*. Rev. ed. Nashville: Abingdon, 1975.
———. *The Story of Christianity*. Vol. 2, *The Reformation to the Present Day*. San Francisco: HarperSanFrancisco, 1985.
Gordon, Peter E. *Continental Divide: Heidegger, Cassirer, Davos*. Cambridge, MA: Harvard University Press, 2010.
Grapotte, Sophie, and Tinca Prunea-Bretonnet, eds. *Kant et Wolff: Héritages et ruptures*. Paris: Vrin, 2011.
Green, Ronald M. *Religion and Moral Reason: A New Method for Comparative Study*. New York: Oxford University Press, 1988.
———. *Religious Reason: The Rational and Moral Basis of Religious Belief*. New York: Oxford University Press, 1978.
Grenz, Stanley, and Roger Olson. *20th-Century Theology: God and the World in a Transitional Age*. Downers Grove, IL: IVP Academic, 1993.
Grube, Dirk-Martin. "Reconstructing the Dialectics in Karl Barth's 'Epistle to the Romans': The Role of Transcendental Argument in Theological Theorizing." *Bijdragen* 69 (2008) 127–46.
Gunton, Colin. *The Barth Lectures*. Edited by Paul Brazier. London: T. & T. Clark, 2007.
Guyer, Paul. *Kant and the Claims of Knowledge*. Cambridge: Cambridge University Press, 1987.
———. "Kant's Intentions in the Refutation of Idealism." *Philosophical Review* 92 (1983) 329–83.

———. *Knowledge, Reason, and Taste: Kant's Response to Hume*. Princeton: Princeton University Press, 2008.
Haas, Alois Maria. "Karl Barths 'Römerbrief' von 1922: Eine Neulektüre." *Philotheos* 12 (2012) 120–32.
Hardy, Lee. "Kant's Reidianism: The Role of Common Sense in Kant's Epistemology of Religious Belief." In *Kant's Moral Metaphysics: God, Freedom, and Immortality*, 233–45. Berlin: de Gruyter, 2010.
Hare, John E. *The Moral Gap: Kantian Ethics, Human Limits, and Divine Assistance*. New York: Oxford University Press, 1996.
Hegel, G. W. F. *Phänomenologie des Geistes*. Bamberg: Goebhardt, 1807.
———. *Phenomenology of Spirit*. Translated by A. V. Miller. Oxford: Oxford University Press, 1997.
———. *Vorlesungen über die Geschichte der Philosophie*. Edited by Karl Ludwig Michelet. Berlin: Duncker und Humblot, 1833–36.
Heidegger, Martin. "Kants These über das Sein." In *Wegmarken*, 445–80. Frankfurt: Klostermann, 1976.
Heim, Karl. *Das Gewißheitsproblem in der systematischen Theologie bis zu Schleiermacher*. Leipzig: Hinrichs, 1911.
Heinrich, Dieter. *Identität und Objektivität: Eine Untersuchung über Kants transzendentale Deduktion*. Heidelberg: Carl Winter Universitätsverlag, 1976.
Herrmann, Wilhelm. *Systematic Theology*. Translated by Nathaniel Micklem and Kenneth A. Saunders. London: Allen and Unwin, 1927.
———. "Zur theologischen Darstellung der christlichen Erfahrung." In *Gesammelte Schriften*, edited by Friedrich Wilhelm Schmidt, 230–53. Tübigen: Mohr, 1923.
Höffe, Otfried. *Immanuel Kant*. Translated by Marshall Farrier. New York: State University of New York Press, 1994.
Hossenfelder, Malte. *Kants Konstitutionstheorie und die Transzendentale Deduktion*. Berlin: de Gruyter, 1978.
Howell, Robert. *Kant's Transcendental Deduction: An Analysis of Main Themes in His Critical Philosophy*. Dordrecht: Kluwer, 1992.
Hume, David. *Enquiry concerning Human Understanding*. Edited by Peter Millican. Oxford: Oxford University Press, 2007.
———. *Treatise of Human Nature*. Edited by David Fate Norton and Mary J. Norton. Oxford: Clarendon, 2007.
Hunsinger, George. *How to Read Karl Barth: The Shape of His Theology*. Oxford: Oxford University Press, 1993.
Insole, Christopher. "Gordon Kaufman and the Kantian Mystery." *International Journal for the Philosophy of Religion* 47 (2000) 101–19.
———. *The Intolerable God: Kant's Theological Journey*. Grand Rapids: Eerdmans, 2016.
———. *Kant and the Creation of Freedom: A Theological Problem*. Oxford: Oxford University Press, 2013.
———. *Kant and the Divine: From Contemplation to the Moral Law*. Oxford: Oxford University Press, 2020.
Inwood, Michael J. *Hegel*. London: Routledge, 1983.
Janke, Wolfgang. *Fichte. Sein und Reflexion—Grundlagen der kritischen Vernunft*. Berlin: de Gruyter, 1970.

Jauernig, Ana. "Kant's Critique of the Leibnizian Philosophy: Contra the Leibnizians, but Pro Leibniz." In *Kant and the Early Moderns*, edited by Daniel Garber and Béatrice Longuenesse, 41–63. Princeton: Princeton University Press, 2008.

Jessop, T. E. "Hume's Limited Scepticism." *Revue Internationale de Philosophie* 30 (1976) 3–27.

Johnson, Keith L. *Karl Barth and the "Analogia Entis."* New York: T. & T. Clark, 2010.

Jones, Paul Dafyyd. "Barth and Anselm: God, Christ, and the Atonement." *International Journal of Systematic Theology* 12 (2012) 257–82.

Josuttis, Manfred. *Die Gegenständlichkeit der Offenbarung: Karl Barths Anselm-Buch und die Denkform seiner Theologie*. Bonn: Bouvier, 1965.

Justin, Gale D. "On Kant's Analysis of Berkeley." *Kant-Studien* 65 (1974) 20–32.

Kalter, Alfons. *Kants vierter Paralogismus*. Meisenheim: Hain, 1975.

Kant, Immanuel. *Critique of Practical Reason*. In *Practical Philosophy*, edited and translated by Mary J. Gregor, 133–272. The Cambridge Edition of the Works of Immanuel Kant. Cambridge: Cambridge University Press, 1996.

———. *Critique of Pure Reason*. Edited and translated by Paul Guyer and Allen W. Wood. The Cambridge Edition of the Works of Immanuel Kant. Cambridge: Cambridge University Press, 1997.

———. *Kritik der reinen Vernunft (1. Aufl. 1781), Prolegomena, Grundlegung zur Metaphysik der Sitten, Metaphysische Anfangsgründe der Naturwissenschaft*. Bd. I.4., *Akademieausgabe von Immanuel Kants Gesammelten Werken*. Berlin: Akademie der Wissenschaften, 1900–.

———. *Kritik der reinen Vernunft (2. Aufl. 1787)*. Bd. I.3, *Akademieausgabe von Immanuel Kants Gesammelten Werken*. Berlin: Akademie der Wissenschaften, 1900–.

———. *Lectures on Philosophical Theology*. Translated by Allen W. Wood and Gertrude M. Clark. Ithaca, NY: Cornell University Press, 1986.

———. *Prolegomena to Any Future Metaphysic*. Edited and translated by Gary Hatfield. Rev. ed. Cambridge: Cambridge University Press, 2004.

———. *Religion within the Boundaries of Mere Reason*. In *Religion and Rational Theology*, edited and translated by Allen W. Wood and George Di Giovanni, 39–216. The Cambridge Edition of the Works of Immanuel Kant. Cambridge: Cambridge University Press, 1996.

Kanterian, Edward. *Kant, God, and Metaphysics: The Secret Thorn*. London: Routledge, 2018.

Kaufman, Gordon. *In Face of Mystery: A Constructive Theology*. Cambridge, MA: Harvard University Press, 1995.

Kaufman, Walter. *An Essay on Theological Method*. Missoula, MT: Scholars, 1979.

———. *God the Problem*. Cambridge, MA: Harvard University Press, 1972.

———. *The Theological Imagination: Constructing the Concept of God*. Louisville: Westminster, 1981.

Kaulbach, Friedrich. *Die Metaphysik des Raumes bei Leibniz und Kant*. Bonn: Bouvier, 1960.

Kelley, J. N. D. *Early Christian Doctrines*. 4th ed. London: T. & T. Clark, 1968.

Kile, Frederick O. *Die theologischen Grundlagen von Schellings Philosophie der Freiheit*. Leiden: Brill, 1965.

Kim, Halla, and Steven Hoeltzel, eds. *Kant, Fichte, and the Legacy of Transcendental Idealism*. New York: Lexington, 2015.

Köhnke, Klaus Christian. *The Rise of Neo-Kantianism: German Academic Philosophy between Idealism and Positivism.* Translated by R. J. Hollingdale. Cambridge: Cambridge University Press, 1991.

Krijnen, Christian, and Andrzej Noras, eds. *Marburg versus Südwestdeutschland: Philosophische Differenzen zwischen den beiden Hauptschulen des Neukantianismus.* Würzburg: Königshausen & Neumann, 2012.

Kronfeld, Arthur. "Geleitworte zum zehnjährigen Bestehen der neue Friesischen Schule." In *Das Wesen der psychiatrischen Erkenntnis*, 46–65. Berlin: Springer, 1920.

Kuehn, Manfred. *Kant: A Biography.* Cambridge: Cambridge University Press, 2001.

———. "Kant's Conception of 'Hume's Problem.'" *Journal of the History of Philosophy* 21 (1983) 275–93.

La Montagne, D. Paul. *Barth and Rationality: Critical Realism in Theology.* Eugene, OR: Cascade, 2014.

Lamm, Julia A. *The Living God: Schleiermacher's Theological Appropriation of Spinoza.* University Park, PA: Pennsylvania State University Press, 1996.

Lange, Friedrich Albert. *Geschichte des Materialismus und Kritik seiner Bedeutung in der Gegenwart.* Iserlohn: Baedeker, 1866.

———. *History of Materialism and Criticism of Its Present Importance.* Translated by Ernest Chester Thomas. 3 vols. 2nd ed. London: Paul, Trench, Trübner, 1892.

Langton, Rae. *Kantian Humility: Our Ignorance of Things in Themselves.* Oxford: Clarendon, 2001.

Lehmann, Gerhard. *Geschichte der nachkantischen Philosophie.* Berlin: Junker und Dünnhaupt, 1931.

Leman, Derek Alan Woodard. "Reason after Revelation: Karl Barth on Divine Word and Human Words." *Modern Theology* 33 (2017) 92–115.

Liebmann, Otto. *Kant und die Epigonen: Eine kritische Abhandlung.* Stuttgart: Schober, 1865.

Liminatis, Nectarios G. *German Idealism and the Problem of Knowledge: Kant, Fichte, Schelling, and Hegel.* New York: Springer, 2008.

Link, Christian. "Karl Barths Römerbrief (1921) als theologisches Signal." *Zeitschrift für dialektische Theologie* 23 (2007) 135–52.

Loades, Ann L. *Kant and Job's Comforters.* Newcastle upon Tyne: Avero, 1985.

Locke, John. *An Essay concerning Human Understanding.* London: Basset, 1690.

Loeb, Louis. *From Descartes to Hume: Continental Metaphysics and the Development of Modern Philosophy.* Ithaca, NY: Cornell University Press, 1981.

Logan, Beryl. "Hume and Kant on Knowing the Deity." *International Journal for Philosophy of Religion* 43 (1998) 133–48.

Lohmann, Johann Friedrich. *Karl Barth und der Neukantianismus: die Rezeption des Neukantianismus im 'Römerbrief' und ihre Bedeutung für die weitere Ausarbeitung der Theologie Karl Barths.* Berlin: de Gruyter, 1995.

Lotze, Hermann. *Metaphysik.* Leipzig: Hirzel, 1841.

Lovejoy, Arthur. "On Kant's Reply to Hume." *Archiv für Geschichte der Philosophie* (1906) 380–407.

Löwith, Karl. *From Hegel to Nietzsche: The Revolution in Nineteenth-Century Thought.* Translated by David Green. New York: Columbia University Press, 1991.

———. *Von Hegel zu Nietzsche: Der revolutionäre Bruch im Denken des neunzehnten Jahrhunderts.* Stuttgart: Kohlhammer, 1940.

Luft, Sebastian, ed. *The Neo-Kantian Reader*. New York: Routledge, 2015.

———. "The Philosophy of the Marburg School: From the Critique of Scientific Cognition to the Philosophy of Culture." In *New Approaches to Neo-Kantianism*, edited by Nicholas de Warren and Andrea Staiti, 221–39. Cambridge: Cambridge University Press, 2015.

Lyden, John Christopher. "Karl Barth's View on the Knowledge of God and Its Relation to the Philosophical Epistemology of Immanuel Kant." PhD diss., University of Chicago, 1989.

Magee, Bryan. *The Philosophy of Schopenhauer*. Rev. ed. Oxford: Clarendon, 1997.

Makreel, Rudolf, and Sebatian Luft, eds. *Neo-Kantianism in Contemporary Philosophy: Collected Essays*. Bloomington: Indiana University Press, 2010.

Malherbe, Michel. *Kant ou Hume: La raison et la sensible*. 2nd ed. Paris: Vrin, 1993.

———. *La philosophie empiriste de David Hume*. Paris: Vrin, 1976.

Mariña, Jacqueline. "Kant on Grace: A Reply to His Critics." *Religious Studies* 33 (1997) 379–400.

Marquardt, F.-W. "Socialism in the Theology of Karl Barth." In *Karl Barth and Radical Politics*, edited by George Hunsinger, 24–49. Philadelphia: Westminster, 1970.

Martin, Wayne. *Idealism and Objectivity: Understanding Fichte's Jena Project*. Stanford: Stanford University Press, 1997.

Marx, Werner. *The Philosophy of F. W. J. Schelling: History, System, and Freedom*. Bloomington: Indiana University Press, 1984.

Matthews, Bruce. *Beyond Presence: The Late F. J. W. Schelling's Criticism of Metaphysics*. Berlin: de Gruyter, 2012.

———. *Schelling's Organic Form of Philosophy: Life as the Schema of Freedom*. New York: State University of New York Press, 2012.

Mauer, Ernstpeter. "Theologische Weichenstellungen in Karl Barths Römerbriefauslegung von 1922." *Zeitschrift für dialektische Theologie* 23 (2007) 209–18.

Maund, Constance. *Hume's Theory of Knowledge: A Critical Examination*. London: Macmillan, 1937.

McCall, Thomas M. "Christology . . . within the Limits of Reason Alone? Kant on Fittingness for Atonement." In *Kant and the Question of Theology*, edited by Chris L. Firestone et al., 213–27. Cambridge: Cambridge University Press, 2017.

McCormack, Bruce. *Karl Barth's Critically Realistic Dialectical Theology: Its Genesis and Development, 1909–1936*. Oxford: Clarendon, 1997.

———. Review of *Karl Barth und der Neukantianismus*, by Johann Sebastian Lohmann. *Journal of Religion* 78 (1998) 129–30.

McFarlane, Andrew G. G. "The Human Person as an Epistemic Agent: The Theological Contours of Creaturely Cognition in Karl Barth's *Church Dogmatics*." PhD diss., University of Edinburgh, 2008.

McGrath, Alister. *Historical Theology: An Introduction to the History of Christian Thought*. 2nd ed. Malden, MA: Wiley-Blackwell, 2013.

McKenzie, David. "Barth's Anselm and the Object of Theological Knowledge." *Foundations* 21 (1978) 272–75.

Michalson, Gordon. *Fallen Freedom: Kant on Radical Evil and Moral Regeneration*. Cambridge: Cambridge University Press, 1990.

———. "Moral Regeneration and Divine Aid in Kant." *Religious Studies* 25 (1989) 259–70.

Miller, George. "Kant and Berkeley: The Alternative Theories." *Kant-Studien* 64 (1973) 315–55.
Mulholland, Leslie. "Freedom and Providence in Kant's Account of Religion: The Problem of Expiation." In *Kant's Philosophy of Religion Reconsidered*, edited by Philip Rossi and Michael W. Wreen, 77–102. Bloomington: Indiana University Press, 1991.
Müller, Hans Michael. "Credo, ut intelligam: Kritische Bemerkugen zu Karl Barths Dogmatik." *Theologische Blätter* 7 (1928) 167–76.
Natorp, Paul. "Kant und die Marburger Schule." *Kant-Studien* 17 (1912) 193–221.
Nelson, Leonard. *Abhandlungen der Fries'schen Schule, Neue Folge*. Göttingen: Vandenhoek & Ruprecht, 1904.
———. "The Critical Method and the Relation of Psychology to Philosophy: An Essay in Methodology." In *Socratic Method and Critical Philosophy: Selected Essays*, translated by Thomas K. Brown III, 105–54. New Haven: Yale University Press, 1949.
———. *Fortschritte und Rückschritte der Philosophie: Von Hume und Kant bis Hegel und Fries*. Göttingen: Öffentliches Leben, 1962.
———. "Die kritische Methode und das Verhältnis der Psychologie zur Philosophie: Ein Kapitel aus der Methodenlehre." *Abhandlungen der Fries'schen Schule* 1 (1904) 1–88.
———. *Progress and Regress in Philosophy: From Hume and Kant to Hegel and Fries*. Edited by Julius Kraft. Translated by Humphrey Palmer. 2 vols. Oxford: Blackwell, 1970.
Noack, Ludwig. *Immanuel Kant's Auferstehung aus dem Grabe: Die Lehre des Alten vom Königsberge*. Leipzig: Wigand, 1861.
Oakes, Kenneth. *Karl Barth on Theology and Philosophy*. Oxford: Oxford University Press, 2012.
———. *Reading Karl Barth: A Companion to Karl Barth's "Epistle to the Romans."* Eugene, OR: Cascade, 2011.
Oberst, Michael. "Kant, Epistemic Phenomenalism, and the Refutation of Idealism." *Archiv für Geschichte der Philosophie* 100 (2018) 172–201.
Oesterle, Hans J. "Karl Barths These über den Gottesbeweis des Anselm von Canterbury." *Neue Zeitschrift für systematische Theologie und Religionsphilosophie* 23 (1981) 91–107.
Ollig, Hans-Ludwig. "Neukantianismus." In *Philosophisches Wörterbuch*, edited by Walter Brugger and Harald Schöndorf, 327. Munich: Karl Alber Freiburg, 2010.
———. *Der Neukantianismus*. Stuttgart: Metzler, 1979.
Olson, Roger. *The Journey of Modern Theology: From Reconstruction to Deconstruction*. Downers Grove, IL: IVP Academic, 2013.
———. *The Story of Christian Theology: Twenty Centuries of Tradition and Reform*. Downers Grove, IL: IVP Academic, 1999.
Österreich, Peter L., and Hartmut Traub. *Der ganze Fichte. Die populäre, wissenschaftliche und metaphysische Erschließung der Welt*. Stuttgart: Kohlhammer, 2006.
Otto, Rudolf. *Das Heilige: Ueber das Irrationale in der Idee des Göttlichen und sein Verhältniß zum Rationalen*. Breslau: Trewandt und Granier, 1917.
———. *The Idea of the Holy: An Inquiry into the Non-rational Factor in the Idea of the Divine and Its Relation to the Rational*. Translated by John Harvey. Oxford: Oxford University Press, 1923.

———. *Kantisch-Fries'sche Religionsphilosophie und ihre Anwendung auf die Theologie*. Tübingen: Mohr, 1909.

———. *The Philosophy of Religion Based on Kant and Fries*. Translated by E. B. Dicker. New York: Smith, 1931.

Palmquist, Stephen. "Kant's 'Appropriation' of Lampe's God." *Harvard Theological Review* 85 (1992) 93.

———. "Kant's Ethics of Grace: Perspectival Solutions to the Moral Difficulties with Divine Assistance." *Journal of Religion* 90 (2010) 530–53.

———. *Kant's Critical Religion*. Aldershot: Ashgate, 2000.

———. *Kant's System of Perspectives*. Lanham, MD: University of America Press, 1993.

Pasternack, Lawrence. "Kant on the Debt of Sin." *Faith and Philosophy* 29 (2012) 30–52.

Pears, David. *Hume's System: An Examination of the First Book of His Treatise*. Oxford: Oxford University Press, 1990.

Peters, Tiemo R. "Das Skandalon Gottes: Der 'Römerbrief' von Karl Barth." *Wort und Antwort* 49 (2008) 136–38.

Peterson, Paul Silas. *The Early Karl Barth: Historical Contexts and Intellectual Formation, 1905–1935*. Tübigen: Mohr Siebeck, 2018.

Pinkard, Terry. *German Philosophy, 1760–1860: The Legacy of Idealism*. Cambridge: Cambridge University Press, 2002.

Pippin, Robert B. *Kant's Theory of Form: An Essay on the "Critique of Pure Reason."* New Haven: Yale University Press, 1982.

Poma, Andre. *The Critical Philosophy of Hermann Cohen*. Translated by John Denton. Albany: State University of New York Press, 1997.

Prichard, Harold Arthur. *Kant's Theory of Knowledge*. Oxford: Clarendon, 1909.

Priest, Stephen. "Descartes, Kant, and Self-Consciousness." *Philosophical Quarterly* 31 (1981) 348–51.

Pugh, Jeffrey C. *The Anselmic Shift: Christology and Method in Karl Barth's Theology*. New York: Lang, 1990.

Quinn, Philip. "Christian Atonement and Kantian Justification." *Faith and Philosophy* 1 (1984) 188–202.

———. "Saving Faith from Kant's Remarkable Antinomy." *Faith and Philosophy* 7 (1990) 418–33.

Ray, Matthew Alun. *Subjectivity and Irreligion: Atheism and Agnosticism in Kant, Schopenhauer, and Nietzsche*. Aldershot: Ashgate, 2003.

Reardon, Bernard M. G. *Kant as Philosophical Theologian*. Lanham, MD: Rowan and Littlefield, 1988.

Reid, Thomas. *Essays on the Intellectual Powers of Man*. Edinburgh: Bell, 1785.

Rockmore, Tom. *Hegel's Circular Epistemology*. Bloomington: Indiana University Press, 1986.

Rockmore, Tom, and Daniel Breazeale, eds. *Fichte and Transcendental Philosophy*. London: Palgrave Macmillan, 2014.

Rossi, Philip, and Michael W. Wreen, eds. *Kant's Philosophy of Religion Reconsidered*. Bloomington: Indiana University Press, 1991.

Rumscheidt, H. Martin. *Revelation and Theology: An Analysis of the Barth-Harnack Correspondence of 1923*. Cambridge: Cambridge University Press, 1972.

———, ed. *The Way of Theology in Karl Barth: Essays and Comments*. Allison Park, PA: Pickwick, 1986.

Runia, Klaas. *Barth's Doctrine of Holy Scripture*. Grand Rapids: Eerdmans, 1962.

Ruschke, Werner M. *Entstehung und Ausführung der Diastasentheologie in Karl Barths zweitem "Römerbrief."* Neukirchen-Vluyn: Neukirchener Verlag, 1987.

Savage, Denis. "Kant's Rejection of Divine Revelation and His Theory of Radical Evil." In *Kant's Philosophy of Religion Reconsidered*, edited by Philip Rossi and Michael W. Wreen, 54–76. Bloomington: Indiana University Press, 1991.

Scharlemann, Robert P. "The No to Nothing and the Nothing to Know: Barth and Tillich and the Possibility of Theological Science." *Journal of the American Academy of Religion* 55 (1987) 57–72.

Schelling, F. W. J. *Philosophical Investigations into the Essence of Human Freedom.* Translated by Jeff Love and Johannes Schmidt. New York: State University of New York Press, 2006.

———. *Philosophische Untersuchungen über das Wesen der menschlichen Freiheit und die damit zusammenhängenden Gegenstände.* Reutlingen: Erstdruck, 1834.

———. *System des transcendentalen Idealismus.* Tübingen: Cotta, 1800.

———. *System of Transcendental Idealism.* Translated by Peter Heath. Charlottesville: University Press of Virginia, 1978.

Schopenhauer, Arthur. *Die Welt als Wille und Vorstellung.* 2 vols. Leipzig: Brockhaus, 1859.

Schwyzer, Hubert. "Subjectivity in Descartes and Kant." *Philosophical Quarterly* 47 (1997) 342–57.

Sedgwick, Sally. "Idealism from Kant to Hegel." In *The Reception of Kant's Critical Philosophy: Fichte, Schelling, Hegel*, edited by Sally Sedgwick, 1–18. Cambridge: Cambridge University Press, 2000.

Sheveland, John. "Tears of Dependence: Anselm and Karl Barth on 'Intelligere.'" *Expository Times* 115 (2004) 181–86.

Shofner, Robert Dancey. *Anselm Revisited: A Study of the Role of the Ontological Argument in the Writings of Karl Barth and Charles Hartshorne.* Leiden: Brill, 1974.

Sieg, Ulrich. *Aufstieg und Niedergang des Marburger Neokantianismus.* Würzburg: Königshausen & Neumann, 1994.

Smit, Houston. "Kant on Marks and the Immediacy of Intuition." *Philosophical Review* 109 (2000) 235–66.

Snow, Dale E. *Schelling and the End of Idealism.* New York: State University of New York Press, 1996.

Spencer, Archie. *The Analogy of Faith: The Quest for God's Speakability.* Downers Grove, IL: IVP Academic, 2015.

Spieckermann, Ingrid. *Gotteserkenntnis: Ein Beitrag zur Grundfrage der neuen Theologie Karl Barths.* Munich: Chr. Kaiser, 1985.

Stanley, Timothy. "Barth after Kant?" *Modern Theology* 28 (2012) 423–45.

———. "Returning Barth to Anselm." *Modern Theology* 24 (2008) 413–37.

Stegemann, Ekkehard W. "'Kritischer müssen mir die Historisch-Kritischen sein!': Karl Barth als Exeget in der zweiten Auflage des Römerbriefs." *Kirche und Israel* 1 (2012) 3–17.

Stern, George. *A Faculty Theory of Knowledge: The Aim and Scope of Hume's First Enquiry.* Lewisburg: Bucknell University Press, 1971.

Stern, Robert. "Metaphysical Dogmatism, Humean Scepticism, Kantian Criticism." *Kantian Review* 11 (2006) 102–16.

Strawson, P. F. *The Bounds of Sense: An Essay on Kant's "Critique of Pure Reason."* London: Methuen, 1966.

Sykes, S. W., ed. *Karl Barth: Studies of His Theological Methods*. Oxford: Oxford University Press, 1980.
Taylor, Charles. *Hegel*. Cambridge, MA: Harvard University Press, 1975.
Thompson, Manley. "Singular Terms and Intuitions in Kant's Epistemology." *Review of Metaphysics* 26 (1972) 314–43.
Thurneysen, Eduard. *Das Römerbriefmansuskript habe ich Gelesen: Eduard Thurneysens gesammelte Briefe und Kommentare aus der Entstehungszeit von Karl Barths Römerbrief II (1920–1921)*. Zürich: TVZ, 2015.
Tillette, Xavier. *Schelling: Biographie*. Paris: Calmann-Lévy, 1999.
Tillich, Paul. "Existential Philosophy." *Journal of the History of Ideas* 5 (1944) 44–70.
Toews, John. *Hegelianism: The Path toward Dialectical Humanism, 1805–1841*. Cambridge: Cambridge University Press, 1980.
Torrance, Thomas F. *Karl Barth: An Introduction to His Early Theology, 1910–1931*. New York: T. & T. Clark, 2004.
Trendelenburg, Adolf. *Logische Untersuchungen*. Berlin: Bethge, 1840.
Turbayne, C. M. "Kant's Refutation of Dogmatic Idealism." *Philosophical Quarterly* 5 (1955) 225–44.
Vaihinger, Hans. *Kommentar zu Kants Kritik der reinen Vernuft*. 2 vols. Stuttgart: Deutsche Verlags Anstalt, 1922.
Vignaux, Paul. "Saint Anselme, Barth et au-delà." *Les quatre fleuves* 1 (1973) 83–95.
Walker, R. C. S., ed. *The Real in the Ideal: Berkeley's Relation to Kant*. London: Routledge, 1989.
Ward, Keith. *The Development of Kant's View of Ethics*. Oxford: Basil Blackwell, 1972.
Warren, Nicholas de, and Andrea Staiti, eds. *New Approaches to Neo-Kantianism*. Cambridge: Cambridge University Press, 2015.
Watson, Gordon. "Karl Barth and St. Anselm's Theological Programme." *Scottish Journal of Theology* 30 (1977) 31–45.
———. "A Study in St. Anselm's Soteriology and Karl Barth's Theological Method." *Scottish Journal of Theology* 42 (1989) 493–512.
Webster, John. *Barth*. 2nd ed. London: Continuum, 2004.
———. "Karl Barth." In *Reading Romans through the Centuries*, edited by Timothy Larsen and Jeffrey P. Greenman, 205–20. Grand Rapids: Brazos, 2005.
Westerholm, Martin. *The Ordering of the Christian Mind: Karl Barth and Theological Rationality*. Oxford: Oxford University Press, 2015.
Westphal, Kenneth. *Hegel's Epistemology: A Philosophical Introduction to the "Phenomenology of Spirit."* Indianapolis: Hackett, 2003.
White, Thomas Joseph. *The Analogy of Being: Invention of the Antichrist or Wisdom of God?* Grand Rapids: Eerdmans, 2010.
Willey, Thomas E. *Back to Kant: The Revival of Kantianism in German Social and Historical Thought, 1860–1914*. Detroit: Wayne State University Press, 1978.
Wilson, Kirk. "Kant on Intuition." *Philosophical Quarterly* 25 (1975) 247–65.
Wilson, Margaret D. "Kant and the Dogmatic Idealism of Berkeley." *Journal of the History of Philosophy* 9 (1971) 459–75.
Windelband, Wilhelm. "Immanuel Kant. Zur Säkularfeier seiner Philosophie (1881)." In *Präludien: Aufsätze und Reden zur Einleitung in die Philosophie*, 135–68. Tübigen: Mohr Siebeck, 1924.
Wolf, Ernst. *Karl Barth: Glaube und Erkenntnis*. Hamburg: Rauhen, 1952.
Wolff, Christian. *Philosophia rationalis, sive logica*. Frankfurt, 1740.

———. *Psychologia empirica*. Frankfurt, 1738.
———. *Theologia naturalis method scientifica pertracta*. Frankfurt, 1736.
Wolterstorff, Nicholas. "Conundrums in Kant's Rational Religion." In *Kant's Philosophy of Religion Reconsidered*, edited by Philip Rossi and Michael W. Wreen, 40–53. Bloomington: Indiana University Press, 1991.
———. "Is It Possible and Desirable for Theologians to Recover from Kant?" *Modern Theology* 14 (1998) 1–18.
———. *John Locke and the Ethics of Belief*. Cambridge Studies in Religion and Critical Thought 2. Cambridge: Cambridge University Press, 1996.
———. *Thomas Reid and the Story of Epistemology*. Modern European Philosophy. Cambridge: Cambridge University Press, 2001.
Wood, Allen. *Kant's Moral Religion*. Ithaca, NY: Cornell University Press, 1970.
———. *Kant's Rational Theology*. Ithaca, NY: Cornell University Press, 1978.
Woolley, J. Patrick. "Kaufman's Debt to Kant: The Epistemological Importance of 'The Structure of the World Which Environs Us.'" *Zygon* 48 (2013) 544–64.
Wundt, Max. *Kant als Metaphysiker: ein Beitrag zur Geschichte der Philosophie im 18. Jahrhundert*. Stuttgart: Enke, 1924.
Yovel, Yirmiahu. *Kant and the Philosophy of History*. Princeton: Princeton University Press, 1980.
Zachhuber, Johannes. *Theology as Science in Nineteenth-Century Germany: From F. C. Baur to Ernst Troeltsch*. Changing Paradigms in Historical and Systematic Theology. Oxford: Oxford University Press, 2013.
Zöller, Günter. *Fichte's Transcendental Philosophy: The Original Duplicity of Intelligence and Will*. Modern European Philosophy. Cambridge: Cambridge University Press, 1998.

www.ingramcontent.com/pod-product-compliance
Lightning Source LLC
Chambersburg PA
CBHW071502150426
43191CB00009B/1403